"To read the text and then g[...] of the arts of expositional preaching. This book will help you with the mechanical, the technical and practical application of biblical preaching."
—Johnny Hunt, Senior Pastor
First Baptist Church, Woodstock, GA

"A classic is born! This volume on preaching is one of the most comprehensive, user friendly, and easily applicated to be found. It is not mere theoretical jargon but has been beaten out on the anvil of personal experience in the study and in the pulpit. Preachers will be gleaning from these timeless truths long after Drs. Akin, Curtis, and Rummage are themselves sitting at the feet of the Prince of all Preachers. Read it and reap!!"
—O. S. Hawkins, President/Chief Executive Officer
Guidestone Financial Resources, Dallas, TX

"This book is a tremendous gift for those who want to teach and preach the Bible. It deals with all the issues in a clear, concise, and challenging way."
—Pastor Mark Driscoll
Mars Hill Church
Acts 29 Church Planting Network, The Resurgence

"These gifted authors have teamed up to provide pastors, students, and other Christians with an outstanding book on the ministry of the Word. With today's misguided stress on being flashy and famous, it is refreshing to read a book that reminds us of our real task of being faithful to speak 'the oracles of God.' Bill Curtis provides an enlightening section on hermeneutics that emphasizes the necessary interpretive principles for exposition. Danny Akin presents a workable and effective plan for developing substantive expositional sermons that exalt King Jesus. Stephen Rummage reminds us of some very important matters on engaging sermon delivery. May God use this book to stir up an army of believers who will proclaim God's Word Christocentrically and winsomely."
—Tony Merida
Pastor, associate professor of preaching, Southeastern Baptist
Theological Seminary, Wake Forest, NC, and author of *Faithful Preaching*

"Best book on preaching I've ever read. It's powerful. It's practical. It's to the point. Oh if I only had it fifty years ago!"
—Dr. John Bisagno, Pastor Emeritus
Second Baptist Church, Houston, TX

"In this well-conceived volume, readers will find superb instruction for the art of biblical exposition and sermon delivery. They also will find much help for the challenging work of interpreting, understanding, and applying the text of Holy Scripture. The authors of this much-needed work bring years of experience, as well as great insight and wisdom, to the wide-ranging subject matter explored in this comprehensive and competent resource. I am confident that *Engaging Exposition* will provide enabling guidance for the next generation of theological students, pastors, and teachers."

—David S. Dockery, President
Union University, Jackson, TN

"Expository preaching is becoming a lost art in the church culture of today. This book is a sterling call to practice biblical exposition that is engaging, elevating, and energizing. No stone is left unturned and no diamond is left unpolished. It is an eloquent exposition of Paul's command, 'Preach the Word!'"

—James Merritt, Senior Pastor
Cross Pointe Church, Duluth, GA

"There are lots of books on preaching that are so dry, tedious, and irrelevant that they douse the fire in a preacher's bones. Not this book. As I read it, I had mixed feelings. I didn't want to put down the book, and yet I was so inspired I wanted to throw it down and go preach! As you read this, you'll find practical counsel, wise instruction, and kindling for the fire inside."

—Russell D. Moore, Dean
The Southern Baptist Theological Seminary, Louisville, KY

"The absence of authentic biblical preaching is killing many churches and producing a generation of starved and immature Christians. For this reason, I welcome the arrival of *Engaging Exposition* by Danny Akin, Bill Curtis, and Stephen Rummage. These men are committed to biblical exposition, and their practical guide to expository preaching will be welcomed by all who yearn for biblical preaching in our churches. This book will be most appreciated by those who bear the responsibility to preach the Word. Preachers will draw great inspiration, sound advice, and solid help from these three gifted preachers. There is a wealth of expository wisdom in these pages."

—R. Albert Mohler Jr., President
The Southern Baptist Theological Seminary, Louisville, KY

"Another book on expository preaching? Yes! However, in Engaging Exposition, Danny Akin, Bill Curtis, and Stephen Rummage cover the critical aspects of exposition that often have gone unstated. This is a refreshing and challenging approach that will enable the contemporary preacher to stay true to the author's intention while making the text leap to life from the page on which it is written."

—Paige Patterson, President
Southwestern Baptist Theological Seminary,
Fort Worth, TX

"Exposition of the Scripture is the core commitment of the church. Unfortunately, exposition is sometimes viewed as antiquated and disconnected from life. So I am grateful for this book's focus on authentic preaching which is engaging, interesting, relevant, and life-changing."

—Jack Graham, Pastor
Prestonwood Baptist Church, Plano, TX

"In this book, three gifted preachers take us step by step down the often difficult and labyrinthine path of biblical interpretation, sermon preparation, and sermon delivery. Regardless of experience level, pastors will benefit from this theologically sound, clearly written and practically applied approach to expositional preaching. Read it and reap the benefits in your own preaching!"

—David Allen, Professor of Preaching
Southwestern Baptist Theological Seminary, Ft. Worth, TX

"So you are called to preach and want to know where to begin? Reading *Engaging Exposition* is the place to start! Akin, Rummage, and Curtis have given us a comprehensive look at preaching in one convenient volume. This work will help raise up a new generation of bold, engaging, biblical preachers."

—Greg Heisler, Professor of Preaching
Southeastern Baptist Theological Seminary
Wake Forest, NC

"In the mind of a preacher, there is an ever-ticking countdown timer, an hourglass that runs out of sand every Sunday as he climbs into the pulpit. The pressure of generating sermons creates a sort of desperation that is always seeking ways to better the exegetical process and polish the expositional delivery. The authors of *Engaging Exposition* have generated an indispensable resource for expositors who desire to learn, grow, and improve the expository process. The encyclopedic scope of this volume will serve as both an introduction for students and a welcome refresher for seasoned preachers. Its breadth on homiletical issues is unequalled."

—Rick Holland, Senior Pastor
Mission Road Bible Church, Kansas City, Kansas
Director of D.Min. Studies, The Master's Seminary

"From the sufficiency of the biblical text to the proficiency of giving voice to that text, this book provides a much needed perspective on the expository sermon. Akin, Curtis and Rummage show that dynamic preaching is not about making the Bible relevant. Rather, they demonstrate that dynamic preaching is about showing people how relevant the Bible already is. This volume strikes a beautiful balance between the sound preparation and the passionate delivery of the expository sermon and it reveals that while what is said in the sermon is of the most importance, how the preacher says it has never been more important."

—Mark Howell, Pastor
Houston Northwest Baptist Church, Houston, TX

Engaging Exposition

Daniel L. Akin
Bill Curtis and
Stephen Rummage

ACADEMIC
Nashville, Tennessee

Engaging Exposition
A 3-D Approach to Preaching

ISBN: 978-0-8054-4668-5

Published by B&H Publishing Group
Nashville, Tennessee

Dewey Decimal Classification: 251
Subject Heading: PREACHING \ SERMONS \ PASTORAL
THEOLOGY

Printed in the United States of America

2 3 4 5 6 7 8 • 18 17 16 15 14
VP

CONTENTS

FOREWORD

I will never forget that night.

I was sitting near the front of a worship service as I watched the guest preacher pace back and forth across the stage. He was a popular speaker in our area, and crowds had come to hear what he had to say. My first clue that something wasn't right was when he started by saying, "I forgot my Bible tonight."

But that didn't deter him. He explained that for days he had prayed about what God wanted him to say to us. He told stories about how he had taken walks in his neighborhood, sat at coffee shops, and reclined in his study. He was funny, witty, and engaging, and he kept the crowd entertained.

When he came to his conclusion, these were his exact words: "I tried to do everything I could to figure out what God wanted me to say, but nothing ever came to my mind. So maybe that means God simply doesn't have anything to say to us tonight." With that, he prayed and walked off the stage.

I sat there with my Bible in my hands, dumbfounded. *God doesn't have anything to say to us tonight?* There I was, holding a library of sixty-six books that are decidedly and definitively the Word of God, and this guy just said God doesn't have a word for us? In my mind I said to this guy, "Just open this book anywhere—to Leviticus, for all I care—and read it, and you've got a word from God. Save yourself the walk around the neighborhood and the cost of your mocha. Just read the book, and God is saying something to us."

I am thankful for that experience, for it burned a permanent brand into my heart and mind. In my life and in the church, we are never without a word from God. At all times, you and I have God's revelation to us in all its power, authority, clarity, and might. We don't have to work to come up with a word from God; we simply have to trust the Word he has already given to us.

This is what exposition is all about: trusting the Word of God to accomplish the work of God among the people of God. As preachers and teachers, we don't have to be creative, innovative, unique or unusual; we simply have to be faithful. Faithful to study the Word of God, faithful to know the God of the Word, and faithful to proclaim it in the world.

For this reason, I am thankful for Danny Akin, Bill Curtis, and Stephen Rummage. In the volume you hold in your hands, they have identified robust theological foundations and have provided valuable practical exhortations for expository preaching. They have clearly wed together responsible hermeneutics with relevant homiletics to guide preachers and teachers from the preparation of a message to the delivery of a sermon. Their words on these pages will drive you to his Word on the pages of Scripture, where you will find an inexhaustible source of truth to treasure in your heart and to tell to the nations. And in the end, my prayer is that you will never, ever, ever find yourself without a God-inspired, Christ-centered, Spirit-empowered, life-changing Word to speak to men and women for the glory of his name.

David Platt

INTRODUCTION

A CRISIS IN TWENTY-FIRST–CENTURY PREACHING: A MANDATE FOR ENGAGING BIBLICAL EXPOSITION

This book reflects a serious concern as well as certain nonnegotiable convictions the three of us hold in common. We believe the church of the Lord Jesus Christ is at a critical point. A crisis is in our pulpits, and this situation is critical. Seduced by the sirens of modernity, preachers of the gospel have jettisoned a word-based ministry that is expository in nature.[1] Skiing across the surface needs of a fallen, sinful humanity, we have turned the pulpit into a pop psychology sideshow and a feel-good pit stop. We have neglected preaching the whole counsel of God's Word. What has resulted? Too many of our people know neither the content nor the doctrines of Scripture. What is the fallout? Not knowing the Word, they do not love or obey the Word. If the Bible is used at all in preaching, it is usually included as a proof-text that is used out of context and has no real connection to what the biblical author is saying. Many who claim and perhaps believe they are expositors betray their confession by their practice.

The words of the prophet Amos were never more piercing as they are now: "'Behold, the days are coming,' says the Lord GOD, 'That I will send a famine on the land, / Not a famine of bread, / Nor a

---

1. We are in complete agreement with Mark Dever's view: "The first mark of a healthy church is expository preaching. It is not only the first mark; it is far and away the most important of them all, because if you get this one right, all of the others should follow." Mark Dever, *Nine Marks of a Healthy Church*, new expanded ed. (Wheaton: Crossway, 2004), 39.

1

thirst for water, / But of hearing the words of the LORD. They shall wander from sea to sea, / And from north to east; / They shall run to and fro, seeking the word of the LORD, / But shall not find it'" (Amos 8:11–12).

Many pastors are guilty of committing ministerial malpractice on their congregation. By what they do, they indicate that they believe we can see people converted and brought to maturity in Christ without the consistent teaching of the Bible. Further, at least implicitly, they question the judgment of God the Holy Spirit is inspiring Scripture as we now have it. By their method and practice, they suggest that the Holy Spirit should have packaged the Bible differently.

A DEFINITION/DESCRIPTION OF BIBLICAL EXPOSITION

If we were limited to 10 words or less, we would define faithful, expository preaching as, "Christ centered, text driven, Spirit led preaching that transforms lives." Expanding this definition into a more full description, we would say,

> Expository preaching is text driven preaching that honors the truth of Scripture as it was given by the Holy Spirit. Its goal is to discover the God-inspired meaning through historical-grammatical-theological investigation and interpretation. By means of engaging and compelling proclamation, the preacher explains, illustrates and applies the meaning of the biblical text in submission to and in the power of the Holy Spirit, preaching Christ for a verdict of changed lives.

We will develop this description throughout this text, providing an equal focus on hermeneutics, homiletics, and delivery. The following seven foundational premises will guide our investigation.

1. *Preaching must be text-driven so that it truly honors what is in the divine revelation.* Expository preaching allows the Scripture text to determine both the substance and the structure of the message. How one structures the Scriptures will

determine how one structures the sermon. The scriptural text drives and determines, shapes and forms sermon development as it relates to the explanation of the biblical text.[2]

2. *Preachers must honor the principle of authorial intent, recognizing that the ultimate author of Scripture is the Holy Spirit, God Himself.* The Bible is best described as the Word of God. Although the Bible has been written in the words of men, we must never forget it is ultimately the Word of God. The divine author's intended meaning as deposited in the text should be honored. David Alan Black notes, "It is within these parameters of authorial intent and grammatical form that faithful biblical interpretation takes place."[3]

3. *Scripture must be interpreted and understood as it was given to the original audience.* The text cannot mean today what it did not mean then. A fundamental principle in preaching is that ". . . the best homiletical outlines of a passage are those that are derived from the text itself."[4] The faithful expositor must not eisegete the text, reading into it the preconceived notions of his imagination or interests. As evangelical expositors, we must continue to affirm that the meaning is one, though the applications are many.

4. *Pulpit proclamation must affirm that the historical-grammatical-theological interpretation will best discover both the truth of the text and the theology of the text.* Doctrinal/theological preaching is noticeably absent in the modern pulpit. Theological and biblical illiteracy is the heavy price being paid. As the preacher both exegetes his text and considers his audience, he should be sensitive to the theological truths the text contains and supports. We believe exegesis must drive theology. Scripture must shape any theological

---

2. Greg Heisler says, "The strength of expository preaching, as opposed to other forms of preaching such as topical, is that expository preaching respects not only the author's original intention, but also the Holy Spirit's placement and sequencing of the text." *Spirit-Led Preaching* (Nashville: B&H, 2007), 22.

3. David A. Black, "Exegesis for the Text-Driven Sermon," in *Text-Driven Preaching*, ed. Daniel L. Akin, David L. Allen, and Ned L. Matthews (Nashville: B&H, 2010), 159.

4. Ibid.

system; a theological system must not shape the use of Scripture.

5. *Effective biblical instruction will take seriously the implications of what Jesus said about the Christological nature of Scripture (John 5:39; Luke 24:25–27,44–47) and develop them.* Call it what you will. Preaching that does not exalt, magnify, and glorify the Lord Jesus is not Christian preaching. Preaching that does not present the gospel and call men and women to repent of sin and place their faith in the death and resurrection of Jesus Christ is not gospel preaching.

   Faithful exposition will be Christological in focus, inner-canonical in context, and inter-textual in building a biblical theology. It will carefully interpret Scripture in the larger context of the grand redemptive story line of Scripture (Creation → Fall → Redemption → Consummation). Applying what can be called a comprehensive Christocentric hermeneutic, we will examine the little narratives and pericopes in light of the larger narrative, that is, the great redemptive narrative centered in Christ.

6. *From beginning to end, from the study to the pulpit, the entire process of biblical exposition must take place in absolute and complete submission to the Holy Spirit.* All that we do in preparation and proclamation of the Bible should take place in humble submission to the Holy Spirit. As we analyze the text, study the grammar, parse the verbs, consult the commentaries, and gather the raw materials for the message, we should seek His guidance and confess our total dependence on Him.

   When we stand to preach and to minister the Word to our people, we must plead for His filling and direction. The interdependence of the Word and the Spirit was a hallmark of the Reformers, and it must be the same with us.

7. *Changed lives for the glory of God is always the goal for which we strive.* Therefore, it is a sin of the most serious sort to preach the Word of God in a boring and unattractive fashion. In the culture in which we live, saturated with multimedia and entertainment, we repeatedly tell our students, "What you say is more important than how you say it, but how you say it has never been more important." The wise preacher will both exegete Scripture and understand his culture.

He understands that he must know each equally well. Bad preaching will sap the life of a church. It will kill its spirit, dry up its fruit, and eventually empty it. If we dare to be honest, we must say that bad preaching is not true preaching. It is preaching not worthy of the name.

Martin Luther threw down the gauntlet and gives us words to guide us and inspire us in our holy assignment. As you reflect on the assignment of preaching God has given you, let these words sink deep into your heart and fill your mind:

Let us then consider it certain and conclusively established that the soul can do without all things except the Word of God, and that where this is not there is no help for the soul in anything else whatever. But if it has the Word it is rich and lacks nothing, since this Word is the Word of life, of truth, of light, of peace, of righteousness, of salvation, of joy, of liberty, of wisdom, of power, of grace, of glory, and of every blessing beyond our power to estimate.[5]

On these convictions the three of us stand. With them serving as foundational pillars, we will explore a three-dimensional approach to teaching and preaching the Word of God for the glory of our Savior and the good of His saints. Engaging exposition is not an option. It is an absolute necessity for the health of the body of Christ.

---

5. Martin Luther, "A Treatise on Christian Liberty," in *Three Treatises* (Philadelphia: Muhlenberg Press, 1943), 23.

SECTION 1

CHAPTER 1

A JOURNEY OF DISCOVERY

A Chinese philosopher once stated that a journey of a thousand miles begins with a single step. Every journey requires three things: a destination, a plan to reach it, and the will to take the first step. In this textbook, you are embarking on a unique journey of discovery in the fields of hermeneutics and homiletics. Your destination is clear—to cultivate the ability to craft and deliver engaging expository sermons. To help you reach your destination, we have developed a plan to guide you on your journey. As you will soon realize, this journey can be challenging, and danger awaits those who take a detour.

When some people prepare for ministry, they only want to learn how to preach. Before we can craft and deliver an expository sermon, however, we must learn how to "correctly [teach] the word of truth" (2 Tim 2:15). John Broadus, the famed Southern Baptist homiletician, described the importance of this task in his classic work *On the Preparation and Delivery of Sermons*:

> For the Scripture to have value for preaching and for the preacher's text to become God's message, the Bible must be interpreted correctly. To interpret and apply his text in accordance with its real meaning is one of the preacher's most sacred duties. He stands before the people for the very purpose of teaching and exhorting them out of the Word of God. He announces a particular passage of God's Word as his text with the distinctly implied understanding that from this his sermon will be drawn. By using a text and undertaking to develop and apply its teachings, he is

solemnly bound to represent the text as meaning precisely what it does mean.[1]

In short, the goal of hermeneutics is to help the pastor-teacher "interpret and apply his text in accordance with its real meaning." Section 1 of this textbook is devoted to helping you learn how to take a biblical text and interpret it correctly, with the goal of developing an expository sermon. It is time to begin your journey of discovery—a journey that begins with a single step.

THE MEANING OF HERMENEUTICS

Hermeneutics has been defined in a variety of ways. The *Concise Encyclopedia of Preaching* provides this definition: "Hermeneutics in general terms is the art of understanding. More specifically, it refers to the method and techniques used to make a text understandable in a world different from the one in which the text originated."[2] David Dockery states, "Hermeneutics is a term from the Greek, *hermeneuien*, meaning to express, to explain, to translate, to interpret. Traditionally, hermeneutics sought to establish the principles, methods, and rules needed in the interpretation of written texts, particularly sacred texts."[3] For the purpose of our discussions in this text, the process of hermeneutics will be defined as the proper use of the principles of interpretation to discover the author's intended meaning of a biblical text, with a goal of applying that meaning to a contemporary audience.

The Dangers of Poor Hermeneutics

Sadly, many prospective pastor-teachers grew up under preachers who struggle to handle the Scriptures either carefully or accurately.

---

1. John A. Broadus, *On the Preparation and Delivery of Sermons*, ed. V. L Stanfield, 4th and rev. ed. (San Francisco: Harper San Francisco, 1979), 23–24.
2. James A. Sanders, "Hermeneutics," in *Concise Encyclopedia of Preaching*, ed. William H. Willimon and Richard Lischer (Louisville: WJK, 1995), 175.
3. David Dockery, "Preaching and Hermeneutics," in *Handbook of Contemporary Preaching*, ed. Michael Duduit (Nashville: Broadman, 1992), 142.

As a result, they continue to emulate the preaching modeled for them, and this perpetuation of poor preaching has dangerous implications for the people of God. Make no mistake—bad hermeneutics leads to bad sermons.

Many pastor-teachers make a number of classic mistakes when approaching the Bible. First, some go to the Scriptures in an attempt to discover something new. "The aim of good interpretation is not uniqueness; one is not trying to discover what no one else has ever seen before."[4] James Rosscup notes, "What a preacher claims a passage says can be very different from what it actually says. His goal should be to ferret out the *indication* of the text, not to foist upon it some *imagination* of his own."[5] Sadly, the attempt to discover something new in the Scriptures is the root of many sects and cults.

Second, some pastor-teachers go to the Scriptures to find support for their own personal interpretations. Grant Osborne defines this fallacy as the proclamation of one's "subjective religious opinions."[6] He states, "The basic evangelical fallacy of our generation is 'proof-texting,' that process whereby a person 'proves' a doctrine or practice merely by alluding to a text without considering its original inspired meaning."[7] Often, a lack of theological training accompanies this tendency. Please understand that we are not calling into question the motives of good men who love God. However, a lack of theological training may contribute to the adoption of certain presuppositions or beliefs that Scripture cannot support. The inability to apply good hermeneutics to one's interpretation often leads to the proof-texting found in much topical preaching.

Third, some pastor-teachers work so hard to be relevant to contemporary culture that they either misuse the biblical text or fail to address it altogether. Walter Kaiser notes,

> Those sermons whose alleged strength is that they speak to contemporary issues, needs, and aspirations often exhibit the

---

4. Gordon D. Fee and Douglas Stuart, *How to Read the Bible for All Its Worth*, 3rd ed. (Grand Rapids: Zondervan, 2003), 16.
5. James E. Rosscup, "Hermeneutics and Expository Preaching," in *Rediscovering Expository Preaching*, ed. J. MacArthur Jr. and the Master's Seminary Faculty (Dallas: Word, 1992), 123.
6. Grant R. Osborne, *The Hermeneutical Spiral*, 2nd ed. (Downers Grove: IVP, 2006), 23.
7. Ibid.

weakness of a subjective approach. In the hands of many practitioners, the Biblical text has been of no real help either in clarifying the questions posed by modern man or in offering solutions. The listener is often not sure whether the word of hope being proclaimed is precisely that same Biblical word which should be connected with the modern situation or issue being addressed in the sermon since the Biblical text often is no more than a slogan or refrain in the message. What is so lacking in this case is exactly what needs to be kept in mind with respect to every sermon which aspires to be at once both Biblical and practical: *It must be derived from an honest exegesis of the text and it must constantly be kept close to the text* [emphasis ours].[8]

In other words, the failure to keep any sermon closely anchored to a text will ultimately result in hindering the text from accomplishing its intended purpose in the lives of the listeners.

Finally, the people of God suffer when pastor-teachers look to discover new interpretations of Scripture, or when they look for Scripture verses to support their own personal ideas about the Bible, or when they place relevance over revelation. Michael Fabarez reminds us of this sobering truth: "Though many intend to base a sermon on a text of Scripture, incompetent handling of the text can lead the preacher to reach unbiblical conclusions and thus waylay his congregants."[9]

The Benefits of Good Hermeneutics

The decision to learn and practice good hermeneutics will benefit the life of the pastor-teacher and his listeners. First, good hermeneutics will keep the pastor-teacher focused on discovering the meaning and significance of a text. John Stott discusses the tension between these two concepts in his classic work *Between Two Worlds*. He notes,

---

8.   Walter C. Kaiser Jr., *Toward an Exegetical Theology* (Grand Rapids: Baker, 1981), 19.
9.   Michael Fabarez, *Preaching that Changes Lives* (Nashville: Thomas Nelson, 2002), 18.

It is essential to keep these two questions both distinct and together. To discover the text's *meaning* is of purely academic interest unless we go on to discern its *message* for today, or (as some theologians prefer to say) its "significance." But to search for its contemporary message without first wrestling with its original meaning is to attempt a forbidden shortcut. It dishonors God (disregarding his chosen way of revealing himself in particular historical and cultural contexts), it misuses his Word (treating it like an almanac or book of magic spells) and it misleads his people (confusing them about how to interpret Scripture).[10]

Good hermeneutics assists the pastor-teacher in discovering the author's intended meaning in a text, whose ultimate author is God the Holy Spirit.

Second, good hermeneutics will assist the pastor-teacher in considering all aspects of a passage's context, while pursuing the author's intended meaning. Since every book of the Bible was written in a unique context, every text has "one primary normative meaning—that which the author intended."[11] To fully understand that meaning, however, the pastor-teacher must understand the context in which the text was written. Kaiser, speaking of the historicity of the Bible, notes that "its words are most frequently . . . directed to a *specific* people in a *specific* situation at a *specific* time and in a *specific* culture."[12] Good hermeneutics enables the pastor-teacher to incorporate a thorough understanding of context when striving to discern the author's intended meaning.

Third, good hermeneutics protects the pastor-teacher from rushing prematurely into the application stage of interpretation. As Stott noted above, the study of a text is incomplete if it fails to assess its significance for today's listeners. However, attempting to discover the significance of a text, without first gaining a thorough understanding of the author's intended meaning, will be equally incomplete. After all, some of our preconceived interpretations are incorrect because our preconceived understandings of a text's meaning are incorrect as well. Consequently, good hermeneutics will force us to

---

10. John R. W. Stott, *Between Two Worlds* (Grand Rapids: Eerdmans, 1982), 221.
11. Dockery, "Preaching and Hermeneutics," in Duduit, *Handbook of Contemporary Preaching*, 147.
12. Kaiser, *Toward and Exegetical Theology*, 37.

make the discovery of the author's intended meaning our first priority, enable us to examine the context fully so that we can arrive at the
intended meaning, and lead us to the proper application of the text
for our listeners.

CHAPTER 2

THE ORIGINS OF BIBLICAL
HERMENEUTICS

For many students, the word *hermeneutics* produces fear and trembling. It conjures up images of brilliant scholars, cloistered in quiet rooms, parsing verbs from original manuscripts by candlelight. Hermeneutics, however, is not a subject for students of the Scriptures to fear. Rather, it provides the framework needed to interpret the Scriptures correctly. In this chapter we will examine the origins of Scripture and trace the historical development of hermeneutics in the church.

DEVELOPMENT OF THE CANON
IN THE EARLY CHURCH

The early church engaged in the oral communication of the gospel following the resurrection and ascension of Jesus Christ to heaven. The book of Acts records the early years of the church and reveals that preaching and teaching took place in an oral context. Over time, however, church leaders began to recognize the need to record the events surrounding the life of Jesus. God used several external factors to motivate them to write. First, the church leaders recognized the need to record the events and teachings of Jesus. Because He was the fulfillment of the Old Testament prophecies concerning the Messiah, the church needed to communicate that message to the world. Second, the church recognized the importance of recording the events of Jesus' life while eyewitness accounts were still available. Third, a number of heretical teachings about Jesus began to infiltrate the early church.[1] This infiltration of heresy motivated church leaders to confront error with the truth of the gospel.

As multiple works were written about Jesus, the church responded by discerning which writings were "God-breathed" and then collecting them for the benefit of the church. Several factors motivated them to begin this process. First, church leaders recognized the need to gather all of the inspired documents into one collection. Initially, all of the gospels and early apostolic letters circulated individually (Col 4:16). Ultimately, nine scrolls were needed to contain all of the writings of the New Testament.[2] A new invention—the codex—emerged in the second century and enabled the church to collect the texts of the New Testament into a more user-friendly format. The codex was the first book, and it foreshadowed today's books. The development of the codex provided an impetus for church leaders to determine which books should be included as part of the New Testament canon.[3]

Second, persecution motivated church leaders to clarify which texts were inspired. Believers could receive the death penalty under Roman law for possessing Christian writings. As a result, believers needed to know which writings to protect. Third, as Christianity became more accepted, church leaders needed to determine with certainty which texts passed the test of inspiration and should be included in the canon. A major test was based on authorship: Was it written by an apostle, or an associate of an apostle? Fourth, the internal evidence in the New Testament Scriptures revealed that

1. Gnosticism, Antinomianism, and the teachings of the Judiazers all threatened the early church. The New Testament writers confronted these heresies.
2. Gerald Cowan, "NT Canon" lecture, Fall 1996, Southeastern Seminary, Wake Forest, NC.
3. The Greek word, κανών had a variety of meanings: "reed," "rod," "measuring rod," "rule," "law," or "standard." It may have originated from a Hebrew word meaning "reed." In time, it came to be used for "an instrument of measurement." As such, it was eventually used to refer to "a rule" or "a standard." This usage was further changed in the church to refer to "the rule of faith" or "the rule of truth." Soon after, it came to represent those books that contained the rule of faith and practice for the church. In this context, κανών was used for the ecclesiastically normative or accepted list of books containing rules of faith. Ibid., Cowan, "NT Canon" lecture.

God intended for these texts to be preserved for the benefit of the church. God used the combination of all of these factors to motivate church leaders to both record and preserve the truth about the life, teachings, and ministry of Jesus.[4]

Early church leaders operated with some basic presuppositions about the nature of the biblical texts contained in the canon. First, they affirmed that the Holy Spirit inspired the New Testament texts.[5] In three distinct New Testament texts, the biblical authors affirmed the supernatural, spiritual nature of Scripture (Col 4:16; 1 Tim 5:18; and 2 Pet 3:15–16). These texts affirmed placing the writings of the New Testament alongside those of the Old Testament as inspired Scripture. Second, the early church affirmed that the New Testament texts themselves claimed to be inspired and infallible. While some scoff at the use of internal evidence as a support for the supernatural nature of Scripture, the New Testament texts have much to say about their own revelation, inspiration, and infallibility (Matt 5:17–18; 2 Tim 3:16; and 2 Pet 1:20–21).[6] Third, the early church believed that God preserved an inspired, infallible text. As a result of rigorous prayer and effort, the early church leaders discerned those books whose writing the Holy Spirit had inspired, and as such, were both truthful and consistent in all areas of faith and practice. The doctrine of inspiration guided the church in the identification of the canon.

The doctrine of biblical inerrancy is an outgrowth of our conviction that the Scriptures are both inspired and infallible. We believe that God can reveal Himself in Scripture by "breathing-out" truth to first-century authors and can preserve those writings so that twenty-first-century readers will know their truth today. We will

---

4. There are a number of excellent works on canonicity. See F. F. Bruce, *The Canon of Scripture* (Downers Grove: IVP, 1988); Philip Comfort, ed., *The Origin of the Bible* (Wheaton: Tyndale, 1992, 2003); Robert L. Plummer, *40 Questions about Interpreting the Bible* (Grand Rapids: Kregel, 2010), 57–67; Paul Wegner, *The Journey from Texts to Translations: The Origin and Development of the Bible* (Grand Rapids: Baker, 1999), 101–51.

5. The church embraced a belief in the inspiration of Scripture in the first century, a belief they inherited from their Hebrew heritage.

6. For more on Jesus' view of the inspiration of the Bible, see J. Wenham, *Christ and the Bible*, 3rd ed. (Grand Rapids: Baker, 1994); Daniel L. Akin, "Sermon: What Did Jesus Believe About the Bible?" *SBJT* 5.2 (Summer 2001): 80–88.

leave a thorough explanation of the doctrine of inerrancy for theology books. Be assured, however, that our views concerning hermeneutics and homiletics are based on our conviction that the Bible is inspired, infallible, and inerrant.[7]

THE DEVELOPMENT OF BIBLICAL HERMENEUTICS

The church entered a new phase in its history when it received the admonition of both Paul and Peter that the new "Spirit-given" texts be read and taught in the churches. Churches moved from simply recounting the oral stories about the ministry and teachings of Jesus to being able to read and study them. This reading and studying ushered in a whole new era of biblical proclamation. As a result, the early church soon recognized that pastor-teachers needed formal training to interpret the Scriptures. In response to this need, two schools emerged during the patristic period of church history: Alexandrian and Antiochian.[8] Two different methods of hermeneutics developed

---

7.   See Wayne Grudem, *Systematic Theology* (Grand Rapids: IVP, 1994) for an excellent section on inerrancy. He says in part, "Inerrancy has always been claimed for the first or *original copies of the biblical documents*. Yet none of these survive: we have only copies of copies of what Moses or Paul or Peter wrote. . . . It must be stated that for over 99 percent of the words of the Bible, we *know* what the original manuscript said. Even for many of the verses where there are textual variants (that is, different words in different ancient copies of the same verse), the correct decision is often quite clear, and there are really very few places where the textual variant is both difficult to evaluate and significant in determining the meaning. In the small percentage of cases where there is significant uncertainty about what the original text said, the general sense of the sentence is usually quite clear from the context. . . . For most practical purposes, then, the *current published scholarly texts* of the Hebrew Old Testament and Greek New Testament *are the same as the original manuscripts*. Thus when we say that the original manuscripts were inerrant, we are also implying that over 99 percent of the words in our present manuscripts are also inerrant, for they are exact copies of the originals." Grudem, *Systematic Theology*, 96. See also David Dockery and David Nelson, "Special Revelation," in *A Theology for the Church,* ed. Daniel L. Akin (Nashville: B&H, 2007), 118–74.
8.   The patristic period refers to the life and times of the early church fathers. Most scholars place the dates for the period from the end of the first century to the fifth century AD.

within these schools. Their influence can still be felt in contemporary theological education today.

The Alexandrian School

This school, located in Alexandria, Egypt, began as a place for the instruction of catechumens but evolved into a place for training teachers and preachers.[9] Clement (c. AD 150–215), the famous teacher and writer, administered the school in the second century.[10] His most famous pupil Origen (c. AD 185–254) succeeded him as the school's director. Origen became a significant leader in the church, and his sermons were routinely preserved through transcription for the benefit of believers.[11] Despite his many positive contributions, he adopted the allegorical method of interpretation, which had a negative influence on the early church. Historian Charles Dargan notes, "While he was not, strictly speaking, the originator of this method, he is perhaps more responsible than anyone else for giving it dignity and enabling it to fasten such a tremendous grip on the pulpit of all ages."[12]

As a result of Origen's influence, this school became identified with the allegorical interpretation of the Scriptures. The proponents of allegorical preaching taught that deeper, spiritual meanings were hidden beneath the literal words of Scripture. These hidden meanings contained the truth of Scripture and could be discovered through the study of the biblical texts. Often, those who practiced allegorical interpretation were limited solely by their own imaginations. Unfortunately, allegory became the dominant method of interpretation in the early church.[13]

---

9. Edwin Charles Dargan, *A History of Preaching*, vol. 1 (Grand Rapids: Baker, 1954), 49.
10. Ibid.
11. Ibid., 50.
12. Ibid., 51. Dargan notes that Origen taught a threefold sense of the Scripture: grammatical, moral, and spiritual (or allegorical). However, he believed that the allegorical sense was the best sense.
13. The allegorical approach to preaching remained the primary model throughout the Middle Ages through the ministries of preachers like Bede, Anselm, Bonaventure, and John Tauler. The allegorical method of interpretation

The Antiochian School

This school, located in the city of Antioch, developed later than the school at Alexandria. Its development was significant because it represented a distinctively different approach to the interpretation of Scripture. Rather than adopting the allegorical approach to interpretation, the Antiochian School taught and emphasized the "literal, historical, and grammatical interpretation of Scripture."[14]

It would be years before the interpretive model of the Antiochian School came to the forefront in the preaching of its greatest proponent, John of Antioch (c. AD 347–407). John became the chief preacher in Antioch in AD 386, and his fame as a preacher spread throughout the region. He was so gifted that he was given the name Chrysostom ("the Golden Mouth"). Chrysostom had been trained under Diodorus, and he was committed to the literal interpretation of Scripture. He believed that allegorical preaching was dangerous because it opened the door for faulty interpretation. Dargan notes that while Chrysostom was known on occasion to utilize a "loose" interpretation of Scripture, he did not "allegorize after the Origenistic fashion."[15]

Chrysostom served as the Archbishop of Constantinople for six years, but he ended his ministry in self-imposed exile. His legacy was one of faithful exposition. He was an advocate of a verse-by-verse approach to preaching, so he generally preached homilies: simple sermons that followed the order of the text. As a result, Chrysostom emphasized that the literal meaning of the text was the most important meaning. His strength in preaching lay in his ability to apply the plain meaning of the text to the existing situations of his people and to do so with such oratorical power that people were compelled to listen. Chrysostom urged others to adopt his philosophy of preaching, but the interpretive model developed in Antioch did not become the predominant one during the patristic era. Consequently, almost

---

remains strong today in some faith traditions that continue to reject the need for instruction in biblical hermeneutics.

14. Dargan, *A History of Preaching,* vol. 1, 51.
15. Ibid., 92.

a thousand years would pass before an emphasis upon the literal interpretation of Scripture would reemerge.[16]

The Reformation

Many scholars identify October 31, 1517, as the beginning of the Reformation. That is the day when Martin Luther (1483–1546) nailed his 95 theses to the church door at Wittenberg, Germany. The concept of *sola scriptura* (Scripture alone) was critical in the development of Luther's theology. He was convinced that Scripture alone contains the truth that is necessary to experience God's forgiveness. As a result of his commitment to the authority of Scripture, he was willing to set aside the teaching and traditions of the Roman Catholic Church.

Luther's high view of Scripture led him to adopt a literal approach to the interpretation of biblical texts. His principles of interpretation have influenced hermeneutics for more than 500 years. Luther advocated three principles of interpretation: (1) Scripture is the only form of revelation and must be interpreted by itself; (2) Every Scripture passage has one simple meaning; (3) Some problems exist in Scripture that cannot be resolved.[17]

Luther began with the presupposition that the Bible is the revelation of God. As a result, he challenged the interpretive methods of Rome, which de-emphasized biblical authority in favor of church teaching and tradition. He rejected this approach and affirmed that Scripture is internally consistent, and external sources should not

---

16. The Antiochian model of preaching had few proponents during the Middle Ages. However, in the years leading up to the Reformation, the preaching of men like John Huss, John Wycliffe, and Girolamo Savonarola began to reflect a commitment to teaching the Scriptures in a literal way. This commitment provided an impetus to have the Bible translated into the languages of the common people.

17. It must be noted that Luther was not always faithful in following a literal hermeneutic. Further, out of a struggle to reconcile some of the biblical texts with one another, he placed Hebrews, James, Jude, and Revelation at the end of his translation of the New Testament. He accepted them as Scripture, but had questions about their value in relation to some of the other New Testament books.

overrule its truth. He even translated the Scriptures into German so that they would be available for his people.

The implications of Luther's methodology were significant. In fact, the development and use of the literal method of biblical interpretation, and the subsequent preaching it produced, were key factors in the success of the Protestant Reformation. Luther was not the only one who was utilizing this method to great effect, however. In Switzerland, John Calvin (1509–64) was developing his own method of biblical interpretation. Dargan notes that Calvin "began his career as an expository preacher while yet a young law student at Bruges. . . . It became the delight and the established method of his life."[18] Calvin made it his habit to preach through books of the Bible, and he delivered his expositions in an extemporaneous way. Luther and Calvin changed the way biblical interpretation was taught and practiced, and they modeled a new approach for those who would follow in the Protestant tradition.[19]

The Modern Era

A renewed interest in the literal interpretation of the biblical texts emerged as a result of the Reformation. The popularity of this interpretive model grew as the Bible was translated into different languages and distributed in Europe and beyond. During the seventeenth century, however, a strong conviction regarding the authority and infallibility of Scripture began to erode in some places. The development of German higher criticism would lead to a hermeneutic that abandoned the concept of a literal, biblical historicity based upon the inspiration of Scripture. Years later, as some scholars rejected historical research in favor of studying the psychological impact of texts upon the reader, numerous reader-driven models of hermeneutics

---

18. Dargan, *A History of Preaching,* vol. 1, 381.
19. Luther and Calvin were joined by numerous others in the practice of communicating the literal meaning of the text. Men like John Knox and Balthasar Hubmaier helped establish the literal interpretation of Scripture as one of the defining aspects of both the Magisterial and Radical branches of the Reformation.

appeared.[20] Despite the development of these new approaches, scholars who embraced biblical inspiration and inerrancy remained committed to the literal interpretation of Scripture.

Modern theories of hermeneutics that embrace the literal interpretation of biblical texts operate with a presupposition of biblical inspiration and inerrancy. In the early modern era, William Perkins contributed significantly to the continuing development of the literal interpretation of Scripture. His interpretive method, contained in his work *The Art of Prophesying*, emphasized four key principles: (1) Read the passage out of the canonical Scriptures; (2) Gain a clear understanding of the passage from Scripture itself; (3) Choose several points of doctrine from the natural sense of the passage; (4) Apply the doctrines, rightly collected, to the life and habit of men in plain language.[21]

Perkins' method was built upon four presuppositions. First, he affirmed that God had inspired the canonical Scriptures. As a result, their claims about truth were essential for the church. Second, he affirmed that a literal interpretation of the text was possible and necessary. Like Luther, Perkins held that the literal meaning of the text was the primary meaning of the text. He favored the clear understanding of literal interpretation, while he rejected allegorical interpretation and the error it could produce in the church. Third, he affirmed that God had given the biblical texts to the church to illuminate the rule of faith. He believed teaching doctrine was important for the health of the church. Fourth, Perkins affirmed that biblical doctrines, once discovered, must be explained and applied to the listener. He understood that explanation without application results in a proclamation that is incomplete and ineffective. Also, he understood the importance of sermon delivery. He advocated preaching in plain language so that his listeners could understand the Scriptures.[22]

---

20. For a brief but helpful discussion of reader-driven hermeneutics, see Plummer, 127–29. For a more detailed and technical analysis, see G. Osborne, *The Hermeneutical Spiral*, rev. and expanded (Downers Grove: IVP, 2006), 465–521.

21. Edwin Charles Dargan, *A History of Preaching*, vol. 2 (Grand Rapids: Baker, 1954), 21.

22. M. William Perkins, *The Works of That Famous and Worthy Minister of Christ in the Universitie of Cambridge, M. William Perkins*, 2:762, located in James

William Perkins' interpretive model influenced the evangelical landscape for more than two hundred years. In 1870, John A. Broadus published a seminary textbook entitled *On the Preparation and Delivery of Sermons*. It remains a significant resource in the field of homiletics and was the standard text for many decades. Like Perkins, Broadus emphasized a literal interpretation of the Scriptures. While the majority of his text is focused on the actual preparation of sermons, he did emphasize three steps in the process of interpretation. First, he challenged pastor-teachers to "study the text minutely." He taught his students to study the vocabulary and grammar of every discourse while looking for key theological concepts. Also, he admonished them to study the text in the original languages if they were able to do so.[23] Second, he urged them to "study the text in its immediate connection." Here, he taught that texts always have meaning in the specific context of the paragraph, chapter, and book.[24] Third, Broadus challenged his students to "study the text in its larger connections."[25] He taught them to remember that every text has a larger historical and theological context that must be considered when engaged in the task of exegesis.[26] He taught his students to allow the totality of biblical truth to assist them in discovering the primary meaning of every discourse.[27]

During the twentieth century, the growth of hermeneutics as a field of study has been exponential. The writings of men like John Stott, Walter Kaiser, Gerhard Maier, Sydney Greidanus, and Grant Osborne have continued to provide valuable insights for those who embrace the literal interpretation of Scripture within the context of biblical exposition. As we make our way through the following chapters, we will stand on their shoulders as we examine the principles of hermeneutics and the process of exegesis.

F. Stitzinger, "The History of Expository Preaching," *The Master's Seminary Journal* (Spring 1992): 22.

23. John A. Broadus, *On the Preparation and Delivery of Sermons*, ed. V. L. Stanfield, 4th and rev. ed. (San Francisco: Harper San Francisco, 1979), 24.
24. Ibid.
25. Ibid.
26. Ibid., 25–26.
27. Ibid., 26–27.

CHAPTER 3

THE AUTHOR'S INTENDED MEANING IN A TEXT

In the study of hermeneutics, discovering the author's intended meaning is essential for those who affirm and embrace the literal interpretation of Scripture. As we will note in the following chapters, we believe that we can discover the author's intended meaning through a careful study of a text's content and context. Gordon D. Fee and Douglas Stuart agree: "The aim of good interpretation is not uniqueness; one is not trying to discover what no one else has ever seen before. . . . Unique interpretations are usually wrong. . . . The aim of good interpretation is simple: to get at the 'plain meaning of the text.'"[1] The discovery of the author's intended meaning is the ultimate goal of hermeneutics and exegesis.

DISCOVERING THE LOCATION OF MEANING

Some of the defining issues in the study of contemporary hermeneutics relate to the location of meaning. When we discuss the locus of meaning in a text, we are attempting to answer one primary question: Where does meaning reside in a biblical text? Recent scholarship in hermeneutics provides three options for determining the

---

1. Gordon D. Fee and Douglas Stuart, *How to Read The Bible for All Its Worth,* 3rd ed. (Grand Rapids: Zondervan, 2003), 16.

location of meaning: behind the text, in front of the text, and within the text.[2]

Behind the Text

Since the seventeenth century, proponents of German higher criticism have been suggesting that meaning lies behind the text. Most proponents of this position have not been seeking the author's intended meaning in a particular text. Rather, they have been studying the Bible like any other literary text and seeking to determine, among other things, questions of authorship, dating, and historicity. German higher criticism was birthed in the era of modernity. When Immanuel Kant and other philosophers suggested that one must separate faith and reason, many scholars began to view and study the Bible as they would any other type of literature. As higher criticism developed, its proponents rejected the concept that the Bible is supernaturally inspired in its entirety. At best, it may contain a "canon within a canon"; at worst, it is just another religious book. Because of their rejection of the doctrine of inerrancy, proponents of higher criticism approached biblical stories as myths or legends. Ultimately, proponents of this method claimed that it was the only valid form of hermeneutics.

Some major weaknesses are associated with the practice of German higher criticism. Its primary weakness involves its rejection of inerrancy. As a result, its proponents viewed the study of biblical history as an end in itself. While we might be tempted to ignore everything associated with higher criticism, one primary lesson for hermeneutics and exegesis can be learned from this methodology—history does matter. German higher criticism emphasized the importance of the unique cultural, historical, geographical, and religious contexts behind every biblical text. Context is one of the key elements for determining the purpose of a biblical text, and

---

2.   In his book *Hearing the New Testament*, Joel Green uses this grid to help us understand where the different schools of hermeneutics look for the meaning of the text. His categories are helpful at this point. Joel B. Green, ed., *Hearing the New Testament* (Grand Rapids: Eerdmans, 1995).

understanding the purpose of a text is one of the keys to determining the author's intended meaning.

In Front of the Text

In recent years, some contemporary hermeneutics methodologies have moved the location of meaning in front of the text.[3] These methodological approaches, which embrace a reader-response hermeneutic, have their origins in the work of Friedrich Schleiermacher (1768–1834). Known as the father of modern theology and hermeneutics, Schleiermacher developed an interpretive approach that he called a *Systematized Hermeneutic*. He was intrigued by the interplay between the psychology of the author and the reader and its implications for interpretation. Martin Heidegger (1889–1976), who taught alongside Rudolph Bultman at Marburg, developed a system of hermeneutics based upon this theory that he called the *Hermeneutical Circle*. He believed the reader had as much influence on the text as the text had on the reader.

Hans-Georg Gadamer (1900–2002), one of Heidegger's students, further developed this theory and rejected the notion of authorial intention altogether. Instead, he believed that the reader and the text were both autonomous. The reader interpreted the text as he interacted with it in the Hermeneutical Circle. Following Gadamer, the structuralist movement rejected surface interpretations of the text in favor of deeper hidden meanings.[4] Today, there are numerous other critical methodologies that locate meaning in front of the text: rhetorical, linguistic, canonical, liberation, and feminist, just to name a few. All of these methodologies emphasize a reader-response approach and locate meaning in the mind of the interpreter.[5]

---

3. For an excellent, but brief, discussion of modern hermeneutics and the key players, see David Dockery, *Biblical Interpretation Then and Now* (Grand Rapids: Baker, 1992), 161–83.
4. The Structuralist Movement was developed through the work of men like Ferdinand de Saussure, Charles Pierce, Paul Ricoeur, and Jacques Derrida. Once again, the influence of the Alexandrian School can be seen.
5. Joel Green in *Hearing the New Testament* and others believe this methodological pluralism is beneficial to biblical interpretation. This method of

Those who locate meaning in front of the text embrace several presuppositions. First, they see the Bible primarily as a literary work. Second, they place a priority upon the reader's response to a text. As a result, they reject, or at best minimize, the notion of authorial intention or the ability on the part of the interpreter to discover it. Third, they accept the probability of multiple meanings within the text, and as a result, they reject the notion that every text contains one primary meaning.

There are numerous weaknesses associated with this approach to hermeneutics. Its primary weakness results from its de-emphasis of authorial intention and its willingness to locate meaning within the mind of the reader. Ultimately, it elevates human experience above biblical revelation. It would be tempting to dismiss these methodologies out of hand, but there is a lesson to be learned here: genre is significant in interpretation. Proponents of methodologies that place the locus of meaning in front of the text recognize the importance of the shape of Scripture. They understand that rhetorical elements are at work in every biblical text. While we would disagree with their interpretations, we will discover in chapters 5 and 6 that the author's choice of genre informs our interpretation of biblical texts.

In the Text

While many have tried to locate meaning behind the text or in front of the text, we believe that the locus of meaning resides within the text. Our position is defined by two basic presuppositions. First, there is one primary meaning in every biblical text—the author's. Second, the author's intended meaning can be discovered by utilizing the proper rules of semantics and syntax.[6]

In 1967, E. D. Hirsch wrote a seminal work entitled *Validity in Interpretation*.[7] He was one of the first to construct a systematic rebuttal to the presuppositions of those tied to Schleiermacher, including

---

interpretation has become the predominant method for adherents to the New Homiletic. We would strongly disagree.

6. Semantics refers to the basic meanings of words, while syntax refers to the way words relate to one another in context.
7. E. D. Hirsch Jr., *Validity in Interpretation* (New Haven, CT: Yale Univ. Press, 1967).

Heidegger, Gadamer, Derrida, and a host of other literary scholars. Hirsch reaffirmed that the author of any text, including any biblical text, has semantic authority over the text. In other words, he is in charge of determining what words to use while writing and how to construct them into sentences, paragraphs, and discourses. Since meaning is unchanging and reproducible, interpreters may discover the author's intended meaning within the text with a high degree of validity.

Hirsch emphasized that every text has both meaning and signifi-cance. While it is true that a text can only have one meaning, it may have different levels of significance for the reader. For Hirsch, the key to determining meaning, then, is found in the text's intrinsic genre. Once the interpreter has located the appropriate language clues, he can arrive at a valid interpretation of the author's intended meaning.[8]

Six attributes define this approach to the locus of meaning. First, it maintains a high view of the inspiration and inerrancy of the Scripture. It acknowledges that God is the source of truth and has spoken to man in an understandable way. Second, it accepts the validity of seeking the author's intended meaning. It presupposes that God enabled men to record His truth in a way that could be inter-preted and applied to the lives of people. Third, it acknowledges that discourse analysis is crucial for discovering the author's intended meaning.[9] As we will see, the biblical authors communicated their messages using different styles and structures of language.

---

8. Ibid., 78–79. Hirsch claims that the key to interpretation is discovering the "intrinsic genre" of every text. Once the type of writing has been discovered, certain linguistic elements always provide clues to the author's meaning. Joining an understanding of genre with an understanding of the author's syn-tax can lead the interpreter to a valid interpretation of the author's intended meaning.

9. For a brief but helpful explanation of the recent development of discourse analysis and text linguistics, see Grant R. Osborne, *The Hermeneutical Spiral*, 2nd ed. (Downers Grove: IVP, 2006), 150–53. He restricts the purpose of dis-course analysis "to the process of determining the structure and meaning inherent in texts and intended by the author" (150–51). One should also con-sult these excellent articles: David Allen, "Preaching a Text-Driven Sermon," in *Text-Driven Preaching*, ed. Daniel L. Akin, David L. Allen, and Ned L. Matthews (Nashville: B&H, 2010), 101–34; David Alan Black, "Exegesis for the Text-Driven Sermon," in id., 135–61. Discourse analysis will be used in

Fourth, the approach of locating meaning within the text recognizes the importance of context for interpretation. As we will discover in chapter 8, understanding the context in which a text was written is pivotal for proper interpretation. Fifth, this approach makes a legitimate distinction between meaning (what the author intended to say to his original audience) and significance (the implications of biblical propositions for contemporary readers). Sixth, it affirms that meaning can be discovered and communicated to others with a high level of validity. As a result, pastor-teachers can preach the word with confidence and authority.

UNDERSTANDING THE TWO HORIZONS

There are three predominant positions in hermeneutics related to the locus of meaning: behind the text, in the text, and in front of the text. As we have noted, we believe that the author's intended meaning is located within the content of the text. However, we must acknowledge that every author lived within a context unique to him. For instance, David wrote during the time of the fledgling monarchy of Israel; Daniel wrote as a captive in Babylon; Paul wrote during the time of the Romans. Each of these men lived within a unique cultural context. As interpreters, we must begin by attempting to understand the author's individual context. In hermeneutics, the cultural context of the author is called the "first horizon."

When we study the Bible, we must acknowledge that our cultural context differs from those of the authors of Scripture. While it is incumbent upon us to study the cultural context of the "first horizon," we must at the same time acknowledge our own context. Scholars in hermeneutics call the context of the reader the "second horizon" (see diagram 3.1).[10]

---

this textbook to determine the structure of a text and the meaning intended by the author through the way he uses language to shape and form a discourse.

10. John R. Stott acknowledges this concept when he writes, "A true sermon bridges the gulf between the biblical and the modern worlds, and must be equally earthed in both." John R. W. Stott, *Between Two Worlds* (Grand Rapids: Eerdmans, 1982), 10.

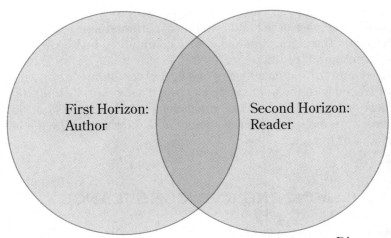

Diagram 3.1

In hermeneutics, the point of connection between the two horizons is the biblical text. As you can see in our second diagram, the biblical text has its origins in the historical context of its author. As readers, the only access we have to the author's intended meaning is the biblical text itself (see diagram 3.2).

Navigating between the two horizons is challenging. In his book *The Two Horizons*, Anthony Thiselton notes,

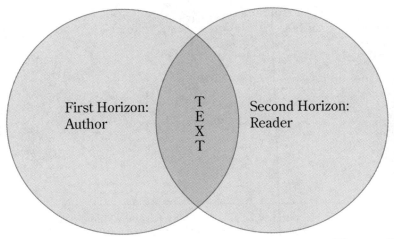

Diagram 3.2

To pay attention to the historical particularities and historical conditionedness of the text remains of paramount importance. . . . However, the modern reader is also conditioned by his own place in history and tradition. . . . Even if, for the moment, we leave out of account the modern reader's *historical* conditionedness, we are still faced with the undeniable fact that if a text is to be *understood* there must occur an engagement between the two sets of horizons . . . namely those of the ancient text and those of the modern reader or hearer.[11]

MEANING AND SIGNIFICANCE

As we continue to develop our diagram, you will notice that we have added the potential loci of meaning posited by the different schools of interpretation (see diagram 3.3).

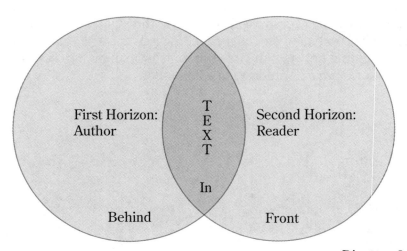

Diagram 3.3

---

11. Anthony C. Thiselton, *The Two Horizons* (Grand Rapids: Eerdmans, 1980), 15. Thiselton attributes the concept of the two horizons to Hans-George Gadamer, the German scholar in the field of philosophical hermeneutics, who believed meaning was discovered within the second horizon as the reader lives in "dialogue" with the text.

As you can see, those who believe that meaning is located *behind* the text, limit their study to the first horizon. Although the text itself is located in the first horizon, proponents of this position do not believe that the author's intended meaning can be discovered through a literal interpretation of a text. Rather, they are committed to the study of the history that influenced the development of the text. Those who believe that meaning is located in front of the text limit their study to the second horizon. They, too, reject the notion that a literal interpretation of a text can reveal the author's intended meaning. As a result, they locate meaning within the experience of the reader and his or her personal responses to the text.

We believe, however, that the author's intended meaning can be discovered *in* the text through a literal approach to interpretation. As we noted above, we believe that an interpreter can discover the author's intended meaning by applying the principles of hermeneutics to the process of exegesis. Before we begin to define and describe this process in the following chapters, however, we must clarify what we mean by the terms "meaning" and "significance." As our expanded diagram now demonstrates, meaning is located within the first horizon, and significance is located within the second horizon (see diagram 3.4).

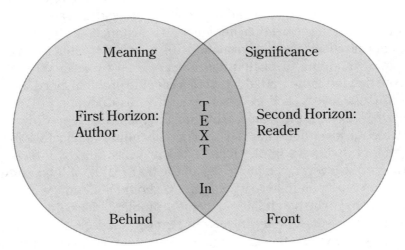

Diagram 3.4

The first goal of hermeneutics is to answer the question, "What is the author's intended meaning?" The answer to this question is located in the first horizon, within the author's text. Since we cannot engage the author about his writings, the biblical text itself must provide the answer to our question. As E. D. Hirsch has reassured us, we can arrive at a valid interpretation of the author's intended meaning if we follow the grammatical and rhetorical guidelines for understanding a written text.

When we speak of the significance of a text, we are dealing with the second horizon. The very first audience of readers shared a cultural context with the author of the text. As such, the author's intended meaning had greater clarity for his original readers. Some of those first readers may have also had the opportunity to discuss the meaning of specific passages with the author himself. As time passed, however, the readers of Scripture drifted further and further away from the historical context of the author. As the readers' culture changed throughout the centuries, the application of the author's intended meaning may have taken on new significances. Remember, the author has one intended meaning, which is true for all people in all places at all times. The significance or application of the text is the factor that may vary.

As people who live in the second horizon of our own twenty-first-century context, our application of certain biblical passages may differ from that of the original audience. For instance, in 1 Corinthians 8, Paul provided the Corinthians with instruction concerning the practice of eating meat that had been offered to idols. When Paul wrote that letter, he was addressing a specific problem faced by first-century believers. We are not faced with this dilemma in Western culture. As a result, Paul's particular admonition regarding meat offered to idols does not have a corresponding application for us (although believers in other parts of our world may still face that problem). However, the main idea of the text (MIT) still has significance in our contemporary context: we should not engage in activities that have the potential to become stumbling blocks in the life of another believer. As you can see, the text continues to have meaning for us today, while its significance for our horizon may differ from that of the original audience. When we speak of significance, we are attempting to accomplish the second goal of hermeneutics, which is to answer this question: "What is the significance of the author's intended meaning?" At the level of application, we must exercise great care and discernment.

To this point, we have identified the options regarding the locus of meaning, defined the two horizons, discussed the relationship between the author, text, and reader, and clarified the ideas of meaning and significance. We must make one final addition to our diagram so that it will reflect the totality of issues related to the process of hermeneutics and exegesis. As you study the final diagram, you will see three key words written beneath the circles (see diagram 3.5).

Interaction of Two Horizons

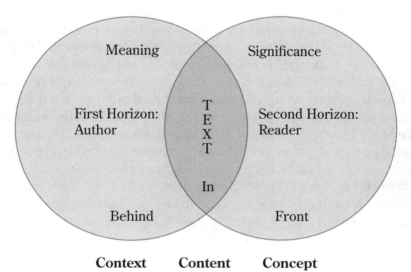

Diagram 3.5

The three words reflect the terms we will use to shape our understanding of exegesis in the following chapters. We have placed the word "context" under the circle that denotes the first horizon of the author. Here, we are acknowledging that the author's cultural, historical, geographical, and theological contexts influenced both his life and his message. We have placed the word "content" under the area of overlap between the two horizons. Here, we are acknowledging that the author's intended meaning must be discovered within the content of his writings. Finally, we have placed the word "concept" under the circle that denotes the second horizon of the reader.

Here, we are acknowledging that it is the task of the interpreter, using the principles of hermeneutics and the practice of exegesis, to discover the author's intended meaning and its significance for the contemporary audience.

As we close this chapter we must add a final and important word. We recognize that interpretation without presuppositions is impossible. We readily concede that the reader-response approach is at least correct at this point. We all unavoidably bring presuppositions, biases, and preconceived ideas to the text. Kevin Vanhoozer rightly notes, "No one reads in a vacuum. Every reading is a contextualized reading."[12] However, we are not bound to or enslaved by our presuppositions. They can be critiqued, altered, and even radically changed. An awareness of our presuppositions is an excellent starting point for doing honest, even humble, hermeneutics. Allowing them to be challenged is essential for doing good hermeneutics and exegesis. We are fallen and flawed. We do not see clearly or read a text with perfect comprehension. However, though we are fallen, we bear the divine image. Though we are sinful, we have the Spirit and are being renewed. With the assistance of the Spirit[13] (His part) and by the means of proven principles of hermeneutics and exegesis (our part), we can grasp genuinely and truly, though not exhaustively, the wonderful truths of the Scriptures deposited by the Divine Author through human instruments. To consider our part, we now move to the next chapter.

---

12. Kevin Vanhoozer, *Is There a Meaning in This Text?* (Grand Rapids: Zondervan, 1998), 382. This work is superb though quite technical. Chapter 7 on "Reforming the Reader" is especially relevant at this point of our discussion. His thesis of "Interpretation as discipleship" (431–41) is essential reading for all who wish to be faithful interpreters of the Scriptures. See also Rob Plummer, *40 Questions About Interpreting the Bible* (Grand Rapids: Kregel, 2010), 127–41.

13. Plummer, *40 Questions About Interpreting the Bible,* 143–50.

CHAPTER 4

BASIC PRINCIPLES OF HERMENEUTICS

I n chapter 2, we traced the development of hermeneutics through-out the history of the church. As we have seen, a significant amount of hermeneutical research is available from scholars who affirm and practice the literal interpretation of Scripture. This scholarship has led to the development of a set of principles that can serve as the foun-dation for sound biblical exegesis. In this chapter, we will define and explain our 10 principles of biblical hermeneutics. These principles will serve as the foundation for our exegesis in the following chapters.

At this point remembering our definition of hermeneutics may be helpful: the proper use of the principles of interpretation to discover the author's intended meaning of a biblical text, with a goal of apply-ing that meaning to a contemporary audience. The following prin-ciples of interpretation are designed to safeguard our exegesis as we seek to discover the author's intended meaning and its significance for our contemporary audience.

THE BIBLE IS THE INSPIRED, INFALLIBLE, AND INERRANT WORD OF GOD[1]

As we noted in chapter 2, the early church had a strong convic-tion about the inspiration and infallibility of the Scriptures. This

---

1. We gladly affirm as a definition and description "The Chicago Statement on Biblical Inerrancy" that was formulated in 1978.

conviction is important because our presuppositions about the Bible affect our interpretation. Gerhard Maier agrees when he states, "The starting point for Hermeneutics must be revelation."[2] Like Maier, we believe the Bible is unique among human writings and must be studied with that in mind.

In his text, Maier affirms some basic truths about the unique task of studying Scripture. First, he states that the Scriptures, rather than our personal experiences, must be our starting point in hermeneutics.[3] In other words, we must begin by asking, "What does this text mean?" rather than, "What does this text mean to me?" Second, Maier states that we must set aside any presuppositions that would hinder us from hearing the biblical texts as anything but what they are—the very words of God.[4] Our failure to do this will affect our ability to discern the author's MIT (Main Idea of the Text).[5] Third, he states that we must allow revelation to shape our theology rather than basing our theology on personal opinion.[6] The failure to allow revelation to shape theology always leads to a divergence of interpretation and the prevalence of doctrinal error. We must approach the Bible with a very clear understanding that it is a unique, divinely inspired, and divinely preserved book. As a result, we will strive to teach it correctly, knowing that it contains "everything required for life and godliness" (2 Pet 1:3).

THE PRIMARY GOAL OF HERMENEUTICS IS THE DISCOVERY OF THE AUTHOR'S INTENDED MEANING

As we discovered in chapter 3, the phrase "author's intended meaning" is one that appears with regularity in the study of hermeneutics. In essence, it affirms our conviction that the ultimate meaning of any passage of Scripture is that which the author intended. We believe

---

2.   Gerhard Maier, *Biblical Hermeneutics* (Wheaton, IL: Crossway, 1994), 34.
3.   Ibid., 33.
4.   Ibld., 34.
5.   This topic is discussed in detail in chapter 10.
6.   Maier, *Biblical Hermeneutics,* 36.

the author's MIT can be discovered through the careful study of the words (semantics), grammar (syntax), and style (genre) that the author used to write his text, as well as through our understanding of the cultural, historical, geographical, and theological contexts that influenced his life.

Fee and Stuart agree with this principle by noting that "the only proper control for hermeneutics is to be found in the *original* intent of the biblical text."[7] In other words, the author's message of truth can be discovered through the literal interpretation of their words, sentences, paragraphs, and books.[8] The practice of this principle will reveal the author's intended meaning and will protect the pastor-teacher from faulty interpretations.

THE AUTHOR'S INTENDED MEANING IN A BIBLICAL TEXT IS FOUND WITHIN COMPLETE UNITS OF THOUGHT

The resurgence of expository preaching has resulted in the development of numerous resources to assist with the process of interpretation. Many of these resources emphasize the study of Hebrew and Greek, which is essential for becoming skilled in the practice of hermeneutics, exegesis, and homiletics.[9] This emphasis upon the original languages has led some interpreters to place a greater importance upon the individual meanings of Hebrew or Greek words than upon the context in which they are found. Indeed, some pastor-teachers interpret entire texts based upon the meaning of a single word. This type of "word-driven" interpretation is flawed. It may result either in missing the author's MIT completely or in rede-

---

7.   Gordon D. Fee and Douglas Stuart, *How to Read the Bible for All Its Worth,* 3rd ed. (Grand Rapids: Zondervan, 2003), 29.

8.   While many passages of Scripture contain figurative language, the majority of Scripture passages should be interpreted literally.

9.   While we believe that the study of Hebrew and Greek is critical for good interpretation, we realize that not every pastor-teacher has the opportunity to study the original languages. For those who cannot, it is essential to use good study resources to gain access to the rich information that can be gleaned from the original languages.

fining theology itself—both of which are unacceptable in biblical interpretation.

As we begin to explain the process of exegesis in chapter 5, understanding this principle is important: the individual words of biblical texts have meaning within sentences, paragraphs, and books.[10] Dictionaries reveal that words may be used in a variety of ways. A word's meaning is determined by its relationship to other words within the context of sentences and paragraphs. The author's choice and combination of specific words becomes his vehicle for delivering content. While understanding the meanings of individual Hebrew and Greek words is valuable in the exegetical process, their ultimate meaning in any biblical text is derived from the context in which they are found.

As early as 1961, scholars were recognizing the danger of using individual word meanings to interpret biblical texts. James Barr wrote the seminal text opposing this type of interpretation. In *The Semantics of Biblical Language*, Barr argued that any approach is flawed that places a higher emphasis upon individual word meanings than the meanings of the words in their written context. He argued further that reading too much theology into individual words was dangerous, primarily because the author may have chosen the words not for their theological meaning, but because they were the best words available to him at the time. Furthermore, Barr reminds us that some words have theological meanings solely because of their usage within the context of individual passages and books. He challenges interpreters to let the text speak without importing their own prejudices into the text.[11] Barr's position is extremely influential. He laid the foundation for all those who would emphasize the importance of interpreting words within their grammatical context.

---

10. Fee and Stuart add, "Indeed this is the *crucial* task in exegesis. . . . Essentially, *literary context* means that words only have meaning in sentences, and for the most part biblical sentences only have meaning in relation to preceding and succeeding sentences" (*How to Read the Bible for All Its Worth*, 27).

11. James Barr, *The Semantics of Biblical Language* (Oxford: Oxford Univ. Press, 1961). Also see Moisés Silva, *Biblical Words and Their Meaning: An Introduction to Lexical Semantics* (Grand Rapids: Zondervan, 1983).

THE AUTHOR'S INTENDED MEANING IN A BIBLICAL TEXT IS ALWAYS DISCOVERED WITHIN ITS OWN UNIQUE GRAMMATICAL CONTENT

Eisegesis is one of the results of poor exegesis. Eisegesis is the practice of reading one's presuppositions and opinions into a biblical text, rather than allowing the text to reveal its own meaning. Interpreters may fall into this trap for a number of reasons. First, they may lack theological training. Without the benefit of instruction, they may scan their concordances for key words and then use selected verses to support a particular topic they plan to discuss. Second, some interpreters may have been exposed to a steady diet of topical preaching. This type of preaching often allows personal preference to drive sermon development at the expense of the meaning of a biblical text. In this approach, verses are chosen and utilized on the basis of perceived content rather than actual context. Third, personal ideology may drive some interpreters more than biblical theology. These interpreters may use individual verses or parts of verses to support their pet positions, despite the lack of biblical support. This type of interpretation, and the preaching it produces, is damaging both to the Scriptures and the church.

We, on the other hand, want to be interpreters who are committed to "correctly teaching the word of truth" (2 Tim 2:15). We are committed to allowing the text to reveal the author's intended meaning as we apply the principles of hermeneutics to the process of exegesis. For this to happen, we must be committed to understanding both the *content* and the *context* of every biblical text. As we will discover in the following chapters, our capacity to discover the author's MIT is tied directly to our understanding of both content and context.

When we think about the grammatical content of a passage, we are focusing our attention upon the literary elements that the author chose to frame his discussion. These elements include the author's choice of specific words and the way he combined them into sentences and paragraphs, as well as the literary genre he selected (i.e., prose, poetry, historical narrative, Wisdom literature, apocalyptic).[12] When we consider this, we can see the dangers of lifting individual clauses or verses out of their specific literary and grammatical construction—it almost insures that the interpreter will misunderstand the content of the passage. While the notion of investigating the grammatical content of a biblical passage may frighten the newcomer to exegesis, this task is essential for discovering the author's MIT.

THE AUTHOR'S INTENDED MEANING IN A BIBLICAL TEXT IS ALWAYS DISCOVERED WITHIN ITS OWN UNIQUE CULTURAL CONTEXT

When we think about the context of a text, we are focusing our attention upon a number of factors that existed when the author recorded his particular content for a particular audience. Some interpreters falsely assume that their work is complete as soon as they have studied the grammatical aspects of a text. To stop at this point, however, is to leave the task of interpretation unfinished. Certainly, understanding the content of a text is important for discovering the author's MIT. However, the biblical authors did not write in a historical vacuum. Rather, they addressed the specific needs of their own day. As a result, understanding the significance of the author's personal context, as best as we can, is important. Failing to understand the context of a text may lead the interpreter to misinterpret the author's content altogether.

Understanding the culture, history, geography, and theology of the writers and their audiences is critical for discovering the historical

---

12. Sidney Greidanus expands our understanding of the importance of this aspect of study when he identifies the key elements for discovering the grammatical content of a passage. He states, "In literary interpretation (broadly conceived as inclusive of grammatical concerns) one commonly raises questions concerning the text's genre of literature, rhetorical devices, figures of speech, grammar, syntax, etc., in order to determine the meaning of words in their immediate context and, ultimately, in the context of the whole document and of the entire Bible" (51).

particularity of biblical texts.[13] Bernard Lonergan states, "The context of the book is the author's *opera omnia*, his life and times, the state of the question in his day, his problems, prospective readers, scope and aim."[14] To devalue these contextual elements is to demean the author's content. As a result, the interpreter must spend the time necessary for discovering the cultural context of the biblical text.[15]

THE AUTHOR'S INTENDED MEANING IN A BIBLICAL TEXT SHOULD BE INTERPRETED LITERALLY, UNLESS THE USE OF FIGURATIVE LANGUAGE SUGGESTS OTHERWISE

Hermeneutics has a famous axiom: "If the plain sense makes good sense, seek no other sense." When we speak about the literal meaning of a text, we are referring simply to the literal interpretation of the words as they are joined together into sentences and paragraphs. In the majority of biblical texts, the authors used plain language to reveal God, communicate His truth, and recount His acts in history. As a result, we can assume that "the writers were normal, rational people who communicated in the same basic ways that we do," only

---

13. Fee and Stuart emphasize this idea when they write, "The historical context, which will differ from book to book, has to do with . . . the *time* and *culture* of the author and his readers, that is, the geographical, topographical, and political factors that are relevant to the author's setting" (*How to Read the Bible*, 26). Osborne rightly notes, "Unless we grasp the whole before attempting to dissect the parts, interpretation is doomed from the start" (Grant R. Osborne, *The Hermeneutical Spiral*, 2nd ed. [Downers Grove: IVP, 2006], 37).
14. Bernard Lonergan, *Method in Theology* (New York: Seabury, 1971), 163.
15. While a text's unique historical context cannot be ignored, it should never drive your exegesis entirely. Osborne calls the historical information "preliminary material" that becomes a filter through which individual texts may be interpreted. See his brief but helpful section in *The Hermeneutical Spiral*, 37–39. The historical context, when it can be conceived, should complement our detailed exegesis. Therefore, the preliminary historical information may be corrected or modified through detailed exegesis.

in different languages and historical contexts.[16] When we study their writings, consequently, we can interpret them literally.

For instance, Moses recounted a pivotal event from his life in Exod 2:11–15. On a trip through Egypt, he saw an Egyptian beating a Hebrew. In his anger, he killed the Egyptian and buried him in the desert. After news of his crime reached Pharaoh, Moses escaped to Midian. As we study this historical narrative, there is no reason to read some deeper, "spiritual" meaning into the text. This account has a plain and simple meaning—namely that Moses murdered an Egyptian, buried him in the desert to hide the evidence, and when his crime was discovered, he ran for his life. Remember, when you are interpreting a biblical text, if the plain sense makes good sense, seek no other sense. This observation does not negate the intriguing issues of *sensus plenoir* or Christological hermeneutics. Both will be addressed in this work. However, accepting the plain sense is a fundamental principle of good hermeneutics.

When you read a text and the literal sense is confusing, you may be encountering figurative language. The biblical authors used figurative language to help increase our understanding of concepts that are difficult to explain or illustrate. Figurative language associates "a concept with a pictorial or analogous representation of its meaning in order to add richness to the statement."[17] Lawrence Perrine states, "On first examination, it might seem absurd to say one thing and mean another. But we all do it and with good reason. We do it because we can say what we want to say more vividly and forcefully by figures than we can by saying it directly. Also, we can say more in figurative statement than we can in literal statement. Figures of speech are another way of adding extra dimensions to language.[18] Figurative language helps make the "abstract concrete."[19]

When a writer incorporates figurative language, often he is using the connotation of a word or words in order to provide a broader

---

16. Howard G. Hendricks and William D. Hendricks, *Living by the Book* (Chicago: Moody Press, 2007), 265.

17. Osborne, *The Hermeneutical Spiral,* 122.

18. Laurence Perrine, *Literature: Structure, Sound, and Sense,* 2nd ed. (New York: Harcourt, Brace, Jovanovich, 1974), 610. Perrine states that rhetoricians have classified as many as 250 separate figures of speech.

19. Ibid., 617.

understanding of the concept he is addressing. The "connotation" of a word is "what it suggests beyond what it expresses: its overtones of meaning."[20] Over time, a word may acquire these connotations by its "past history and associations, by the way and the circumstances in which it has been used."[21] We are familiar with the way words acquire new levels of meaning in our own culture. Years ago, the word "hot" meant that something was "warm to the touch." That meaning is the denotation of the word. In recent years, however, "hot" has become a word that describes the enhanced quality of a particular object—like one's car. As a result, "hot" has a new connotation. Our understanding of the connotation of the words will help us discover the author's MIT when examining poetry, wisdom literature, and some apocalyptic literature.

Connotation is especially important to poets. It allows them to explore and enrich their content, and to do so with an economy of words. Consider one of the connotations that David used in writing Psalm 23. He wrote, "The LORD is my shepherd." When we read this, we immediately recognize that the literal sense does not make good sense. Since God is a spirit, He cannot be a literal shepherd. David is using the connotation of a shepherd to give us an important metaphor for God. Like a shepherd, He provides ("there is nothing I lack"), He cares ("He lets me lie down in green pastures"), He directs ("He leads me beside quiet waters"), He encourages ("He renews my life"), and He guides ("He leads me along the right paths for His name's sake"). All of these traits are connotations we derive from our understanding of the word "shepherd." When you are interpreting a biblical text and the literal sense does not make good sense, most likely you are encountering figurative language.

Interpreters must exercise great caution when interpreting the figures of speech found in Scripture, however. As Grant Osborne notes, "The major difficulty in interpreting figures of speech is that languages develop their associative relations independently; therefore, metaphorical language in Hebrew or Greek often does not correspond at all to English expressions."[22] As a result, we must be ready to study the historical and inner-canonical contexts of the text so that

---

20. Ibid., 585.
21. Ibid.
22. Osborne, *The Hermeneutical Spiral*, 123.

we can discern the way the author uses the figure of speech. Once we discover that use, we must be careful that our explanation of that idiom in our own language is faithful to the text under consideration.

THE AUTHOR'S INTENDED MEANING IN A BIBLICAL TEXT SHOULD BE INFORMED BY THE WRITINGS OF OTHER BIBLICAL AUTHORS ON THE SAME CONCEPTS

As we study the totality of Scripture, we will encounter many reoccurring theological concepts. After all, the Bible is a progressive revelation of God's redemptive purposes in the world. As a result, we should expect to encounter these theological concepts as they are revealed and developed in the Scriptures.

When we study specific biblical texts, we must be aware of any theological concepts developed by the author and their purposes within the overall structure of his text. Because the purpose of every biblical book differs, no two authors may deal with the same theological concepts. If they do use the same concepts, they may not deal with them to the same degree or for the same purpose. Because an author may not completely explain every theological concept he mentions, we must be prepared to let other biblical texts inform our understanding when they share the same theological concepts. This type of interpretation is what we mean by inner-canonical hermeneutics. Gerhard Maier refers to this process as "harmonization." He states,

> If the statement is correct that God spoke by the prophets of the Old Testament, by his Son, and by the apostles . . . and if it is moreover true that revelation has God as its one de facto author . . . ; then it is in fact the duty of the interpreter to do justice to *this* unity of the entire Bible. That is, it is his duty to attempt to demonstrate as far as *possible* . . . this unity in faith and the veracity that the Holy Spirit grants. We arrive here at a point, then, where we see that the inspiration and unity of Scripture, together with the interpreter's stand toward . . . the faith, shape the direction that interpretation will take.[23]

---

23. Maier, *Biblical Hermeneutics,* 207. He further states, "That person who cannot affirm the inspiration and unity of Scripture, who demands that the interpreter

In other words, we begin with a presupposition that a unity of theological concepts within the Scriptures exists, and we must allow our understanding of those concepts to influence our interpretation of individual texts. As a result, adopting the following guidelines will help us understand and teach theological concepts.

First, the interpretation of shorter texts is always influenced by our interpretation of longer texts that share the same theological concept. Unfortunately, many an error in doctrine has resulted from an interpreter who built a whole theology on a brief text (often taken out of its context), while ignoring the clear teaching of a lengthier text on the same concept. For instance, some people could use 1 Cor 15:29 to substantiate the practice of baptizing "for the dead." This verse states, "Otherwise what will they do who are being baptized for the dead? If the dead are not raised at all, then why are people baptized for them?" In this text, Paul references baptism for the dead as evidence for the resurrection of believers. Because this practice is mentioned only once in the entire New Testament, however, it would be unwise to build a theology around it.

Second, interpreters must distinguish between "descriptive" and "prescriptive" texts in Scripture. When we speak about a text being "descriptive," we are saying that it is describing the current condition of a person or thing. In 1 Cor 15:29, Paul is describing a type of baptism that some early believers were practicing. When we speak about a text being "prescriptive," we are saying that it prescribes a specific course of action or condition of attitude. In the example above, Paul is not prescribing this practice as a function of the church because it is not taught anywhere else in Paul's writings or those of the other New Testament authors. Understanding the difference between descriptive and prescriptive texts is helpful here. Fee

---

be an ostensibly 'neutral' scientist who eschews the faith—that person likewise labors under factors that shape his interpretation!" Vanhoozer adds, "My thesis is that the "fuller meaning" of Scripture—the meaning associated with divine authorship—emerges only at the level of the whole canon" (Kevin Vanhoozer, *Is There a Meaning in This Text?* [Grand Rapids: Zondervan, 1998], 264).

and Stuart add clarity to the distinction between prescriptive and descriptive texts when they state, "Unless Scripture explicitly tells us we must do something, what is only narrated or described does not function in a normative way—unless it can be demonstrated on other grounds that the author intended it to function in this way."[24]

Third, the interpretation of obscure biblical texts should be influenced by texts more fully developed on the same subject. Clearly, 1 Cor 15:29 is challenging to interpret. Paul is not defending or affirming this practice, despite his use of it to argue for the resurrection believers will share with Christ.[25] Fee and Stuart state, "We do not know and probably never will know *who* was doing it, *for whom* they were doing it, and *why* they were doing it. The details and the meaning of the practice, therefore, are probably forever lost to us."[26] Building a theology of baptizing for the dead on the basis of this one verse would be an interpretive mistake. As interpreters, we should choose substantial biblical texts, rather than obscure ones, to inform our theology and enhance our teaching.

THE AUTHOR'S INTENDED MEANING IN A BIBLICAL TEXT MAY HAVE A FULLER MEANING, BUT THAT MEANING CAN ONLY BE DETERMINED ON THE BASIS OF SUBSEQUENT BIBLICAL REVELATION AND THE WHOLE CANON

As interpreters, we are searching for the author's intended meaning in every Old and New Testament text. Since God's revelation is progressive, we must acknowledge that the Old Testament writers did not have the benefit of New Testament revelation. Granted, God allowed certain Old Testament authors like Daniel and Isaiah to have glimpses into the future outworking of His redemptive plan, but they did not have all of the particulars. Paul describes this truth in Eph 3:1–7,

> For this reason, I, Paul, the prisoner of Christ Jesus on behalf of you Gentiles—you have heard, haven't you, about the

---

24. Fee and Stuart, *How to Read the Bible for All Its Worth,* 118–19.
25. Ibid., 68–70.
26. Ibid., 69.

administration of God's grace that He gave to me for you? The *mystery* was made known to me by revelation, as I have briefly written above. By reading this you are able to understand my insight about the *mystery* of the Messiah. *This was not made known to people in other generations as it is now revealed to His holy apostles and prophets by the Spirit*: the Gentiles are co-heirs, members of the same body, and partners of the promise in Christ Jesus through the gospel. I was made a servant of this gospel by the gift of God's grace that was given to me by the working of His power [emphasis ours].

Paul stated that the mystery of the gospel and its global application were revealed to him after the ascension of Jesus. We cannot of our own accord, therefore, force New Testament revelation about the gospel upon Old Testament texts. Walter Kaiser says it this way, "It is a mark of *eisegesis*, not *exegesis*, to borrow freight that appears chronologically later in the text and to transport it back and unload it on an earlier passage simply because both or all the passages involved share the same canon."[27]

However, the Bible is one book with one divine author. It does tell one great story framed in a "grand redemptive narrative." All the "little narratives" have their place in the "big narrative." Further, some Old Testament passages are specifically declared in the New Testament to have some level of "fuller meaning." In the field of hermeneutics, we refer to this level as the *sensus plenior* of the text. Greidanus writes, "In the history of interpretation this phenomenon of meanings beyond the author's original intention has been called the *sensus plenior*, the fuller sense."[28] Raymond Brown defines *sensus plenior* as "that additional, deeper meaning, intended by God but not clearly intended by the human author, which is seen to exist in the words of a biblical text (or group of texts, or even a whole book) when they are studied in the light of further revelation or development in the understanding of revelation."[29]

---

27.   Walter C. Kaiser Jr., *Toward an Exegetical Theology* (Grand Rapids: Baker, 1981), 82.
28.   Greidanus, *The Modern Preacher and the Ancient Text,* 111.
29.   Raymond E. Brown, "The 'Sensus Plenior' of Sacred Scripture," S.T.D. Dissertation(Baltimore, St. Mary's, 1955), 92, 145–46; quoted in Greidanus, *The Modern Preacher and the Ancient Text,* 72.

Brown is emphasizing a couple of very important aspects of *sensus plenior*. First, some texts of Scripture have a fuller meaning than the human authors understood while they were writing. Second, these fuller meanings are not the result of allegorical interpretation, but they are revealed by subsequent revelation. Greidanus expands our understanding of this process:

> The idea of the fuller sense is related to the Reformation's principle of comparing Scripture with Scripture. Both the idea of *sensus plenior* and that of *anologia Scriptura* are grounded in the conviction that the Old Testament and the New Testament belong together and are basically one book because they are written by the same primary Author on the same topic. From this unity of the Bible and the rule that a text must be understood in its context, it follows that a biblical text must be interpreted in the context of the whole Bible. And this is exactly what the principle of comparing Scripture with Scripture requires: after establishing the original intent and meaning of the text, interpreters must verify or, if necessary, expand the meaning of the text in the light of the whole canon. Thus comparing Scripture with Scripture nudges interpreters beyond the immediate purpose of human authors to the overall purpose of the primary Author.[30]

Greidanus emphasizes that individual texts must be interpreted within the larger context of the entire canon. This approach must be especially used when we study the Old Testament. As interpreters, we study the Old Testament from a New Testament context. We do not read the Old Testament as Jewish rabbis do. We read the Bible, all of it, as Christian Scripture. As a result, we are able to see a foreshadowing of New Testament teaching and theology within the texts of the Old Testament. However, since the authors of the Old Testament did not have the benefit of New Testament revelation, we must be careful and not read the New Testament back into their historical context. We must place the emphasis upon discovering the

---

30. Greidanus, *The Modern Preacher and the Ancient Text,* 112.

legitimate instances of *sensus plenior*, drawing particularly from the patterns and principles provided for us in the New Testament.[31]

Some young interpreters, upon discovering the nuances of progressive revelation, might be tempted to question the relevance of the Old Testament. If the fullness of God's revelation is revealed in the New Testament, why do we continue to place an emphasis on the Old Testament at all? Greidanus addresses that very question:

> This relation [between Old and New Testaments] does not make the earlier revelation obsolete, for it is the foundation of later revelation and, as part of the canon, remains authoritative for the church. It does mean, however, that on the one hand the earlier (Old Testament) revelation must be compared with later revelation for its fuller sense and possibly its divergence from later (New Testament) revelation. On the other hand, New Testament revelation can be properly understood only against the background of Old Testament revelation. Consequently, the idea of progressive revelation affirms the indispensability of both the Old and New Testament revelation while at the same time it underscores the necessity to interpret Old Testament revelation in the light of New Testament revelation. This broader context for understanding a

---

31. Jonah is just such an example. In the Old Testament account, Jonah requested to be cast into the sea to spare the lives of the crew with whom he was sailing. Upon entering the water, "The Lord appointed a great fish to swallow Jonah, and Jonah was in the fish three days and three nights" (Jonah 1:17). Jonah recognized that he was experiencing God's judgment for his disobedience. When his repentance was complete, "The Lord commanded the fish, and it vomited Jonah onto dry land" (Jonah 2:10). If you had asked Jonah if the time he spent in the fish foreshadowed the time that Jesus would remain in the grave following his crucifixion, he would have been clueless about your question. He had no idea that his ordeal was anything other than a painful act of God's discipline. In the New Testament, however, Jesus revealed to His followers that Jonah was, indeed, a spiritual "type," and that the days he spent in the great fish had a "fuller sense." When the scribes and Pharisees approached Jesus to make a mocking request for a "sign," Jesus replied, "An evil and adulterous generation demands a sign, but no sign will be given to it except the sign of the prophet Jonah. For as Jonah was in the belly of the great fish three days and three nights, so the Son of Man will be in the heart of the earth three days and three nights" (Matt 12:39–40). In this account, Jesus reveals that Jonah's "entombment" foreshadowed Jesus' own time in the grave. Because the New Testament confirms that Jonah is a "type" of Jesus, we can feel confident to describe it as such in our interpretation of the Jonah passage.

biblical text inevitably broadens the scope of interpretation from the immediate purpose of human authors to the ultimate purpose of God.[32]

Here, Greidanus reinforces the significance of both the Old and New Testaments for the church. Because revelation is progressive, we find that the New Testament informs the Old Testament and reveals legitimate instances of *sensus plenior.* However, we also recognize that the Old Testament informs the New Testament, something some expositors miss or neglect too often.

While specific Old Testament examples of *sensus plenior* can be identified only on the basis of New Testament revelation, we cannot deny that the Old Testament foreshadows the redemptive work of Jesus. This leaves us with a significant question: How do we identify and interact with the foreshadowing of Jesus that we find in the Old Testament, while avoiding the temptation to invent "types" and the allegories that accompany them? Bryan Chapell provides helpful insight for us at this point. He states, "Christ-centered preaching rightly understood does not seek to discover where Christ is mentioned in every text but to disclose where every text stands in relation to Christ."[33] This insight, then, provides us with the help we need. When we interpret the Old Testament, we aim not to discover new types of Christ; rather, we aim to determine how a particular text may contribute to our understanding of God's redemptive plan accomplished through Jesus.[34]

32. Greidanus, *The Modern Preacher and the Ancient Text,* 113.
33. Bryan Chapell, *Christ-Centered Preaching* (Grand Rapids: Baker, 1994), 279.
34. For those wishing to read more on *sensus plenoir,* we would commend Vanhoozer, *Is There a Meaning?,* 263–65 and especially Douglas Moo, "The Problem of *Sensus Plenoir"* in *Hermeneutics, Authority, and Canon,* ed. D. A. Carson and John Woodbridge (Grand Rapids: Baker, 1986, 1995), 179–211. For more on a Christological hermeneutic for preaching, see Sinclair Ferguson, *Preaching Christ from the Old Testament* (London: The Proclamation Trust, 2002); Edmund Clowney, *Preaching Christ in All Scripture* (Wheaton: Crossway, 2003); Graeme Goldsworthy, *Preaching the Whole Bible as Christian Scripture: The Application of Biblical Theology to Expository Preaching* (Grand Rapids: Eerdmans, 2000); Sidney Greidanus, *Preaching Christ from the Old Testament: A Contemporary Hermeneutical Method* (Grand Rapids: Eerdmans, 1999); Dennis Johnson, *Him We Proclaim: Preaching Christ from All the Scriptures* (Phillipsburg: P&R, 2007). We would also commend, in this context, the

THE AUTHOR'S INTENDED MEANING IN A BIBLICAL TEXT WILL NEVER BE IN CONTRADICTION TO HIS OWN WRITINGS OR THE REST OF THE CANON

Despite the individual nature of the parts, we affirm that the Scriptures comprise a single whole whose parts can never contradict themselves. At the core of this conviction is an even greater conviction about God, who is the ultimate "Author" of the canon. Maier provides four reasons why we can hold to this conviction. First, he notes that the Holy Spirit "permeates it [the canon] and constitutes it as a unity" (2 Tim 3:16).[35] Second, the texts of Scripture summon people to faith in God on the basis of its unified message.[36] Third, the Bible provides a framework for human history within the context of redemptive history.[37] Fourth, the unity of Scripture is a prerequisite for the defense of truth against error.[38] Maier does us a great service by reminding us that we can have confidence in the absolute truth of God's revelation and our capacity to trust it for every area of faith and practice. Our confidence is rooted in the character of the sovereign Author of the Bible—not the capability of its human authors.

Because the Bible has a contextual unity, it will not contradict itself. As we have noted, our interpretation must result from a careful analysis of the text. This results from the study of the content of the text, but it is also grounded in the context in which the content was written. Kaiser writes, "Good exegetical procedure dictates that the details be viewed in light of the total context. . . . The ability to state what each section of a book is about and how the paragraphs in each section contribute to that argument—is one of the most critical steps."[39] He then lists several layers of biblical context.

He calls the first layer the "immediate context." This layer refers to the relationship between a particular text and the "section of the

---

preaching ministry of Tim Keller, pastor of Redeemer Presbyterian Church in New York City.
35. Maier, *Biblical Hermeneutics,* 191.
36. Ibid.
37. Ibid., 192.
38. Ibid.
39. Kaiser, *Toward an Exegetical Theology,* 69.

book in which it is found."[40] He calls the second layer the "sectional context," which refers to the actual context of a particular text within its own literary context. It is "the connection of thought that runs through a passage, those links that weave it into one piece."[41] He calls the third layer the "book context." This layer refers to the overall context of a particular book and the way in which an individual text functions within the author's purpose for the entire book.[42] He calls the fourth layer the "canonical context." This layer refers to the fact that every text has a place not only within the individual book but also within the context of the entire canon.[43] Because God is the ultimate Author of Scripture, we can expect to find unity in the immediate, sectional, book, and canonical contexts as well.

THE AUTHOR'S INTENDED MEANING IN A BIBLICAL TEXT HAS A THEOCENTRIC/ CHRISTOLOGICAL PURPOSE, AND AS A RESULT, IT HAS SIGNIFICANCE FOR ALL PEOPLE, IN ALL PLACES, AT ALL TIMES

Once the interpreter has discovered both the content and the context of a biblical text, his final task involves verbalizing his understanding of the author's intended meaning. This task is the goal of hermeneutics and provides the moment of truth in exegesis. The author's intended meaning will always be theocentric—it will reflect the great truths about God and His Christ. After all, the Bible is first and foremost a record of God's redemptive plan for the world. The great redemptive themes of love, grace, mercy, justice, regeneration, repentance, faith, and reconciliation can be found throughout the entire Bible. These themes are revealed progressively, however. As a result, we find them revealed first in the Old Testament covenant relationship between God and Israel, where the system of animal sacrifice foreshadowed the atonement of

---

40. Ibid., 83.
41. Ibid., 71.
42. Ibid., 77.
43. Ibid., 81.

Jesus. In the New Testament, we find the mystery of His substitutionary atonement fully revealed in the relationship between Jesus and the church, where both Jew and Gentile are united in him.[44]

In recent years, the church has experienced a significant increase in man-centered preaching. This type of preaching, which places its primary emphasis upon the "felt needs" of the listener, often substitutes psychology for exposition. Greidanus states, "In contrast to anthropocentric interpretation, therefore, theocentric interpretation would emphasize that the Bible's purpose is first of all to tell the story of God. In relating that story, the Bible naturally also depicts human characters—not, however, for their own sake but for the sake of showing what God is doing for, in, and through them."[45] Our awareness of the theocentric nature of Scripture will help ensure that our interpretation and preaching are God-centered.

At the conclusion of the exegetical process, the interpreter should be able to state the author's MIT in a concise, past tense statement of theological truth: truth that is applicable to all people, in all places, at all times. Regardless of the time and effort an interpreter has spent studying a biblical text, his work is incomplete if he cannot clearly state its theocentric and Christological truth claim.

These 10 principles, which serve as the foundation for our exegesis, are important to keep in the forefront of our thinking when we study the Bible. In the remaining chapters of section 1, we will provide a system of study that will equip you to discover the meaning and significance of any biblical text, and in so doing, lay the foundation for a solid, expository sermon.

---

44. Greidanus, states, "One of the most important questions we can ask in interpreting a passage is, 'What does this passage tell us about God and his coming kingdom?'" (*The Modern Preacher and the Ancient Text,* 114).
45. Ibid., 117–18.

CHAPTER 5

DISCOVERING THE AUTHOR'S METHOD OF COMMUNICATION—PROSE

A s we noted in previous chapters, hermeneutics is the proper use of the principles of interpretation to discover the author's intended meaning of a biblical text, with a goal of applying that meaning to a contemporary audience. In the following chapters, we will focus our attention on the process of interpretation, which is called "exegesis."

In its broadest sense, "The word 'Exegesis,' despite its dauntingly technical connotations, simply means 'interpretation.' Every close reading of a text—any text—is an act of exegesis."[1] Ultimately, exegesis refers to the process of discerning the truth of Scripture by allowing a text to reveal its meaning and significance, rather than reading the interpreter's bias into it. While hermeneutics, then, refers to the proper use of a set of specific principles of interpretation, exegesis refers to the proper use of a set of specific procedures to discover the correct interpretation of a text. For the purpose of our discussions in this textbook, the process of exegesis will be defined as the use of the appropriate grammatical and contextual resources to determine the author's intended meaning of the text

---

1.   Richard B. Hays, "Exegesis," in *Concise Encyclopedia of Preaching*, ed. William H. Willimon and Richard Lischer (Louisville: WJK, 1995), 122.

and its significance for today's readers, as guided by the appropriate principles of hermeneutics.

As we begin the process of exegesis, we must inspect the content of the biblical text. When we speak of "content," we are talking about the author's use of semantics, syntax, and genre. We must begin the exegetical process by studying the Scriptures, as opposed to commentaries, so that external sources do not prejudice our interpretation before we have taken the time to inspect the text itself. As you will see, there is a time and a place for the use of external sources, but it should always follow our own close inspection of the biblical text. Once the content has been thoroughly examined, we will turn our attention to the multiple layers of context that influenced the author.

When we think about the grammatical content of a passage, we are focusing our attention upon the literary elements that the author utilized to present his information. This process begins by determining the literary genre (or style) chosen by the author to communicate his intended meaning to his audience. Next, it requires the ability to discover the distinct units of thought that carry the author's meaning throughout the book. Finally, it requires observing the author's choice of specific words (semantics) and the way he combined them into sentences and paragraphs (syntax) within the text.[2] As we begin the process of exegesis, we are embarking on a four-step process for discovering the author's MIT (see diagram 5.1 on page 58).

The first step in biblical exegesis is the inspection of the text. "Inspect" means to look closely at, or into, something. The interpreter's task is to inspect carefully the totality of the biblical text under consideration. In the field of journalism, reporters use a formula to ensure that they include all of the necessary information in their stories. The "reporter's formula" seeks to answer the following questions: Who, What, When, Where, How, and Why? Journalists

---

2.   Sidney Greidanus, *The Modern Preacher and the Ancient Text* (Grand Rapids: Eerdmans, 1988), 51. He states, "In literary interpretation (broadly conceived as inclusive of grammatical concerns), one commonly raises questions concerning the text's genre of literature, rhetorical devices, figures of speech, grammar, syntax, etc., in order to determine the meaning of words in their immediate context and, ultimately, in the context of the whole document and of the entire Bible."

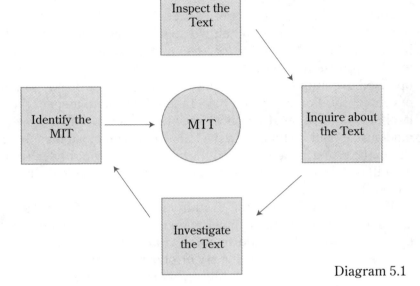

Diagram 5.1

inspect all of the information they gather, with the goal of answering these questions. Just as the answers to these questions help reporters communicate the specific facts of an event, they can also be used to help us understand both the content and the context of a biblical text. In this chapter, we will focus on how the text was written.

HOW WAS THE TEXT WRITTEN?

In recent years, the study of the unique styles of biblical literature has received a renewed emphasis. In literature, the word used to refer to a unique style of writing is "genre." Genre is defined as "a kind of style, especially of art or literature (e.g., novel, drama, satire)."[3] In exegesis, the study of genre provides valuable insights for the interpreter.[4] Also, the genre may help the interpreter discern

---

3. *The Oxford American Dictionary of Common Usage* (1999), s.v. "Genre."
4. Kevin Vanhoozer states that finding the literary form of a text is of utmost importance, because genre provides a literary context for the text, and that context contributes to the discovery of the author's intended meaning. Kevin J. Vanhoozer, "The Semantics of Biblical Literature: Truth and Scripture's

between the need for a literal or figurative reading of the text. Kaiser writes, "Often the key to the use and function of language is the literary form in which it was cast."[5]

Hermeneutics scholars have invested a great deal of effort in cataloguing the variety of genres that can be found in Scripture, which range from the simple to the complex.[6] For the sake of this introduction to hermeneutics and exegesis, we will limit our description of biblical genres to five specific categories: prose, poetry, historical narrative, wisdom literature, and apocalypse.[7] As we examine these major categories, we would do well to remember Grant Osborne's advice: "Genre plays a positive role as a hermeneutical device for determining the *sensus literalis* or intended meaning of the text. Genre is more than a means of classifying literary types; it is an epistemological tool for unlocking the meaning of individual texts."[8] We will begin our study of genre with the predominant literary style found in Scripture—prose.

Prose

In its simplest and broadest understanding, prose is any genre of writing that is not poetry. It is often described as the style of everyday speech. Generally, prose refers to the kind of writing used in novels, newspapers, speeches, letters, and contracts. It may incorporate poetic language, but it does not conform to the rules of poetry.[9] Within the field of biblical studies, prose would be used to describe those texts known as historical narratives (OT History, Gospel,

---

Diverse Literary Forms," in *Hermeneutics, Authority, and Canon*, ed. D. A. Carson and John D. Woodbridge (Grand Rapids: Zondervan, 1986), 80.

5. Walter C. Kaiser Jr., *Toward an Exegetical Theology* (Grand Rapids: Baker, 1981), 94.

6. For instance, Grant Osborne identifies seven different genres in *The Hermeneutical Spiral*, 2nd ed. (Downers Grove: IVP, 2006), while Howard Hendricks and William Hendricks identify 14 different genres in *Living by the Book* (Chicago: Moody Press, 2007).

7. Kaiser, *Toward an Exegetical Theology*, 91–94.

8. Grant R. Osborne, "Genre Criticism—Sensus Literalis," *Trinity Journal* 4/2 (1983): 24.

9. The form of poetry known as "blank verse" is a style that incorporates the use of metaphor into prose style, while avoiding poetic forms.

Acts), speeches (OT Prophets, New Testament sermons), parables (Gospels), and letters (Epistles). The majority of the Bible is written in prose.

A couple of aspects about prose are noteworthy at this point. First, texts written in this style are often descriptive in nature. Writers use prose to state facts, describe events, provide interpretations, and tell stories. Second, an author's use of prose as his primary genre does not mean that he did not incorporate other genres into his writing. For instance, Moses used prose to record the narrative of the Exodus. Yet, in chapter 15, he records a victory poem. Third, the types of prose are not as easily compartmentalized as we might like. For example, when we think of parables, we tend to think immediately of the Gospels. However, parables are found throughout the Scriptures. Within the historical narrative of David's reign in Israel, for example, we suddenly encounter Nathan's parable (2 Sam 12:1–4). Fourth, some types of biblical prose are so distinctive that they have their own genre designation, such as historical narrative, epistle, and apocalypse.

Historical Narrative

As we noted above, prose is the predominant genre in the Bible. Historical narrative is one of the styles of prose that appears most frequently. Given its ubiquitous nature in Scripture, we will examine it as a separate genre here.

When we discuss the historical narratives found in Scripture, we must remember Greidanus' words:

> The Bible contains not history but history writing. . . . In other words, what we find in the Bible are not the events themselves but particular interpretations of certain events. Like all history writers, the biblical authors had to select carefully which remembered or recorded events they would write about and which aspect of these events they would highlight. . . . The focus of the writers is not on the economic side of the events, nor on the social or political sides; their interest is concentrated on a deeper level of meaning: God's covenant, God's coming kingdom, the religious-theocentric dimension. At this point the biblical authors leave ordinary history writing far behind, and their claims that *God* was

at work for a specific purpose, say in the fall of Jerusalem or the crucifixion, are "beyond the realm of verification by historians"[10]; these claims can be accepted only by faith. The biblical interpretations of events are worthy of acceptance by faith.[11]

Historical narratives provide far more than just the recounting of historical facts. Rather, as Greidanus notes, every historical narrative has a spiritual focus and dimension. Maier concurs, "God made the creation. God is the ultimate ground of history. God revealed himself in history in such a way that his revelation could be discerned even in the midst of a fallen human race. When we speak of the historical nature of the Bible, we have in mind precisely that crossover of the eternal divine revelation into the present space-time world (*transition revelationis*). This crossover, in which the eternal enters the temporal and itself assumes the characteristics of a temporal phenomenon, is a mystery."[12] The mystery of God at work in human history is what we are seeking to discover when we study historical narratives.

As we turn toward the practical issues of interpreting narratives, we must pause first to identify those parts of Scripture that should be included in this category of texts. When we think about historical narratives, we think immediately of the Historical Books: Joshua, Judges, Ruth, 1–2 Samuel, 1–2 Kings, 1–2 Chronicles, Ezra, Nehemiah, and Esther.[13] However, it would be a mistake to think

---

10. Gordon Wenham, "History and the Old Testament" in *History, Criticism and Faith: Four Exploratory Essays*, ed. Colin Brown (Downer's Grove, IL: IVP, 1976), 13–75, quoted in Greidanus, *The Modern Preacher and the Ancient Text*, 88.

11. Greidanus, *The Modern Preacher and the Ancient Text*, 86–88.

12. Gerhard Maier, *Biblical Hermeneutics* (Wheaton, IL: Crossway, 1994), 210.

13. Paul House, "Preaching in the Historical Books," in *Handbook of Contemporary Preaching*, ed. Michael Duduit (Nashville: Broadman, 1992), 283. House notes that "this ordering offers the reader two rather complete histories of Israel. The first stretches from Joshua to 2 Kings, and the second encompasses 1 Chronicles through Esther. The two accounts tell many of the same events, yet have different purposes, which allow the readers to see more than one perspective of what happened." House also notes, "This list follows the Latin Bible, and differs from the Hebrew order. The Hebrew text includes the same books, but places them in a different sequence, and also calls them 'former prophets'" (291).

that these books contain the only narratives in Scripture. In truth, any text of Scripture that contains a story is a narrative, whether it is a literal event or a parable. As you can see, if prose is the predominant writing style in Scripture, historical narrative is the predominant writing style in prose.

When we turn our attention to the unique writing style of historical narratives, we must be sure to understand the basic elements included in every narrative. At this point Osborne provides us with some valuable categories for studying narratives.[14] First, we must understand our primary concern is with the text, not the author. While we must understand the various contexts that influenced the writer, which we will identify in a later chapter, we must never lose sight that the text itself is of first importance. Second, we must work to understand the point of view that the author uses when writing his story. Every author is writing from a specific point of view, and "this point of view guides the reader to the significance of the story and determines the actual 'shape' that the author gives to the narrative."[15]

Third, we must identify the plot of the story. Every story has several key plot elements. Perrine identifies these key plot elements as conflict (the source of the story), protagonist (the main character in the story), antagonist (the forces or people arrayed against the protagonist), suspense (what will happen to the protagonist), peripeteia (surprise turning point in the story), and the denouement (the final resolution of the story).[16] Our ability to identify these key plot elements will greatly improve our ability to interpret a historical narrative.

Fourth, we must be able to identify the characters and their traits as they are revealed in the story. Often we are given insights into the characters by their descriptions in the text. For instance, we see John the Baptist described as wearing "a garment of camel's hair and a leather belt around his waist" (Matt 3:4 NASB), which immediately suggests that he lived on the fringe of society. In other places, we must infer aspects of the characters from the text. For instance, when the angel appeared to Gideon, he found him hiding in a wine press to keep the Midianites from discovering him. The angel's

---

14. Osborne, *The Hermeneutical Spiral*, 200–221.
15. Ibid., 204.
16. Laurence Perrine, *Literature: Structure, Sound, and Sense*, 2nd ed. (New York: Harcourt, Brace, Jovanovich, 1974), 4351.

ironic greeting, "The LORD is with you, mighty warrior," implies that Gideon was acting more like a frightened child than a valiant warrior (Judg 6:11–12). Whether the traits of a character are revealed explicitly or implicitly, we must take the time to fully understand the characters in the narrative.

Fifth, we must grasp the setting of the story. Often, the setting is as significant to the narrative's meaning as any other aspect. In the parable of the Good Samaritan, the setting for the narrative is the dangerous road between Jerusalem and Jericho. Understanding the setting is pivotal to the plot. Later, we will discuss the significance of geography to the context of a biblical passage, but nowhere is it more significant than in the study of historical narratives.

Sixth, we must look for the implied or explicit commentary of the author. In other words, we must understand that the author had an intended meaning for the story. He included it in his book for a reason. Sometimes the author will tell you why he has recorded the narrative. John provides his purpose when he says, "but these have been written so that you may believe that Jesus is the Christ, the Son of God; and that believing you may have life in His name" (John 20:31 NASB). Often, however, we must labor to discover the author's MIT by examining the devices he used to tell his story. His use of "irony, comedy, symbolism and other literary devices . . . guides the reader through the drama of his story."[17] In the narrative about Jesus and Nicodemus, Jesus responds to a question by saying, "Are you a teacher of Israel and don't know these things?" (John 3:10). If we listen closely, we can hear the irony in Jesus' question. It reveals the spiritual illiteracy that characterized even the most fervent of Pharisees, and it works in the narrative to underscore the supremacy of Jesus' teaching as the Son of Man.

Historical narratives are by far the most common example of prose in the Bible. Yet for all of their abundance, many pastor-teachers fail to spend time preaching these amazing texts. Because historical narratives are challenging to understand and interpret, many pastor-teachers fail to preach them with regularity. With time and effort, however, these narratives will yield an amazing treasure of truth for the church.

---

17. Osborne, *The Hermeneutical Spiral,* 210.

Apocalyptic

Apocalyptic literature is perhaps the most challenging of all biblical literature to interpret.[18] This difficulty is due primarily to its use of symbols to represent future events. *Apacolupsis* means to "unveil" or "reveal." At its core, apocalyptic literature deals with the *eschaton*, or end times. When we think of the apocalyptic literature in the Bible, our minds turn first to Revelation. While this unique book is an epistle that contains prophecy, its content is primarily apocalyptic. However, it would be a mistake to assume that Revelation is the only evidence of apocalyptic literature in the Bible. Ezekiel, Daniel, Zechariah, and parts of Isaiah also contain this type of writing.

Kaiser notes that there are some generally accepted features of apocalyptic writing: "(a) rich symbolism involving angels, demons, and mixed features of animals, birds, and men; (b) a formalized phraseology indicating that the revelation came by a vision or dream; (c) frequent conversations between the prophet/seer/apostle and a heavenly being who disclosed God's secret to him; (d) cosmic catastrophes and convolutions; (e) a radical transformation of all of nature and the nations in the near future of that day; and (f) the imminent end of the present age and the establishment of the eternal kingdom of God."[19]

We encounter all of these elements when we study the apocalyptic texts in Scripture. We must remember, however, that when we study these texts we are dealing with more than simple fantasy or myth—we are dealing with truth. As a result, our interpretation of these writings requires our utmost diligence.[20] What makes apoca-

---

18. Apocalyptic language clearly is not the style of everyday speech. We place our discussion of it here for the sake of simplicity. Interpreting it, we readily acknowledge, is not simple. Further attention of this genre will be given in chapter 7.
19. Kaiser, *Toward an Exegetical Theology,* 93–94.
20. Grant R. Osborne, *Revelation* (Grand Rapids: Baker Academic, 2002), 14–15. Osborne notes that "the fundamental perspective of the book [Revelation] is the exhortation to endure persecution on the basis of the transcendent reality of God's kingdom in the present as grounded in God's control of the future.... The judgment of the wicked and the vindication of the saints are important elements in apocalyptic and dominate Revelation as well.... The recurring theme of the letters is repentance, for only this makes it possible to be an overcomer. The basis of it all is the determinism of the book. God is triumphant."

lyptic literature so challenging for interpreters is the preponderance of symbolism and imagery. Today, many pastor-teachers strive to "explain" every symbol or to predict the exact manner in which the *eschaton* will occur. Osborne notes,

> This does not mean that prophecy and apocalyptic should not be applied to the current situation nor that their "fulfillment" should not be sought. Rather, it means that the interpreter should seek first the "author's intended meaning" in the original context before delineating the way that the prophecies apply to our time. . . . At the same time the purpose of esoteric symbols in apocalyptic is to turn readers from the actual event to its theological meaning. In other words, readers are expected to see the hand of God in the future but are not supposed to know the exact sequence of events—that is, they are not given a description of what will actually happen. In short, we have no blueprint in Scripture for current events, but rather theological signs which tell us *in general* that God is going to draw history to a close. Symbols are literal in that they point to future events but not so literal that they tell us exactly how God is going to accomplish his purposes.[21]

Interpreting apocalyptic literature is a challenging endeavor. We must work diligently to discover the author's MIT. Then, with great care, we share its truth with our contemporary audience. As we encounter the elaborate symbolism of apocalyptic literature, however, we must acknowledge that we can only go so far in our finite thinking. When we reach the end of ourselves, we must acknowledge our limited understanding and place our confidence in the work of an infinite, sovereign God.

---

21. Osborne, *The Hermeneutical Spiral*, 283.

CHAPTER 6

DISCOVERING THE AUTHOR'S METHOD OF COMMUNICATION — POETRY

As we noted in chapter 5, prose is the primary literary style found in the Bible. Nevertheless, poetic styles are in Scripture too. Walt Kaiser notes that poetry "is important enough to occupy about one-third of the Old Testament."[1] The bulk of biblical poetry is contained in the book of Psalms. Psalms are musical poems. In this chapter, we will continue our study of genre by examining the use of poetry both in the Psalms and the wisdom writings.

POETRY

Unlike prose, poetry is a medium of communication that uses figurative language to explore the intricacies of life. Perrine states, "Poetry might be defined as a kind of language that says *more* and says it *more intensely* than does ordinary language."[2] Through its creative use of rhyme and meter, along with its use of figurative language, poetry has the capacity to provide an extraordinary view of ordinary

---

1. Walter C. Kaiser Jr., *Toward an Exegetical Theology* (Grand Rapids: Baker, 1981), 92.
2. Laurence Perrine, *Literature: Structure, Sound, and Sense*, 2nd ed. (New York: Harcourt, Brace, Jovanovich, 1974), 553.

things. To fully understand poetry, we must first understand some of the key devices that poets use in their craft.

Fee and Stuart note that there are different types of psalms. First, there are laments, which express various emotions characterized by "struggles, suffering, or disappointment." Second, there are "psalms of thanksgiving," which are the opposite of laments. Third, there are "psalms of praise," which center on the goodness of God and His provision for His people. Fourth, there are "historical psalms," which focus on God's works in history. Fifth, there are "psalms of celebration and affirmation," which affirm God's work among the people of Israel. Sixth, there are "wisdom psalms," which celebrate the virtues of living a wise life. Seventh, there are "psalms of trust," which remind the reader of the faithfulness of God, regardless of the situations of life.[3]

Fee and Stuart continue by stating that Old Testament poetry also takes different forms. In other words, every type of psalm has its own distinct literary form that follows a set of basic rules. For instance, every lament psalm includes the following basic elements: (a) address, (b) complaint, (c) trust, (d) deliverance, (e) assurance, and (f) praise.[4] As a result, once we understand the form of a lament, we can expect to find these elements in any lament psalm. The interpreter's understanding of the various poetic forms is critical for good exegesis.

Next, Fee and Stuart affirm that every Old Testament psalm has a distinct function.[5] In other words, the psalms were written to accomplish something in the life of the reader. Primarily, "[The Psalms] served the crucial function of making connection between the worshipper and God."[6] Given the unique seasons of the human soul, different psalms were written to address different needs. Osborne notes, "Semitic poetry had its origin in the religious life of the people, both corporate and individual. Prose was inadequate to express the deep yearnings of the soul, and poetry as an emotional, deep expression of faith and worship became a necessity. The many types of religious

---

3.   Gordon D. Fee and Douglas Stuart, *How to Read the Bible for All Its Worth,* 3rd ed. (Grand Rapids: Zondervan, 2003), 212–15.

4.   Ibid., 215.

5.   Ibid., 210–11.

6.   Ibid., 210.

needs called for different types of hymns. Hebrew poetry was not recreational but was functional in the life of the nation and its relationship with Yahweh."[7] Understanding the function of a psalm will aid in its interpretation.[8]

Additionally, we should note various patterns in the Psalms. While an in-depth study of those patterns is outside the scope of this text, we must understand the primary pattern found in Old Testament poetry—semantic parallelism. Kaiser describes semantic parallelism as of "major importance both for identifying the literary form and for getting at its meaning."[9] He further states, "The basic idea of parallelism is that two or more lines of poetry express either a synonymous idea by use of an equivalent but different word, or an antithetic idea by some type of contrast. The parallelism may be semantic (dealing with meaning) or grammatical (pertaining to form)."[10] Again, understanding the patterns used in Hebrew poetry is vital to proper interpretation.

Finally, Fee and Stuart affirm that every psalm must be read as a complete literary unit.[11] Sadly, many pick and choose specific verses out of individual psalms for personal edification or for preaching a sermon. However, those individual verses have meaning as they relate to the other verses in the psalm. Osborne concurs by urging, "Study the psalm as a whole before drawing conclusions. The thought flow of the psalm is critical to its meaning. . . . The Psalms intend to be understood as literary units, for they were written individually on single occasions. Therefore, it is even more true of poetry (than of prose) that the whole is key to the parts."[12]

---

7.   Grant R. Osborne, *The Hermeneutical Spiral*, 2nd ed. (Downers Grove: IVP, 2006), 231.

8.   Osborne further notes that while the Psalms "make no actual theological statements . . . their very God-centeredness is highly theological" (Ibid., 237). In a way, the Psalms take the unique season of the human soul (lament, thanksgiving, praise, etc.) and communicate humanity's greatest need—God's presence and provision." Osborne's short section on the "Theology of Psalms" is helpful on this issue (250–51).

9.   Kaiser, *Toward an Exegetical Theology*, 92.

10.   Ibid. Kaiser provides an excellent, in-depth analysis of the use of poetry in biblical exposition on pages 211–31. For additional information, consult Osborne, *The Hermeneutical Spiral,* 221–41.

11.   Fee and Stuart, *How to Read the Bible for All Its Worth,* 209–10.

12.   Osborne, *The Hermeneutical Spiral,* 241.

Despite the predominance of the Psalms as Old Testament poetry, Scripture contains many other examples of poetry. In particular, Job, Proverbs, Ecclesiastes, and Song of Solomon all contain poetry. While poetry is predominantly found in the Old Testament, examples of poetry are located in the New Testament as well. For instance, many scholars believe that Phil 2:5–11 may represent a Christian hymn from the first century.

Poetry is often difficult to interpret because it contains so much figurative language. Poets may incorporate the use of figurative language in numerous ways.[13] One of the primary figurative devices found in Scripture is the simile. Similes, like metaphors, are "used as a means of comparing things that are essentially unlike. The only distinction between them is that in simile the comparison is *expressed* by the use of some word or phrase, such as *like, as, than, similar to, resembles, or seems.*"[14] For instance, in Psalm 1 the Psalmist said of the righteous man, "He is *like* a tree planted beside streams of water." Here, the writer is using figurative language to connect the attributes of a well-watered tree (growth, strength, stability) with the life of a righteous man.

While similes *express* the comparison, metaphors *imply* the comparison. That is, "The figurative term is *substituted for* or *identified with* the literal term."[15] We have already noted that Psalm 23 provides a metaphor of God as a shepherd. However, scores of metaphors can be found in Scripture. One cluster of famous metaphors for God is found in Psalm 18. Here God is compared to a rock, a fortress, a mountain, and a stronghold (vv. 1–2). All of these metaphors are used to describe God as the source of stability and safety in dangerous times.

Personification is a third type of figurative language found in Scripture. In personification, objects, animals, or ideas are given human attributes.[16] In the Psalms, God's actions are often given human comparisons. In Psalm 18 we read that God "shot His arrows and scattered them." Clearly, archery is a human activity, but here,

---

13. The use of a good book about literary interpretation, like the one written by Lawrence Perrine, will provide an in-depth explanation of these devices.
14. Perrine, *Literature: Structure, Sound, and Sense,* 610.
15. Ibid.
16. Ibid., 612.

God is perceived as "shooting" the lightning as an archer would shoot his arrows. Objects in creation are assigned human attributes in Scripture as well. Psalm 98:8 states, "Let the rivers clap their hands; / let the mountains shout together for joy." In this example, the rivers and mountains are given human attributes to reinforce the truth that all creation exists to proclaim the glory of God.

Paradox is yet another form of figurative language. "A paradox is an apparent contradiction that is nevertheless somehow true. It may be either a situation or a statement."[17] The Scriptures contain numerous examples of the use of paradox. In fact, Jesus used paradox often. He said, "whoever is greatest among you must become like the youngest, and whoever leads, like the one serving" (Luke 22:26); "For whoever wants to save his life will lose it, but whoever loses his life because of Me will find it" (Matt 16:25); "it is easier for a camel to go through the eye of a needle than for a rich person to enter the kingdom of God" (Matt 19:24). These verses join ideas that are difficult to reconcile. Yet after consideration, we discover the truth they contain.

Irony is another form of figurative language that occurs in Scripture, although it is not as common as those listed above. Irony is "saying the opposite of what one means."[18] As we noted earlier, a classic example of irony can be seen in Jesus' conversation with Nicodemus. Jesus asked, "Are you a teacher of Israel and don't know these things?" (John 3:10). Clearly, Nicodemus *was* a teacher of Israel, but that was not Jesus' point. Jesus was saying that Nicodemus was *not* a teacher in the sense he needed to be because he did not understand the spiritual basics that Jesus was discussing with him. In addition to understanding these figurative devices, we must be careful not to over-exegete figurative language in Scripture. A commitment to allow the context to determine the meaning will put us well on our way to understanding Scripture's rich use of figurative language.[19]

---

17. Ibid., 649.
18. Ibid., 653. Perrine notes that irony is often confused with sarcasm and satire, but it does not have to carry those negative connotations with it.
19. For further reading, see Osborne's helpful and more thorough section on figures of speech (*The Hermeneutical Spiral,* 121–30).

WISDOM

Wisdom literature in the Bible is often associated with the books of poetry. In fact, the books of wisdom often utilize poetics. For the sake of our study, however, we will examine Wisdom literature as a separate genre. While all of Scripture may be described as containing God's wisdom for His world, the books of Job, Proverbs, and Ecclesiastes are unique in their discussion and treatment of God's principles of wisdom for His people.

Walter Kaiser notes that there are two types of wisdom writings. The first are writings of a "reflective or a philosophical type of wisdom that tends to carry a sustained argument across a large body of text."[20] Numerous texts would fit into this category. We would include the books of Job and Ecclesiastes in this group, along with the first nine chapters of Proverbs. While it is often classified as a book of poetry, Walter Kaiser describes Song of Solomon as wisdom literature and includes it in this category.[21] Similarly, he includes the Sermon on the Mount as a sustained treatise on principles of wisdom in the kingdom of God.[22]

The second type of wisdom writing that Kaiser examines is a "prudential type of wisdom writing consisting of smaller units of thought which are disconnected and often isolated contextually."[23] He includes Proverbs 10–31, some select Psalms, and the book of James in this category.[24] As you can see, while we focus our attention on the Old Testament wisdom books, examples of wisdom literature can be found sprinkled liberally throughout the Bible.

---

20. Kaiser, *Toward an Exegetical Theology,* 92–93.
21. For a popular treatment of this book that seeks to expound God's marital wisdom in the Song of Solomon, see Daniel L. Akin, *God on Sex* (Nashville: B&H, 2003); Tommy Nelson, *The Book of Romance* (Nashville: Thomas Nelson, 1998).
22. Kaiser, *Toward an Exegetical Theology,* 93. See also D. A. Carson, *The Sermon on the Mount: An Evangelical Exposition of Matthew 5–7* (Grand Rapids: Baker, 1978).
23. Kaiser, *Toward an Exegetical Theology,* 93.
24. Ibid. He cites Psalms 1, 37, 49, and 112 as examples of wisdom writing in the Psalms.

In his book *The Hermeneutical Spiral,* Osborne provides a wonderful overview of the 10 forms that wisdom writing may take.[25] First, he defines the proverb, the most prominent form of wisdom writing, as a "brief statement of universally accepted truth formulated in such a way as to be memorable," which will function uniquely based on its goals.[26] Second, he describes wisdom sayings. These differ from typical proverbs in that they may not be prescriptive in nature. Rather, they suggest possible outcomes based on potential choices. Third, he discusses the riddle. Used rarely in Scripture, the riddle was a key form of wisdom literature in the ancient world. He believes that Judg 14:10–18 is the only clear example of riddle in the Bible, but speculates that riddles may have been the source of numerical proverbs (i.e., Prov 6:16–19 and select parts of Proverbs 30). Fourth, Osborne discusses the admonition in wisdom literature. This form of wisdom writing presents the hearer with a wise course of action and immediately provides positive or negative reinforcement by revealing a potential outcome based upon the choice made. Fifth, he examines the use of allegory in wisdom literature. Allegory, as a literary device, involves communicating a deeper meaning through the use of symbols or a story. While it is rarely used in the Scriptures, it can be found in places like Eccl 12:1–7, where a variety of striking images portray old age and the decay of the body.

Sixth, Osborne notes that hymns and prayers can be found in wisdom literature. Often, these prayers are written as poetry. Certainly, the same is true for the hymns. Most of these examples are found in Job.[27] Seventh, he discusses the dialogue. The dialogue is found primarily in Job but is used in Proverbs as well. This type of wisdom writing chronicles a conversation between people, with the goal of attaining wisdom or understanding. Eighth, he examines the confession. Found primarily in Ecclesiastes, this form of wisdom writing functions as an autobiography of sorts, where life's lessons are recounted—both the good and the bad. Ninth, he mentions the wisdom literature called *onomastica.* This type of wisdom writing,

---

25. Osborne, *The Hermeneutical Spiral,* 247–50.
26. Ibid., 247. Osborne notes these forms as instruction, wisdom sayings, admonition or prohibition, counsel, numerical, synonymous or antithetical, and factual or experiential.
27. Ibid., 249. He notes Job 5:9–16; 9:5–12; 12:13–25; 26:5–14,28.

found rarely in Scripture recounts the attributes of God (cf. Job 38). Tenth, Osborne discusses beatitudes. They are found throughout Scripture, but are most noted for their use in the Sermon on the Mount (Matt 5:3–12). Beatitudes provide examples of the kind of wise choices that result in the blessing of God.

Wisdom literature is one of the most challenging genres to interpret correctly. Because of their practical nature, we can easily lose sight of the theology that supports them. For instance, the book of Proverbs contains practical advice on everything from marriage to personal finances. However, every proverb is built upon this truth: "The fear of the Lord is the beginning of knowledge" (Prov 1:7). We can see clearly, then, that the foundation for every aspect of practical wisdom is an authentic relationship with God. As interpreters, we must be careful that our teaching reflects this truth when we deal with wisdom literature.

CHAPTER 7

DEVELOPING A GENRE-SPECIFIC OUTLINE

Once we have determined the genre of a biblical text, we must analyze the structure of the text. The second step of the inspection process is the development of an outline. Today, some pastor-teachers minimize or neglect this aspect of exegesis altogether. We remain convinced, however, that the practice of outlining remains one of the key components for discovering the author's MIT. Remember, the author wrote with a specific purpose in mind. To accomplish this purpose, he chose words, developed sentences, and organized those sentences into a specific format. In this process the author intended to communicate meaning. As an interpreter, your ability to understand the author's organizational strategy will help you discover his MIT. As we think about the use of the Reporter's Formula, we seek to answer the following question: "What did the author write?"

DISCOVERING THE AUTHOR'S CONTENT

Discourse analysis requires an assessment of the author's syntax and semantics.[1] We will demonstrate several outlining strat-

---

1. In addition to works cited in chap. 3, n. 13, we recommend David Alan Black, "Discourse Analysis: Getting the Big Picture," in *Linguistics for Students of*

egies that you can use in your analysis of the different genres found in Scripture. These strategies are designed to accomplish several tasks. First, they will help you develop a "genre-specific" outline of a biblical text. Second, they will help you identify the key events, people, and language cues (key words and sentences) necessary to interpret a text. Third, they will help you discover the key theological themes revealed in the text. Fourth, they will provide you with the framework necessary to understand the various contextual elements in the text, which will help you discover the author's MIT.

ANALYSIS OF HISTORICAL NARRATIVE

As we noted in chapter 5, prose is the most prevalent genre in the Bible. Prose is used most notably in the historical narratives and the Epistles. We will use different tools to help us analyze and outline their styles. A number of key elements require examination when interpreting historical narratives. We will use 1 Samuel 17 as an example as we explain how to develop a narrative outline.

Setting

Interpreters must begin with the setting of the story when they analyze a historical narrative. Setting refers to the circumstances and location where an event takes place. For instance, in the account of David's fight with Goliath, the setting of the story is a conflict between Israel and Philistia. The fight itself occurs at Socoh, in Judah. The Philistines were camped between Socoh and Azekah, in Ephes-dammin, while Israel was camped beside a stream in the Elah valley. Following the fight, the Israelites chased the Philistines along the way to Shaaraim, all the way to Gath and the gates of Ekron.

New Testament Greek (Grand Rapids: Baker, 1995) and David Alan Black and David S. Dockery, ed., *Interpreting the New Testament: Essays on Methods and Issues* (Nashville: B&H, 2001). Both are more technical works but still usable for pastors and students with a working knowledge of the languages.

Characters

Every story revolves around a cast of characters. Generally, every story has a protagonist (the hero) and an antagonist (the enemy). In historical narratives the protagonist is slightly different. Ultimately, God is the hero of every narrative in the Bible. This perspective must never be forgotten. The human characters described in the Bible are participants in God's redemptive plan for humanity. Ultimately, understanding the characters and their role within the story is important for discovering truth about God. The Samuel narrative includes a number of primary and secondary characters. Of course, David (protagonist) and Goliath (antagonist) are the primary characters in the story, but King Saul is also an important character. The story has a number of secondary characters, including David's father, Jesse, and David's brothers, Eliab, Abinadab, and Shammah. Finally, the armies of Israel and Philistia are group characters. Every character in the story provides clues to the story's meaning.

Point of View

In narratives, point of view refers to the perspective of the person telling the story. This perspective, in turn, leads us to consider why he is telling the story. Authors can tell a story in a number of ways, but most historical narratives are told from the omniscient point of view. In other words, "The story is told by the author, using third person, and his knowledge and prerogatives are unlimited."[2] Our understanding of the inspiration of Scripture also means that the biblical writers recorded the events as God willed.

Identification of the Plot

Once you have discovered the setting, characters, and point of view of the story, it is time to identify the plot. This exercise is simple. Read the account and place the events in their proper order. This

---

2.   Laurence Perrine, *Literature: Structure, Sound, and Sense*, 2nd ed. (New York: Harcourt, Brace, Jovanovich, 1974), 175.

ordering will help you get a sense of the development of the story over time, including the introduction of the characters and the problem. The more familiar you are with the historical narratives, the more likely you are to skip this step. You should exercise caution before assuming that you know the plot of the story. Remember, the key to interpreting a narrative is not simply to tell the story. The key is to discover what the story reveals about God and His relationship to His people. The principles contained in historical narratives must often be inferred because they are not stated explicitly. We will find those principles embedded in the details of the plot.

The analysis of the plot should reflect the important aspects of the story. In the Samuel narrative, the plot unfolds like this: (a) the Philistines invade Israel and challenge a member of the Israelite army to a duel with their great warrior Goliath; (b) Saul and his army are paralyzed by fear; (c) Jesse sends his son David to provide food for his brothers and check on their welfare; (d) David finds his brothers and hears the challenge from Goliath; (e) David hears about the reward offered to the man who can kill Goliath; (f) David confronts the soldiers with a penetrating question; (g) David's brother, Eliab, becomes angry with David over his remarks; (h) Saul sends for David and hears about his desire to fight the giant; (i) David recounts his victories against wild animals and proclaims his confidence in God's protection; (j) David tests and rejects Saul's armor in favor of his sling and some stones gathered from the river; (k) David proclaims victory in the power of God and kills Goliath; and (l) Israel defeats Philistia.

These events comprise the plot of 1 Samuel 17. Each of the plot elements reveals important information about the true meaning of the story. This is more than a story about a young man who kills a giant. It is an exposé that reveals Saul's lack of faith in God and the spiritual impotence of Israel. It reminds us that people, perhaps even those in our own family, are prepared to stand in the way of our own journey of faith. It is a testimony to the power of God, which is greater than the perceived strength of any enemy. It is a story about David and his victory over evil, which anticipates a greater Son of David and His ultimate victory over evil when He crushed a head, the head of Satan (Rom 16:20). You might miss some of these principles if you fail to discover the plot, or to consider the story in the full canonical context of Scripture.

Identification of the *Peripeteia*

The *peripeteia* is the "turning-point moment" in a narrative. This event abruptly changes the direction of the story and begins moving it toward its denouement, or conclusion. Finding that sudden, unexpected turning point is critical because that event often sheds light upon the primary meaning of the story. Finding the *peripeteia* in the story may be a challenging task for the interpreter. In this story, the turning point occurs when David refuses to wear Saul's armor. After all, what soldier would decline the opportunity to use advanced technology in battle? David's decision to abandon the armor is shocking—just as it is intended to be. Instead, David faces Goliath clothed only in his shepherd's attire and his confident assurance in the power of God. This attire and demeanor help reveal the primary theological theme of the story.

Identifying the Theological Themes

Once you have looked at all of the different aspects of the narrative, you are ready to begin identifying the theological themes. As noted above, most historical narratives yield their theological truths via inference. With that in mind, the interpreter must pause to consider the theological themes. First Samuel 17 includes a number of theological themes: fear vs. faith, weakness vs. strength, and self-reliance vs. reliance upon the power of God. Each theme can be found throughout the narratives of Scripture. Yet, all of these themes are subordinate to the primary theme—God alone has the power to deliver His children from their enemies. Remember also to ask how does this "little narrative" fit into the "Grand Redemptive Narrative" of the whole Bible? Diagram 7.1 provides an example of a narrative outline.

ANALYSIS OF EPISTLES

The Epistle is the one of the predominant types of prose found in the New Testament. Epistolary literature is propositional in nature and requires a careful analysis of both its linguistic and literary

Text: 1 Samuel 17

Setting	Characters	Point of View
• Socoh and Azekah, in Ephes-dammin; • valley, called Elah; • Shaaraim, all the way to Gath and the gates of Ekron	• David, Saul, Goliath; • Jesse and David's brothers, Eliab, Abinadab, and Shammah; • Armies of Israel/Philistia	• Samuel, omniscient, third person

Plot

Philistines/Goliath appear, • Israel paralyzed by fear, • David arrives to check on brothers, • David hears Goliath's challenge, • David hears about reward, • David challenges the army, • Eliab angry with David, • Saul sends for David, • David recounts exploits and confidence in God, • David rejects Saul's armor in favor of slingshot, • David proclaims God's power and kills Goliath; • Israel defeats Philistia.

Peripatia	Theological Themes
•David rejects Saul's armor in favor of his slingshot.	• fear vs. faith; • weakness vs. strength; • self-reliance vs. reliance upon God; • God alone can deliver His children from their enemies.

Diagram 7.1

contexts. Developing a structural diagram of the epistle is critical for this process.

Interpreters must remember several characteristics as they outline epistles. First, the author's MIT is not found in individual words or even sentences—it is found in studying the whole discourse as it relates to the parts (e.g., a paragraph, a sentence, a clause, a phrase, and a word). Second, epistles were written to address localized situations and problems. They are occasional documents addressing particular persons and specific issues. Consequently, they tend to be thematic. Third, the authors of the Epistles are developing theological arguments that address a local church context. As a result, the writing is propositional, and the themes are tied together through logical development. Outlining any of the epistles is challenging because it requires knowledge of grammar. When you outline a portion of an epistle, there are 7 areas need consideration. We will examine them as we provide a brief analysis of Phil 2:5–11.[3]

Scope of the Text

Locating the parameters of the text is critical when outlining the Epistles. This delineation helps ensure that every text is being studied in its context. Thankfully, many Bible translations provide headings designed to reveal these parameters. Rather than relying upon the work of others, however, interpreters should verify the parameters on their own by using the language clues they find in the text.

In Phil 1:27–2:4, Paul develops the theme of humble unity in the Spirit. This unity aids in the expansion of the gospel (1:27), provides courage in the face of persecution or suffering (1:28–30), and results in mutual appreciation within the church (2:1–4). In 2:5, Paul's thought shifts from an admonition to the church to a description of the incarnation of Jesus. Verse 5, then, serves as the pivotal link between two distinct sections. It refers back to the call for humility within the church found in 2:3–4 and urges the church to model it as an attribute of Christ. Also, it looks forward to 2:6–11, which provide a beautiful description of Christ as the divine prototype of authentic humility.

Discovering not only where a text begins but also where it ends is important. In 2:12, you suddenly encounter the words, "So then." These words serve as a verbal cue that Paul is preparing to move into another discourse. In 2:12–18, he will begin to challenge the Philippian believers to let the reality of their salvation be seen through the tangible actions of their lives. This analysis allows us to approach 2:5–11 with the confidence that it is a complete unit of thought.

---

3. Also, see the fine discussion on the epistles in Gordon D. Fee and Douglas Stuart, *How to Read the Bible for All Its Worth,* 3rd ed. (Grand Rapids: Zondervan, 2003), 311–41; Sidney Greidanus, *The Modern Preacher and the Ancient Text* (Grand Rapids: Eerdmans, 1988); Thomas Long, *Preaching and the Literary Forms of the Bible* (Philadelphia: Fortress, 1989), 107–26; Grant R. Osborne, *The Hermeneutical Spiral*, 2nd ed. (Downers Grove: IVP, 2006), 312–22.

Identification of the Independent Clauses

As we noted earlier, prose is characterized by a stylized, grammatical structure that is used to convey meaning. The basic unit of thought in grammar is the sentence, and every sentence (or independent clause) is constructed through the combination of a subject and predicate.[4] Writers of prose use independent clauses to convey meaning. As a result, if you can discover the independent clauses, you can discover the primary units of thought in the text.

As you begin to study verses 5–11, you will discover five independent clauses in this order: (a) "[You] make your own attitude that of Christ Jesus" (2:5),[5] (b) "[Jesus] did not consider equality with God as something to be used for His own advantage" (2:6), (c) "He emptied himself" (2:7), (d) "He humbled Himself" (2:8), and (e) "God also highly exalted Him and gave Him the name that is above every name" (2:9). These independent clauses represent the primary units of thought in this text.

Identification of the Dependent Clauses

As you read verses 5–11, you will realize that there are more words than the ones identified above. These additional words represent the dependent clauses. Dependent clauses provide descriptions or explanations of the independent clauses. As you study verses 5–11, you will find these dependent clauses: (a) "existing in the form of God" (2:6), (b) "by assuming the form of a slave" and "taking on the likeness of men" (2:7), (c) "and when He had come as a man in His external form" (2:7) and "by becoming obedient to the point of death—even to death on a cross" (2:8), (d) "for this reason God also" (2:9), and (e) "so that at the name of Jesus every knee should bow—of those in heaven and on earth and under the earth—and every tongue should confess that Jesus Christ is Lord, to the glory of God the Father" (2:10–11). These dependent clauses are important

---

4.   The subject provides the topic of the sentence, while the predicate describes what the subject is doing or being.

5.   Place "brackets" around understood subjects or subjects that represent the antecedent of a pronoun. These insertions will aid you with clarity as you outline.

because they expand our understanding of the author's main ideas as revealed through the independent clauses. The independent and dependent clauses are identified in diagram 7.2 below.

Scope: Philippians 2:5–11

Independent Clauses	Dependent Clauses
• [You make your own attitude that of Christ Jesus	
	• existing in the form of God
• Who . . . did not consider equality with God something to be used for His own advantage	• assuming form of a slave; taking on likeness of men;
• He emptied Himself	• when . . . form; by becoming obedient . . . cross
• He humbled Himself	
	• for this reason; so that . . . Earth; every tongue . . . Lord; to the glory . . . Father.
• God also highly exalted Him and gave Him the name that is above every name	

Transitional cues: "who (6)"; "instead (7)"; "for this reason (9)"; "so that (10)"

Diagram 7.2

Producing a Structural Diagram of the Text

The process of discovering both the independent and dependent clauses will provide you with the information you need to develop a structural diagram. This diagram will help you discover the natural divisions within the text. Your ability to recognize the natural divisions will increase your ability to discover the author's MIT. You will see the structural diagram of Phil 2:5–11 in diagram 7.3 on the next page.

Structural Diagram: Philippians 2:5–11

Make your own attitude that of Christ Jesus [cf. 2:1–4].

who [Christ Jesus] . . . did not consider equality with God as something to be used for His own advantage.

> existing in the form of God

Instead He emptied Himself

> by assuming the form of a slave,

> taking on the likeness of men

. . . He humbled Himself

> . . . And when He had come as a man in His external form . . .

> by becoming obedient to the point of death—even to death on a cross

For this reason [2:6–8] God also highly exalted Him and bestowed to Him the name which is above every name (result—vv. 6–8)

> so that . . . , EVERY KNEE SHOULD BOW—of those who are in heaven and on earth and under the earth—

> and that every tongue should confess that Jesus Christ is Lord

> . . . at the name of Jesus . . .

> to the glory of God

Transitional Cues: "who" (2:6); "Instead" (2:7); "For this reason" (2:9); "so that" (2:10)

Diagram 7.3

Identification of Transitional Clues in the Text

You should begin to see the author's MIT taking shape after you have produced your structural diagram. Generally, a text will have one main idea and some supporting concepts. The author often reveals these supporting concepts through his use of transitions. Not every text will contain these clues, but many will. For instance, Phil 2:5–11 has four transitional clues: (a) the relative pronoun "who" (2:6) that links "Christ Jesus" (2:5) with the phrase "equality with God" (2:6), and enables us to examine the Christological implications of this text; (b) the adverb "Instead" (2:7), which clarifies that Christ Jesus was willing to set aside some of the benefits of his "equality with

God" for the purpose of the incarnation; (c) the subordinating conjunction "For this reason" (2:9), which reveals why God has chosen to exalt Christ above all of creation; and (d) the subordinating conjunction "so that" (2:10), which demonstrates the future action of all creation in response to the exaltation of Jesus. Remember, the biblical authors used transitional clues like these to develop their arguments.

Identification of Key Words and Concepts

An author's MIT is always discovered through the analysis of a biblical text. Even though every text is constructed with words, the author chose those words under the inspiration of the Holy Spirit. As a result, it is essential to understand the meaning and significance of those words.

Space does not permit a lengthy treatment advocating the pursuit of a workable knowledge of Hebrew and Greek. Suffice it to say, if you are going to devote your life to Christian proclamation, it is critical that you take the time to learn the biblical languages, if at all possible. Your ability to discover the key words in a biblical text, especially in the Epistles, is vital for discovering the author's MIT.

At this stage, all that is required is the ability to recognize and define the words that appear to carry the meaning of the text. You will want to identify those words for additional study in the second stage of exegesis. As you look at Phil 2:5–11, a number of key words and phrases stand out: "attitude," "existing," "form," "advantage," "emptied Himself," "slave," "likeness," "external form," "humbled," "obedient," "cross," "name," "knee should bow," "tongue," "should confess," and "Lord." Since every one of these words is significant, you will need to discover their meanings as you complete your study of this text. Diagram 7.4 on the next page provides an example of how to identify key words.

Identification of Key Theological Themes

Every biblical text is designed to reveal something about God and humanity. As you identify the key elements in an epistolary text, you must keep in mind that theological themes are present. The author may address several theological themes in a text, either by stating or inferring them. Your task is to discover them.

Philippians 2:5–11 is one of four great Christological passages in the New Testament, and it provides one of the essential descriptions of the person and work of Jesus.[6] As a result, you would expect to find a number of theological themes, and you would be correct. There are at least four distinct themes: (1) the full deity of God the Son; (2) the incarnation of the Son; (3) the substitutionary, atoning death of Jesus on the cross; and (4) the exaltation of Jesus. Diagram 7.4 provides an example of how to identify the theological themes found in a text.

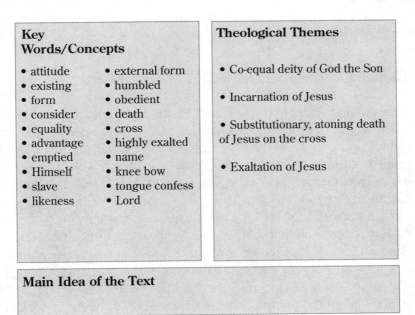

Key Words/Concepts		Theological Themes
• attitude	• external form	• Co-equal deity of God the Son
• existing	• humbled	
• form	• obedient	• Incarnation of Jesus
• consider	• death	
• equality	• cross	• Substitutionary, atoning death of Jesus on the cross
• advantage	• highly exalted	
• emptied	• name	
• Himself	• knee bow	• Exaltation of Jesus
• slave	• tongue confess	
• likeness	• Lord	

Main Idea of the Text

Diagram 7.4

ANALYSIS OF POETRY

The development of a thematic outline will help you discover the author's MIT when you encounter poetry in the Scriptures. In chapter 6 we noted that it is essential to consider rhyme, meter, and the use of figurative language when interpreting poetry. We will use

---

6. The others are John 1:1–18; Col 1:13–23; and Heb 1:1–14.

Psalm 4 as an example of how to address these areas when analyzing a poem.[7]

Poetry Type and Pattern

A variety of poetic styles can be found in the Scriptures. Determining the type and pattern of a poem is one of the most challenging aspects of studying poetry, especially for young interpreters. For instance, Psalm 4 is a Psalm of trust—it reminds the reader of God's faithfulness in life's trials. If you do not know what type of Psalm you are studying, leave this area of your analysis sheet blank until you do your investigation in stage three.

Producing a Thematic Structural Diagram

When dealing with poetry, you are not attempting to identify the plot as you would in studying a narrative. You are not concerned with producing the kind of intensive structural diagram required by the Epistles. Rather, you are attempting to trace the development of the poem's themes and movement. As a result, you want to produce an analysis of the poem that will identify these.

For instance, in Psalm 4, David addresses several primary themes: (a) God is righteous, and He hears the prayers of His people (4:1); (b) man's natural inclination is to participate in destructive activities (4:2); (c) God's people fear and trust Him (4:3–5); and (d) God alone is the source of provision and safety for His people (4:6–8). Once you have identified the primary themes, the MIT will begin to surface.

7.　On poetry also consult Long, *Preaching and the Literary Forms of the Bible,* 43–52; Osborne, *The Hermeneutical Spiral,* 223–41. For Psalms, see Richard Belcher Jr., *The Messiah and the Psalms* (Scotland: Christian Focus, 2006); Mark Futato, *Interpreting the Psalms* (Grand Rapids: Kregel, 2007); Patrick Reardon, *Christ in the Psalms* (Ben Lomond: Conciliar Press, 2000).

Identification of Figurative Language

As we discovered in chapter 6, poets use figurative language to describe the issues and emotions of life. Furthermore, the theological content of poems is often contained in their poetic devices. Consequently, interpretation requires an ability to understand a poem's figures of speech and their connotations.

Psalm 4 is a straightforward poem. At first glance, it does not appear to have much figurative language, but a closer inspection will reveal a couple of poetic elements. First, David uses the phrase "exalted men" to refer to the people around him (4:2). More importantly, he uses it in contrast to those who are "the faithful" (4:3). Second, David uses personification to describe how God had set faithful people apart for himself (4:3) and had put joy into David's heart (4:7). The act of "setting something apart" implies the use of hands. So, too, does the act of "placing something somewhere"— even if David is referring to a feeling like joy. Third, David uses irony to describe the difference between his joy and the joy of the exalted men. For those who are separated from God by sin, nothing brings more joy than the abundance of material things, like grain and new wine (4:7). In the scope of eternity, however, those are worthless to pursue (4:2). David's joy, in contrast to the exalted men's, was immaterial; it resulted from the fullness of peace and safety he had received from God. God graciously and intentionally placed this joy into David's heart (4:7–8).

Identification of the Theological Themes

As is true for every other genre, biblical poetry is about God and humanity. Consequently, it contains theological themes about God and His work among His people. The thematic structure that you develop on your analysis sheet will reveal the theological themes in the poem. We already identified the primary themes above. Trusting God is the over-arching theological theme of Psalm 4. He can be trusted to hear our prayers, to set us apart to fulfill his purposes, to infuse our hearts with joy, and to provide safety and security as we follow Him. Diagram 7.5, on the next page, provides an example of a poetry outline.

Text: Psalm 4

Thematic Structure—Psalm

- God is righteous, and He hears the prayers of His people (v. 1).

- Man's natural inclination is to participate in destructive activities (v. 2).

- God's people fear God and trust in Him (vv. 3–5).

- God alone is the source of provision and safety for His people (vv. 6–8).

Psalm Type/Pattern	Figurative Language	Theological Themes
Psalm of Trust	• Imagery: son of men • Personification: God places (hand imagery) • Irony: joy is not found in possessions but rather in close communication with God	• prayer • natural man • fear of the Lord • trust God

Diagram 7.5

ANALYSIS OF WISDOM LITERATURE

Wisdom literature is a genre that incorporates both narrative and poetic elements. When you are studying in either Job or Ecclesiastes, use the narrative analysis form in the appropriate places, and apply the appropriate criteria. When you are studying Song of Solomon, Proverbs, and the poetic parts of Job, use the poetry analysis form and apply the appropriate criteria. Because of the similarities between poetry and wisdom literature, we will not devote an entire section to the analysis of wisdom literature here.[8] Diagram 7.6, on the next page, provides an example of a wisdom literature outline.

---

8.   For further study on Wisdom literature, see Fee and Stuart, *How to Read the Bible,* 225–48; Goldsworthy, *Preaching the Whole Bible,* 183–95; Osborne, *The Hermeneutical Spiral,* 242–57.

Text: Job 42:1–6

Thematic Structure—Wisdom/Poetry

• God is sovereign and always accomplishes His will (v. 2).

• God's knowledge is limitless and dwarfs the knowledge of man (v. 3).

• Man's response to the sovereign knowlege and purpose of God must always be repentance and surrender (vv. 4–6).

Psalm Type/Pattern	Figurative Language	Theological Themes
	• conceals my counsel with ignorance	• God's sovereignty • God's wisdom • faith & repentance

Diagram 7.6

ANALYSIS OF APOCALYPTIC LITERATURE

Similarly, the genre of apocalyptic literature is very challenging to interpret.[9] Because of its unique forms and language, apocalyptic literature incorporates both narrative and poetic elements. As is the case with Wisdom literature, use the analysis form that works best

---

9. On this genre of biblical literature, see Fee and Stuart, *How to Read the Bible,* 249–64; Graeme Goldsworthy, *Preaching the Whole Bible as Christian Scripture: The Application of Biblical Theology to Expository Preaching* (Grand Rapids: Eerdmans, 2000), 212–21; Bruce Metzger, *Breaking the Code: Understanding the Book of Revelation* (Nashville: Abingdon, 1993); J. Ramsey Michaels, *Interpreting the Book of Revelation* (Grand Rapids: Baker, 1992); Osborne, *The Hermeneutical Spiral,* 275–90; M. Tenney, *Interpreting Revelation* (Grand Rapids: Eerdmans, 1957).

for the text under consideration, whether narrative, epistolary, or poetic. Diagram 7.7 provides an example of how to outline a portion of an apocalyptic writing.

Text: Revelation 7:9–17

Setting	Characters	Point of View
• Throne room in heaven;	• Jesus (Lamb) • 24 Elders • 4 living creatures • multitude of people before the throne • John	• John as he recounts his vision

Plot
• John sees a multitude of people before the throne, clothed in white robes, waving palm branches and singing, • The 24 Elders and 4 living creatures join in the worship, • John is questioned by an Elder about the multitude but has no answer, • The Elder tells John they represent the souls of the saints from all the nations, • The Elder describes God's blessings for the martyrs.

Peripatia	Theological Themes
• The revelation of the identity of the multitude	• God's sovereignty • worship • justice • reward for the saints

Diagram 7.7

As you can see, every biblical genre requires a unique model of outlining. This outlining will ensure that you properly identify the key elements used by the author in his writing. Rushing through the inspection stage may rob you of the joy and significance you will find in letting a text "speak." Your haste, often influenced by personal presuppositions, may hinder you from "hearing" the text in the way God intends. Instead, make the commitment to study the Scriptures carefully. Your close inspection of every biblical text will help you discover the author's MIT.

CHAPTER 8

THE SIGNIFICANCE OF CONTEXT

T he inspection stage of exegesis is finished once we have identified the genre and developed a genre-specific outline. These
two elements are required to properly examine the content of a text.
When this stage is completed, the second phase of the exegetical
process begins (see diagram 8.1).

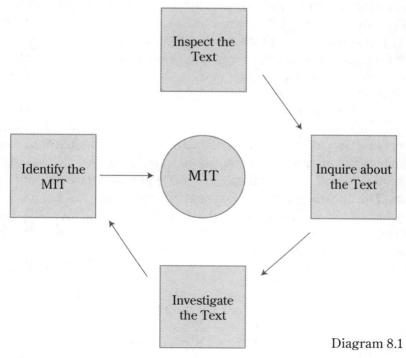

Diagram 8.1

Stage 2 is the inquiry stage. The word "inquire" means to ask a question. In this stage, our attention shifts from observing the content of a text to inquiring about its context.

Consider again our diagram about the Two Horizons (see diagram 8.2). As you can see, the context of a biblical text is linked to the world of the author in the first horizon. Understanding the author's context is critical for understanding his content. Consequently, you must be prepared to study the particularized context of every biblical text.

When interpreters think about the context, they are focusing their attention upon the unique cultural, historical, geographical, and theological factors that existed when the author recorded his particular content for a particular audience. Some interpreters falsely assume that their work is finished as soon as they have inspected the content of a text. To stop at this point, however, is to leave the task of exegesis half-finished. Certainly, understanding the content of every biblical text is vitally important for discovering the author's MIT. Similarly, since the biblical authors addressed the specific needs of their own day in their writings, the significance of the historical context of every biblical text cannot be overstated. A failure to understand the context of a text may lead the interpreter to misinterpret the author's content. Kaiser concurs, "It is exceedingly important that the interpreter complete a thorough investigation of the Biblical book's author, date, cultural, and historical background."[1] Interpreters must spend the time to discover, as best they can, the various contextual elements of every biblical text.

In chapters 5 and 6, we answered the question, "How?" This question is related to the rhetorical design of a text. The genre of a text provides the answer to this question. In chapter 7, we answered the question, "What?" This question is related to the literary design of a text. The outlining process is designed to uncover the unique literary features that the author used to help us grasp his meaning. Both of these questions are linked, ultimately, to the content of a text. Four other questions, borrowed from the Reporter's Formula, can also help us discover the context of the text: Who? When? Where? Why?

---

1.   Walter C. Kaiser Jr., *Toward an Exegetical Theology* (Grand Rapids: Baker, 1981), 50.

WHO?—THE CULTURAL CONTEXT

The cultural context is a crucial element interpreters should consider as they begin to inquire into the results of their initial inspection of a text. The author and readers of every biblical book lived in a particular context—often it was the same, but sometimes it was very different. For instance, most biblical authors of the Old Testament books wrote specifically to the Hebrews. Paul, on the other hand, wrote letters to churches that were increasingly Gentile, and he addressed the unique cultural situations they faced as new believers. When attempting to discover the cultural context of a biblical text, you should consider three specific areas: the author, the actors, and the audience.

Interaction of Two Horizons

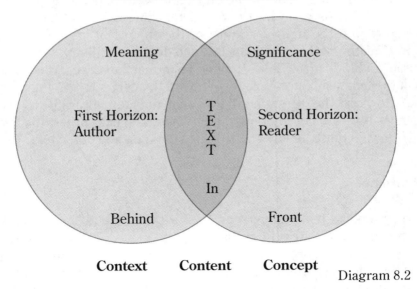

Diagram 8.2

Author

One's assessment of the cultural context begins with the author. In most cases, you will know who the biblical author is with a great deal of historical certainty. In other cases, opinions on authorship may vary. Nevertheless, the internal information in the book will often provide you with information about the author's culture. The author's personal circumstances can also add great insight into his particular place in the culture. For instance, Job's flawed understanding of God's blessings influences the entire book as he grapples with his sudden, personal crisis. There are three questions to ask about the author and his place in the culture: (a) Who wrote the book? (b) What do we know about him? (c) How did his unique experience in his culture shape his purpose in writing?

Actors

This heading may seem strange, but as you remember from our study in chapter 5, much of the Bible is written as historical narrative. Every author had to make choices about which characters or personalities to include in the story and what dialogue and events to highlight. As a result, the characters themselves often provide insights into the unique culture of the time. For instance, David and Goliath provide a window into the different military cultures of Israel and Philistia. When studying historical narratives, you should ask the following questions: (a) Who are the characters in the story? (b) How are they described? (c) What unique, culturally relevant factors are revealed by how the characters speak, dress, and act? (d) How do those factors contribute to the meaning of the text?

Audience

Every biblical text was written with a specific audience in mind. Often, understanding the cultural context of the audience is the key to understanding the meaning of a text. Consider the conclusion to 2 Thessalonians. In 2 Thess 3:6–15, Paul confronts the unwillingness of some Thessalonian believers to work. Some scholars believe that the church's misconceptions about the imminent return of Christ had produced this behavior. The interpreter's understanding of this unique culture within the church at Thessalonica will aid in discovering the author's MIT. When analyzing the audience, you should focus on these questions: (a) Who is the primary audience for this text? (b) What is the unique cultural setting for this audience? (c) What cultural issues are discussed in the text? (d) How are those cultural issues addressed in the text?

WHEN?—HISTORICAL CONTEXT

History is a second contextual element to consider as you continue the inquiry stage. The author and readers of every biblical book lived at a specific time in history. As a result, every biblical event took place in a specific historical context. Because every historical age is unique, knowledge of world affairs may provide unique insights into the text. Several areas need consideration when assessing a text's historical context.

Time

Biblical accounts need to be placed into the world calendar whenever possible. While biblical interpreters are focused primarily on God's redemptive plan for the world as revealed in Scripture and God's Messiah, His plan is accomplished within the context of human history. In fact, God uses world events, even the choices of pagan nations, to accomplish His will on earth. For example, Habakkuk struggles to understand God's use of the Babylonians to judge Israel for their idolatry. When analyzing the time of a text, you should ask these questions: (a) When is this story or event occurring in secular history? (b) Does any event in secular history influence the story or event? (c) Where does this story or event fit in redemptive history? (d) How does this story or event contribute to our understanding of redemptive history? However, when precise historical information is not possible, it does not negate the legitimacy of the text or hinder accurate interpretation since the location of meaning resides within the text, not behind it or in front of it (see chap. 3).

Political Climate

In every historical age political realities influence people and nations. These political realities are often the backdrop against which, or because of which, certain biblical events occur. God routinely accomplishes His will through the political drama and intrigue of pagan nations. The significance of politics can be seen through Haman's scheme to destroy the Jews (Esther) or the Roman tax that took Joseph and Mary to Bethlehem (Luke 2:1–5). When considering the political climate in any biblical text, consider the following questions: (a) What is the dominant nation during this time? (b) What, if any, is Israel's relationship to this nation? (c) Are there any unique, localized, political issues in play in the text? (d) Does politics have a direct impact on the characters or events depicted in the text?

Religious Climate

There is a religious context in every nation. The Bible reveals God's redemptive plan accomplished through the nation of Israel. As you study Scripture, however, you will discover that Israel had encounters with nations who had unique religions and gods. Israel's monotheistic worship of Yahweh, one they did not always consistently practice, was unique in the ancient world. It often brought them into conflict with the nations around them. Often, an interpreter must understand the religious climate of the other nations to grasp the scope of an event. For example, the plagues of Egypt were not just judgments upon Pharaoh; they were God's direct assaults upon the false gods of the Egyptians. When you study the historical context of a book or passage, you should ask these questions about the religious climate: (a) What religion did a nation practice? (b) What gods did they worship, and what does history reveal about those gods? (c) How did their religious beliefs differ from those of Israel? (d) Did the religious climate of this nation influence the characters or events in the text?

WHERE?—GEOGRAPHICAL CONTEXT

Geography is the third contextual element to consider as you continue the inquiry stage. This contextual element is often overlooked in biblical interpretation. Just as every biblical event occurred within a specific cultural and historical context, it also occurred in a specific region of the world. Understanding these regions often increases an interpreter's understanding of the events themselves. As you study the geographical context, pay close attention to the following locales: cities, regions, and countries.

Cities

People have been living in cities since the days of Cain. Most ancient cities were constructed because of their proximity to water, food, trade routes, and natural defenses. As an interpreter, your knowledge of the cities mentioned in the Bible can provide you with important contextual information. For instance, when Jonah arrived in Nineveh, we are told that it was an "extremely large city, a three-day walk" (3:3). This verse has led to several assumptions about the size of the city, including whether it took three days to walk across it or around it. When you encounter the cities mentioned in the Bible, you should ask the following questions: (a) Where was the city located? (b) What was the size and scope of the city? (c) Were there any unique features or historical landmarks associated with the city? (d) Has the city been discovered through modern archaeology? (e) Does the city exist today?

Regions

Every city was located in a specific region of a country. Each region was unique, for the people often spoke different languages or dialects, engaged in different types of commerce, and even warred against one another at different times. Understanding the regions in which cites were located can provide the interpreter interesting and helpful information. The region of Samaria is a classic example. Because the Samaritans had created their own system of worship, the Jews despised them and would not travel through their region. This knowledge provides great insight into Jesus' decision to enter Samaria and witness. When you are studying a region mentioned in a biblical text, you should ask the following questions: (a) Where is the region located in a nation? (b) What cultural factors define the region? (c) Is the region unique in some way topographically, industrially, militarily, or religiously?

Countries

Every region is located in a specific country. These countries relate to one another in unique ways, sometimes as allies and sometimes as enemies. Often, the relationships between these nations change as a result of treaties or intermarriage. Egypt is a prime example of this type of relationship. Pharaoh provided Joseph's family with land and provisions during a time of famine. Later, of course, a subsequent Pharaoh enslaved Jacob's descendents. Primarily, Egypt was an enemy of Israel; at other times, however, Egypt was an ally. You should ask the following questions when you encounter the nations mentioned in the Bible: (a) What nation is mentioned? (b) Where is that nation geographically in relation to Israel? (c) What is the relationship of that nation to Israel? (d) Is that nation used by God to further His redemptive plan for the world in any way?

WHY?—THEOLOGICAL CONTEXT

Theology is the final contextual element to consider as you conclude the inquiry stage of exegesis. This task is one of the most challenging aspects of your interpretive work. Since the Bible is first and foremost a book of theology, every event in the Bible has a theological purpose, even if that purpose is hard to discern. In Esther, for example, God is never even mentioned. However, His providence is on bold display as He preserves his people from the threat of slaughter. When you begin analyzing the theological context, you should consider the following areas: the text, the book, and the canon.

The Text

As we noted earlier, all biblical interpretation must begin at the level of the individual text. You will discover the theological context as you reflect upon the significance of the content and the context of every biblical text. Furthermore, you will discover that the individual texts in a book are working together to communicate the message of the entire book. Finally, the theological themes you discover in individual texts will be connected to the primary thesis of the book as well. For instance, in Eph 2:1–10, Paul provides an explanation of what happens when someone becomes a Christian. In this text, he addresses the following theological themes: (1) the bondage of the will (2:1–3), (2) regeneration (2:4–5), (3) God's grace in salvation (2:6–9), and (4) God's grace in sanctification (2:10). All of these theological truths support Paul's predominant theme in Ephesians: God's grace is demonstrated through the salvation and sanctification of His saints as he is glorified in the building of His church.

When searching for the theological context of a text, you should ask the following questions: (a) What theological themes are mentioned? (b) What theological themes are implied? (c) Which of the stated theological themes are developed? (d) What do the theological themes reveal about God and his redemptive plan in Christ?

The Book

Every book in the Bible contributes uniquely to the unfolding of God's redemptive plan through history—from creation to the eternal state. As a result, your task as an interpreter is to discover the theological themes that each unique book develops. Some books may examine a single theological theme. Jude, for instance, emphasizes the need to remain faithful in the face of a church-infecting apostasy. Books like Ephesians, however, address a number of theological themes: grace, election, predestination, redemption, adoption, and the Spirit's work in producing church unity, family unity, and protection in spiritual warfare. Recognizing theological themes is critical to biblical interpretation. Consider again Eph 2:1–10. The theological context of this text is a part of the larger context of Ephesians chapters 1–3. These chapters form the theological basis for this text—God's grace at work in salvation. Chapters 4–6 examine the theological implications of this book—God's grace at work in sanctification. As you can see, understanding the larger theological purpose of the book is helpful at the level of interpreting the particular text.

When inquiring into the theological context of a book, you should consider the following questions: (a) What are the dominant theological themes? (b) Does one theological theme appear to predominate over the others? (c) What is the primary theological purpose of the book?

The Canon

Every individual book is part of the canon. As a result, you must attempt to discover how the truths revealed in a particular book fit within the totality of Scripture. Our study of the principles of hermeneutics revealed that Scripture never contradicts itself.[2] Every text in the canon is revealing truth about God and His plans for creation. Furthermore, every text adds important information to the developing story of redemption.

As a result, you must think broadly in terms of what Kaiser calls the "canonical context." Kaiser affirms that every text not only has a purpose within its own individual book, but it also has a role within the context of the truth of the entire canon.[3] Because God is the ultimate author of Scripture, you can expect to find a unity of theology in the totality of Scripture, from the level of the particular text to the individual book to the entire canon.[4]

When you are contemplating a particular text within the theological context of the canon, you should ask the following questions: (a) How would the reader have understood this theological theme within his own canonical context? (b) Does this theological theme have some level of correspondence within either the Old Testament or the New Testament? (c) How does this theological theme point to Jesus or reveal Jesus?

Unlocking the meaning of any biblical text depends upon the interpreter's ability to inspect its content and inquire into its unique context. Even at this stage, however, the interpreter is not prepared to identify the MIT. Before that assessment can occur, the interpreter must discover the answers to the questions raised through the first two stages of exegesis.

---

2.   Hermeneutical principle 9 states, "The author's intended meaning in a biblical text will never be in contradiction to his own writings or the rest of the canon."
3.   Kaiser, *Toward an Exegetical Theology,* 53.
4.   An excellent work that addresses this issue is Michael Lawrence, *Biblical Theology in the Life of the Church* (Wheaton: Crossways, 2010).

CHAPTER 9

DISCOVERING THE AUTHOR'S LANGUAGE CLUES IN A TEXT

To this point, we have learned about the inspection and inquiry stages of the exegetical process. Now it is time to move into stage three—the investigation stage.

"Investigate" means to examine something systematically. This stage provides the interpreter with the opportunity to discover the answers to all of the questions raised during both the inspection and inquiry stages. In this stage you will consult a variety of academic resources to help you decipher the author's language clues. Today, interpreters have many scholarly studies available to assist them in their studies. These scholarly resources are available in both print and electronic formats. We will not take the time to cover these resources in this textbook, because the topic has been developed fully elsewhere[1] (see diagram 9.1 on p. 102).

In chapter 7, we provided an example of an analysis of Phil 2:5–11. Now, we will unpack this analysis and see how the investigation stage might look. It is helpful to begin at the semantic level. As a result, we will begin by investigating the key words that we have

---

1. James Stitzinger provides an excellent overview of this topic. James F. Stitzinger, "Study Tools for Expository Preaching," in *Rediscovering Expository Preaching,* ed. Richard L. Mayhue and Robert L. Thomas (Dallas: Word, 1992). Also, consult Daniel L. Akin, *Building a Theological Library*, a booklet that is updated every two years. It can be downloaded at www.danielakin.com.

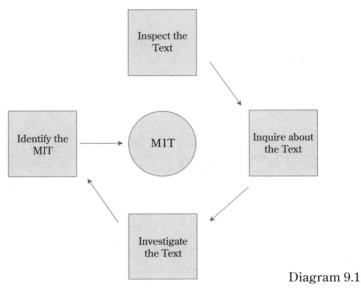

Diagram 9.1

identified. Here is the second part of the Philippians 2 analysis from chapter 7 (see diagram below).

Key Words/Concepts		Theological Themes
• attitude	• external form	• Co-equal deity of God the Son
• existing	• humbled	
• form	• obedient	• Incarnation of Jesus
• consider	• death	
• equality	• cross	• Substitutionary, atoning death of Jesus on the cross
• advantage	• highly exalted	
• emptied	• name	• Exaltation of Jesus
• Himself	• knee bow	
• slave	• tongue confess	
• likeness	• Lord	

Main Idea of the Text

CONTENT INVESTIGATION

It is imperative to have some good resources to help you discover the Greek (or Hebrew) words in a text. A good interlinear Bible, keyed with the Greek vocabulary, or a helpful electronic site or software can help you with this study.[2] Once we have identified the key words in the content of a text, the first step in the investigation stage is to gain an understanding of their meanings.[3] Here is what the notes might look like on a challenging text like Phil 2:5–11.[4]

Verses 5–6

- attitude: *phrōneitē* (imperative/2P); "to think," "to mind," "to be of an opinion," "frame of mind." **Note: command to have a certain mind-set.**
- existing: *huparchōne* (pres/part/sing); "to begin," "to come into existence," "to exist," "to be." **Note: to be in a state of continuing existence.**

---

2. The standard lexicon for biblical Greek is *A Greek-English Lexicon of the New Testament and Other Early Christian Literature*, ed. Frederick W. Danker, 3rd ed. (Chicago: Univ. of Chicago Press, 2000), and an invaluable supplement to *BDAG* is *Greek-English Lexicon of the New Testament: Based on Semantic Domains*, ed. Johannes P. Louw and Eugene A. Nida, 2 vols. (New York: United Bible Societies, 1988). The standard lexicon for biblical Hebrew is *Hebrew and English Lexicon of the Old Testament with an Appendix Containing Biblical Aramaic*, ed. F. Brown, S. R. Driver, and C. A. Briggs (Oxford: Clarendon Press, 1907). These are technical works, but provide the best definitions of words by taking the word's context into consideration.
3. The words in italics refer to the actual Greek words, and the words within quotation marks provide their meanings. The parentheses denote the grammatical information. The notes, written in a bold font, denote the thoughts of the interpreter.
4. Two Greek language resources were used to investigate the meanings of the key words in Phil 2:5–11: Kurt Aland, Matthew Black, et al., eds., *Analytical Greek New Testament* (Grand Rapids: Baker, 1981); Harold K. Moulton, ed., *The Analytical Greek Lexicon Revised* (Grand Rapids: Zondervan Publishing House, 1978). We would also commend Cleon Rogers Jr. and Cleon Rogers III, *The New Linguistic and Exegetical Key to the Greek New Testament* (Grand Rapids: Zondervan, 1998).

- form: *morphē* (simple noun); "form," "the image by which a person or thing is seen." **Note: This word seems to relate to essence vs. a simple external appearance (same word in v. 7—"form of slave").**
- something . . . advantage: *harpagmos* (simple noun); "robbery," "eager seizure," "a thing retained with an eager grasp or eagerly claimed." **Note: Jesus did not eagerly seize upon his own rights and position within the Trinity.**
- consider: *hēgēsato* (ind/aor/mid); "to take the lead"; "to preside, govern, rule"; "to consider or esteem." **Note: Jesus did not attempt to supersede the authority of His Father in regards to the incarnation.**
- equality: *isos* (adj); "equal," "like," "on an equality." **Note: Although Jesus is equal in essence within the Trinity, He embraced a functional subordination.**

Verse 7

- emptied: *ekenōsen*; (aor/ind/act); "to empty, evacuate"; "to divest oneself of one's prerogatives"; "to abase oneself." **Note: Jesus responded to the will of His Father. He "Himself" (see below) laid aside the free exercise of His divine rights to participate in the incarnation.**
- Himself: *heauton*; (pronoun); "himself." **Note: This was an action by Jesus.**
- slave: *doulos* (noun); "slave" or "servant." **Note: Jesus' incarnation was a redemptive act of service; His ministry was an act of service. When one is omnipresent, one's delimitation to time and space is the equivalent of slavery to a body.**
- likeness of men: *homōiomati anthrōpōn* (nouns); "resembling men." **Note: Jesus looked like any other male human being; He embraced of a real human nature and body.**
- external form: *schēma* (noun); "external show," "guise," "appearance." **Note: Jesus was human in every way from the physical perspective. This word is contrasted with "form" in verse 6.**

Verse 8

- humbled: *etapeinosen* (ind/aor/act); "to humble, abase"; "to humble oneself." **Note: This word, joined with "heauton" (see on previous page), reveals that just as Jesus "emptied" Himself of His divine prerogatives, so too did He "humble" Himself to the greatest degree, even to the point of death on a cross.**
- obedient: *hupēkoos* (adj); "to obey," "to render submissive acceptance," "to be submissive." **Note: Jesus demonstrated his humility through obedience. One must be willing to come under the full authority of another to obey them.**
- death: *thanatos* (noun); "to die," "to be dead." **Note: Jesus was completely, humanly dead after His crucifixion. There is no room for swoon theory here.**
- cross: *stauros* (noun); "a stake"; "a cross"; "by implication, the punishment of the cross; crucifixion." **Note: Jesus died in a specific way—Roman crucifixion.**

Verse 9–11

- for this reason: *dio* (conj); "wherefore," "therefore." **Note: This transitional clue provides the rational for the exaltation of Jesus in verses 9–11; it is specifically because of His humility/obedience to the sovereign plan of the Father in redemption.**
- highly exalted: *huperupsōsen* (aor/ind/act); "to exalt supremely." **Note: God the Father has given Jesus a position above everything and everyone else that exists anywhere in God's creation (excluding the Trinity).**
- name: *onoma* (noun); "name," "proper name of a person," "specificity." **Note: God has declared that there is no greater name in all of creation than Jesus. We note that some believe the name given is "Lord."**
- so that: *hina* (conj); "that," "in order that," "so that." **Note: This clause demonstrates the result of the action of God giving Jesus the name above all names. One day, by virtue**

of that name, and the person and position it represents, all people will bow.

- knee should bow: *gonu; kampsē* (noun; aor/sub/act); "knee"; "to bend, bow"; "to inflect (the knee)." **Note: These words described the classic meaning of bowing before a sovereign or superior.**
- tongue . . . confess: *glossa; exomologēsētai* (noun; aor/sub/mid); "tongue," "agree," "bind oneself," "promise," "to confess or profess openly." **Note: Just as knees will bow automatically, so, too, will tongues openly confess that Jesus Christ is Lord. They will do this to the ultimate glory of the Father, who accomplished his redemptive plan through His Son, Jesus Christ.**
- Lord: *kurios* (noun); "lord," "master"; "owner," "possessor"; "potentate," "sovereign," "deity." **Note: Jesus is sovereign king over all of creation.**

CONTEXT INVESTIGATION

Numerous resources are available to assist you with discovering the contextual issues in a biblical text. These resources include Bible dictionaries, handbooks, surveys, theology texts, and commentaries. It is often helpful to select one excellent commentary set and then supplement it with individual commentaries as necessary. When studying a text, a collection of four to five good commentaries is the irreducible minimum. With these resources in hand, the interpreter can begin tackling the contextual issues in a text. In chapter 8, we identified the contextual questions to ask of every biblical text. The investigation stage is the time to ask and answer those questions. We will continue to use Phil 2:5–11 as our example. The contextual notes for this text might look like these.

WHO?—CULTURAL CONTEXT

- Author: Paul (There was unanimous consensus in the early church that Paul wrote this letter).
- Actors: N/A (This text is not a historical narrative.)
- Audience: Church at Philippi

WHEN?—HISTORICAL CONTEXT

- Time:
  - ⇒ AD 60–63: Paul wrote the letter during his first imprisonment in Rome. (The references "imperial guard" [Phil 1:13] and the "saints in Caesar's household" [4:22] both suggest Rome.)
  - ⇒ Option 2: Paul wrote the letter during his two-year captivity in Caesarea. (However, the items listed above are not consistent with his Caesarean captivity.)
  - ⇒ Option 3: Paul wrote the letter from Ephesus. (This option is a minority position and does not meet the test of Option 1 or 2.)
  - ⇒ NOTE: We believe that Rome is the best option as the location.[5]

- Political Climate:
  - ⇒ Nero was Caesar from AD 54–68.
  - ⇒ Nero was noted for being tyrannical and paranoid. Ancient records suggest he killed his mother and stepbrother and killed Christians as punishment for burning Rome (historians lay that at Nero's feet).
  - ⇒ Facing assassination, Nero committed suicide at the age of 31. Rome's relationship with the Jews and Christians was tenuous during this time.[6]

- Religious Climate:
  - ⇒ **In Rome:** While the Jews were allowed to practice their religion in Israel (specifically within the Temple area), Christianity was outlawed in the Roman Empire. In order to avoid a death sentence in Jerusalem, Paul used his right as a Roman citizen to appeal his legal case to Caesar. During his imprisonment (Acts 28:30–31), Paul was able to receive guests and continue his ministry, primarily through his writing. A number of people in Nero's household had

---

5.   John MacArthur, *The MacArthur Bible Handbook* (Nashville: Thomas Nelson, 2003), 407.

6.   *The Hutchinson Dictionary of World History* (Surrey: Oxon Helicon Publishing Limited, 2004), eBook, 1270.

been converted to Christianity, ostensibly through Paul. Although it cannot be proved, many scholars believe that Paul was beheaded during the latter reign of Nero, after a fourth missionary journey and second Roman imprisonment, presumably during the persecution that followed the burning of Rome in AD 64.

⇒ **In Philippi:** The city of Philippi appeared to have a very small Jewish population, as they did not have enough Jewish men to have a synagogue (since 10 men were required) at the time that Paul arrived (Acts 16). Some devout women worshipped by the river, where on his second missionary journey Paul saw Lydia converted. Paul was unjustly beaten and imprisoned in Philippi (where as a Roman citizen he was entitled to due process). The Philippian jailer and his family were converted during that event.[7]

WHERE?—GEOGRAPHICAL CONTEXT

- City:
  - ⇒ Philippi was named for Philip II of Macedon, who was the father of Alexander the Great.
  - ⇒ Philippi became a part of the Roman Empire in the second century BC.
  - ⇒ Philippi gained fame as a result of perhaps the most famous Roman battle, which pitted the forces of Antony and Octavian against Brutus and Cassius. Antony and Octavian were victorious, and their victory ended the republic and initiated the Empire.
  - ⇒ As a Roman colony, Philippi had all of the rights and privileges as Rome itself.

- Region:
  - ⇒ Philippi was located near the end of the *Via Egnatia* between Thessalonica and the coastal region of Neapolis.
  - ⇒ This region was well known for its gold and silver mines.

---

7. MacArthur, *Handbook,* 408.

- Country:
  - ⇒ Philippi was located in the Roman province of Macedonia along the *Via Egnatia*, a pivotal trade route between Rome and the East.
  - ⇒ When Paul was trying to head to the East with the gospel, he was prevented by the Holy Spirit in a vision, where a man from Macedonia called to Paul for help (Acts 16:6–10).
  - ⇒ On his second missionary journey, once he arrived in Macedonia, Paul visited Philippi first.
  - ⇒ Philippi is the first city in Europe to hear the gospel from Paul.[8]

WHY?—THEOLOGICAL CONTEXT

- Co-equal deity of God the Son with God the Father
  - ⇒ "form [morphe] of God"; "The idea is that, before the Incarnation, from all eternity past, Jesus preexisted in the divine form of God, equal with God the Father in every way. By His very nature and innate being, Jesus Christ is, always has been, and will forever be fully divine."[9]
  - ⇒ "equality (isos) with God"; "In Philippians 2:6 the word *isos* teaches that Jesus is God's equal."[10]
  - ⇒ Council of Nicaea (AD 325): homoousios; Christ exists as God "from all eternity," and He is "of one substance with the Father."[11]

- Incarnation of Jesus:
  - ⇒ "form of a slave, taking on the likeness of men"; "Although He continued to fully exist as God, during His incarnation He refused to hold on to His divine rights and prerogatives."[12]

8. Ibid.
9. John MacArthur, *Philippians* (Chicago: Moody, 2001), 122.
10. James M. Boice, *Philippians* (Grand Rapids: Baker, 2000), 116.
11. Timothy George, "The Nature of God: Being Attributes, and Acts," in *A Theology for the Church,* ed., Daniel L. Akin (Nashville: B&H, 2007), 211–13.
12. MacArthur, *Philippians,* 124.

⇒ "He emptied himself of all of its prerogatives. . . . completely of every vestige of advantage and privilege, refusing to assert any divine right on His own behalf."[13]

⇒ hamoiomati anthropon; "refers to that which is made to be like something else, not just in appearance but in reality. Jesus was not a clone, a disguised alien, or merely some reasonable facsimile of a man. He became exactly like all other human beings, having all the attributes of humanity, a genuine man among men."[14]

⇒ "Paul writes that the one who was in the form of God and was God's equal from all eternity took the form of a man at a particular moment in history. He took upon himself the nature of a servant; he was made in human likeness" (cf. Gal. 4:4).[15]

⇒ "The witness of the New Testament is that God indeed became one of us in the person of Jesus Christ. The Old Testament promised that he would come, and the New Testament testifies that he came. The New Testament records a varied and complementary witness to the God who took on humanity, the Word who became flesh" (John 1:14). A quintessential quartet stands out in what they teach concerning both the deity and humanity of Jesus. The texts are John 1:1–18; Phil 2:5–11; Col 1:15–23; 2:9–10; and Heb 1:1–4.[16]

- Substitutionary, atoning death of Jesus on the cross:
  ⇒ "In His stepping downward, Jesus was willing to suffer humiliation and degradation even to becoming obedient to the point of death. . . . The Father did not force death upon the Son. It was the Father's will, but it was the Son's will always to perfectly obey the Father. He had a free choice. Had He not had a choice, He could not have been obedient."[17]

---

13. Ibid., 126.
14. Ibid., 130.
15. Boice, *Philippians,* 120.
16. Daniel L. Akin, "The Person of Christ," in *A Theology for the Church* (Nashville: B&H, 2007), 492.
17. MacArthur, *Philippians,* 133–34.

⇒ "Jesus submitted even to death on a cross. There were many ways by which He could have been killed. He could have been beheaded, such as John the Baptist was, or stoned or hanged. But He was destined not for just any kind of death but for death on a cross."[18]

⇒ "In God's infinite wisdom, death on a cross was the only way of redemption for fallen, sinful, and condemned mankind."[19]

⇒ "The cross is the central figure of the New Testament. . . . the cross of Christ is in a real sense the central theme of the Old Testament. . . . The cross stands as the focal point of the Christian faith."[20]

⇒ "This is what Jesus Christ came to do. He came to remove our sin, bearing it in his own person. Sin separates men from God, but Jesus removes that sin. He was made sin for us. . . . The second reason for Christ's death is that he died to satisfy divine justice. The justice of God calls for the punishment of sin, and the punishment of sin is death. Jesus paid that penalty by dying in our place, satisfying divine justice and leaving nothing for us but God's heaven."[21]

⇒ "Jesus Christ, the Son of God, was born to die. Unlike any other person who has ever lived, he came into this world for the expressed purpose of dying on the cross as the perfect sacrifice for the sins of the world."[22]

⇒ "According to Paul, what happens in the propitiatory sacrifice of Christ on the cross is a grand exhibition of God's righteousness in which whoever comes to God by faith in Jesus is justified, and more importantly, he is justified justly."[23]

- Eternal Exaltation of Jesus:
  ⇒ "The humble, incarnate Savior has been exalted as the almighty and sovereign Lord. Because of that, believers

---

18. Ibid., 134.
19. Ibid., 135.
20. Boice, *Philippians,* 124–25.
21. Ibid., 126–27.
22. Paige Patterson, "The Work of Christ," in Akin, *A Theology for the Church,* 545.
23. Ibid., 563–64.

have the assurance that their redemption is certain and that their place in heaven is secured forever. He is also to be obeyed as divine Lord, and honored and worshiped throughout all time and eternity."[24]

⇒ "highly exalted": "God lifted up His beloved Son in the most magnificent way possible. It involved four steps upward: His resurrection, His ascension, His coronation, and His intercession."[25]

⇒ "name above every name": "Whoever is Lord is over everyone else—and that is precisely the point in so titling the Savior—has absolute supremacy and the right to be obeyed as divine Master."[26]

⇒ "Jesus is God's Messiah. He is God's Son. He is the Son of man. He is our prophet, priest, and king, the Alpha and Omega, the door, the Beloved, and many other names. But the title 'Lord' is above them all. It is at the name of Jesus Christ as lord that every knee shall bow."[27]

⇒ "The future has a name: Jesus of Nazareth. Like all doctrines of the faith, eschatology is an outworking of Christology. God's final purpose with his creation is to 'bring everything together in the Messiah, both things in heaven and things on earth in Him'" (Eph 1:10).[28]

While not every text may require the same level of in-depth word study or theological analysis as Phil 2:5–11, many will. The simple truth is that exegesis takes time. Remember that the goal of exegesis, and ultimately of hermeneutics, is to let the text speak for itself. We want to discover the author's MIT. Before we conclude our exegesis of Phil 2:5–11, let us reflect on our journey to this point.

In stage one of the exegetical process, we inspected the text and focused our attention on its *content*. We began by determining the genre of the text. Genre is important because it may yield valuable

---

24. When you actually write your sermon manuscript, in-text citations are the easiest means of tracking your key sources. We model this method in this section of "Eternal Exaltation of Jesus," MacArthur, *Philippians*, 139.

25. Ibid., 140.

26. Ibid., 143.

27. Boice, *Philippians*, 131–32.

28. Akin, *A Theology for the Church*, 892–93.

interpretive clues. Next, we outlined the text, using a genre-specific outline. Outlines help us discover the main ideas that are being developed by the author. Finally, we took the time to analyze the author's language usage in order to identify the key words and concepts he addressed, whether explicitly, implicitly, or through figurative language.

In stage two of the exegetical process, we inquired about the text and focused our attention on its *context*. We identified the specific contextual elements that must be examined and provided a series of questions to be asked about each one. The answers to these questions provide us with a solid understanding of the context in which the author and his readers lived. We use these questions to guide our research in the third stage of the process.

In stage three of the exegetical process, we investigated the text itself, answering the questions we raised through our study of the text's content and context. Here, we discovered the meaning of the key words and researched the contextual areas as well.[29] The process of exegesis, informed as it is by the principles of hermeneutics, requires a close inspection of the text. This inspection provides the information necessary to discover the author's MIT. Determining the author's MIT and its implications for the contemporary audience is the final stage of the exegetical process. We will examine this stage in chapter 10.

---

29. In the notes above, you can see that we have included a significant amount of information about the location and history of Philippi. If you were preaching a "stand-alone" sermon on Phil 2:5–11, you should do this type of in-depth, contextual research. Of course, if you were teaching through the entire book of Philippians, you would do much of this general work at the beginning of your study. Then, you would incorporate information about the particular contextual issues you encounter as you preach through the text.

CHAPTER 10

IDENTIFYING THE MAIN IDEA
OF THE TEXT

A s we conclude section 1, revisiting our primary definitions for hermeneutics and exegesis may be helpful. Hermeneutics is the proper use of the principles of interpretation to discover the author's intended meaning of a biblical text, with a goal of applying that meaning to a contemporary audience. In this textbook, we have identified 10 principles that provide the foundation for our exegesis. These principles will protect us from the danger of eisegesis and the faulty interpretations it produces.

Exegesis is the proper use of the process of interpretation to discover the author's intended meaning of a biblical text, with a goal of applying that meaning to a contemporary audience. Our exegetical model requires the interpreter to inspect, inquire, and investigate every biblical text. When these steps have been completed, it is time to identify the author's MIT. This step is the fourth and final stage of the exegetical process. We must be able to clearly identify and state the MIT before we are ready to identify its significance for the contemporary audience (see diagram 10.1 on page 115).

STATING THE MAIN IDEA OF THE TEXT

Much has been written about the importance of stating the main idea of the text, or what some call the textual idea, in a clear and

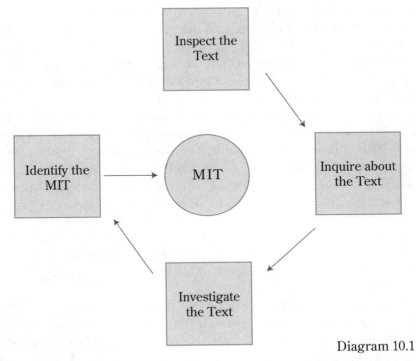

Diagram 10.1

concise manner. Wayne McDill believes that the main idea of the text should be written as a past-tense sentence.[1] Wording the MIT in the past-tense helps the interpreter remain focused on the meaning of the text rather than its significance at this point. We must identify first what the text meant when it was written.

As you attempt to identify the MIT, several textual clues may help you. First, attempt to discover if the MIT is stated overtly. Often, especially in the Epistles, the author clearly states the MIT. For instance, consider Eph 4:17–24. Paul clearly states the MIT in verses 17 and 24 when he writes, "You should no longer walk as the Gentiles walk, in the futility of their thoughts. . . . Put on the new man, the one created according to God's likeness in righteousness and purity of the truth." This text then prescribes the steps necessary to accomplish this.

---

1. Wayne McDill, *The 12 Essential Skills for Great Preaching* (Nashville: B&H, 1994), 88.

Second, in the event the author's MIT is not stated overtly, look for the repetition of key words. When the author repeats the same words or cognates, he is emphasizing their importance. The MIT may be linked to that repetition. In Eph 6:18–20, Paul mentions prayer five times. Clearly, he is emphasizing its significance within the context of spiritual warfare.

Third, in the absence of an overt declaration or the repetition of key words, look for a dominant theme or image to reveal the author's MIT. This strategy is an excellent one for dealing with historical narratives and parables, and even with Psalms. In Luke 9:57–62, for instance, we see Jesus recruiting workers for a short-term mission of proclamation. Jesus responds to a number of interesting excuses during the recruitment process. As you study this discourse, there is neither an overtly stated exegetical idea nor the repetition of key words. Rather, this theme recurs throughout it: The concerns of life may hinder one's journey of faith. This theme is Luke's MIT in this discourse.

Now, consider Phil 2:5–11 in light of the three textual clues listed above. First, we must look to see if the main idea is overtly stated. As we look at the discourse, verse 5 provides us with a prescriptive statement in the form of a present imperative. When we look at the greater context, however, we recognize that the humiliation and exaltation of Jesus receives the greatest attention in this text, not the readers. A quick perusal of 2:6–11 fails to reveal an overt main idea, but it is clearly linked to verse 5 and the idea of the mind of Christ. The second step would be looking for the use of repetitive words or cognates. Looking back at our outline, we notice that no words or cognates are repeated in this text. However, the idea of humility in 2:8 is also addressed in 2:3, providing us a clue for future investigation.

The final step is to examine the text for a dominant theme or image. This analysis requires us to look at the text itself as well as the larger context in which it is found. Remember, 2:5 serves as a bridge between 1:27–2:4 and 2:6–11. When we pause to consider those verses, a couple of ideas become apparent. First, the exegetical idea of 1:27–2:4 is found in 1:27, "Live your life in a manner worthy of the gospel of Christ." Paul explains that idea in the following verses. When we look at his teaching, we will note that "rivalry" and "conceit" are the two attitudes that can derail gospel-worthy living.

In 2:3, we find a word that ties this section to 2:5–11: "humility." Paul states, "Do nothing out of rivalry or conceit, but in humility consider others as more important than yourselves." Suddenly, the larger context has provided a link to our text—the repetition of the word "humility." The word "humility," in turn, places 2:5 into its proper place as a bridge verse, and the word "attitude" becomes very significant to both discourses. Suddenly, we feel the text opening before us. Additional work must be done, however. At this point, we must once again turn our attention to the first part of our outline (see diagram 10.2).

In chapter seven, we learned that the author's use of independent clauses provides insights into his MIT. As we look at the outline above, there are five independent clauses in this text. The first clause is the bridge verse found in 2:5. It is also an imperative, a word of command. It introduces the concept of attitude, which clearly references the "conceit," "rivalry," and "humility" mentioned in 2:3. The second clause introduces the notion of "equality." This theme resonates throughout 1:27–2:4. In those verses, Paul challenged the church to work "side by side," "focus on one goal," and "consider others as more important than yourselves." Later in 4:2–3, this theme reappears as he tries to reconcile two ladies, calling them to "be of the same mind in the Lord." These phrases emphasize the equality of believers in ministry. The third and fourth clauses reveal two specific actions by Jesus that were necessitated by his incarnation and sacrificial death. These clauses point back to 2:4, where Paul challenged the church to "look out for the interests of others." The last clause reveals the final result of Jesus' sacrificial death—his exaltation above all of creation.

At this point, we are close to identifying Paul's MIT in Phil 2:5–11. As interpreters, we have found it beneficial to make a list that clarifies the main concepts in a text. This list is based upon our understanding of the independent clauses and the significant words and themes that connect them to the larger context. As we consider the larger context in which 2:5–11 is located, several truths have become apparent: (a) Paul challenged the church to relate to one another in a spirit of equality—this attitude eliminates any personal posturing based upon rivalry or conceit. (b) Paul's solution to this problem is the cultivation of a personal humility that places value upon the interests of others. (c) Jesus is the model for this attitude. (d) Although

Scope: Philippians 2:5–11

Make your own attitude that of Christ Jesus [cf. 2:1–4]

<u>who</u> [Christ Jesus] . . . did not consider equality with God as something to be used for His own advantage,

⮕ existing in the form of God

<u>Instead</u> He emptied Himself

⮕ by assuming the form of a slave,

⮕ taking on the likeness of men.

. . . He humbled Himself

⮕ . . . And when He had come as a man in His external form . . .

⮕ by becoming obedient to the point of death—even to death on a cross.

<u>For this reason</u> [2:6–8], God also highly exalted Him and gave Him the name that is above every name [result—vv. 6–8]

⮕ <u>so that</u> . . . , EVERY KNEE SHOULD BOW—of those who are in heaven and on earth and under the earth—

⮕ and every tongue should confess that Jesus Christ is Lord

⮕ . . . at the name of Jesus . . .

⮕ to the glory of God

Transitional Cues: "who" (2:6); "Instead" (2:7); "For this reason" (2:9); "so that" (2:10)

Diagram 10.2

Jesus is equal with God, He embraced the "functional subordination" that was inherent in the incarnation. (e) Jesus' incarnation demonstrated a willingness to "look out for the interests of others" at His own expense. (f) Jesus demonstrated authentic humility by obeying the will of His Father to the point of His own death on the cross. (g) Jesus has been exalted over all creation as a result of His personal atonement for the sins of humanity.

With this information before us, it is time to identify the MIT of Phil 2:5–11. Once again, 2:5 is significant because it provides a bridge between 1:27–2:4 and 2:6–11. It places the emphasis upon one's personal attitudes. Our next step is to consider the attitudes of Jesus that are identified. As we look at the independent clauses, humility is the only attitude that is mentioned. When we note that humility is mentioned in 2:3 and 2:8, we may conclude that Paul's primary point of emphasis in this particular text is the humility of Jesus, which serves as the model for humility in the church.

All that remains is to develop a past-tense statement of the MIT. The goal is not that every interpreter arrive at a statement that is worded exactly the same. The goal is to include all of the information necessary to answer the question raised in chapter 3: "What is the author's intended meaning?" Here is an example of how we might word the MIT: *Jesus demonstrated an authentic humility for us to imitate, by setting aside the privileges of deity through His incarnation and obeying God to the point of death on the cross.* This statement emphasizes the MIT, which is Jesus' humility, while demonstrating the way He modeled it for the church. Notice how it appears on our final, exegetical chart (see diagram 10.3).

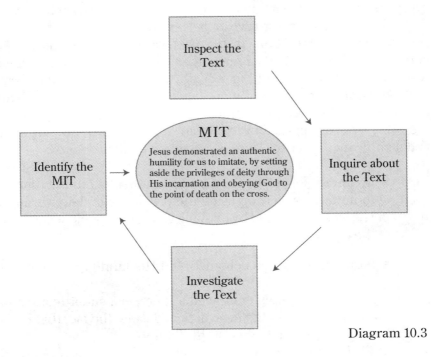

Diagram 10.3

Once we have stated the textual idea, it is time to answer the second question raised in chapter 3: "What is the significance of the author's intended meaning?" Only at this point in the process of exegesis are we ready to reflect upon the significance of the text for the contemporary audience. Michael Fabarez reminds us of this step when he states, "Meaning is discovered as I rightly understand the truth presented in a passage of Scripture; significance is discovered as I rightly determine the impact that truth is intended to make on my congregation."[2] As we attempt to answer this second question of hermeneutics, the goal is to identify the key areas of application for the contemporary audience.

Depending upon the genre, the application may be overtly stated or simply inferred. Often, the application of the text is clear when we study the Epistles. The application of texts in other genres, like historical narratives, may be more difficult to identify. As we seek to identify the significance of a text, we may ask yet another question: What is the author *saying* about the MIT? Often this question will help us discover the application of the text. Keep in mind that while every text has one primary meaning, it may have several applications.

At this point, we must revisit the text to consider what Paul is *saying* about the MIT both in the primary text and in the larger context. In Phil 2:5–11, Paul notes that humility was at the core of Jesus' incarnation, ministry, and death, and that Jesus' willingness to demonstrate perfect humility resulted in his exaltation above all creation. Once we have determined what the author is saying about the MIT, we are prepared to finish our assessment of the meaning and significance of a text. Here is one way it could be stated:

⇒ Meaning: Jesus demonstrated an authentic humility for us to imitate, by setting aside the privileges of deity through His incarnation and by obeying God to the point of death on the cross.

⇒ Significance: Jesus demonstrated His humility in four tangible ways:
   1) Jesus willingly embraced a functional subordination to the Father in the incarnation, despite the fact that He is a co-equal member of the Trinity.
   2) Jesus willingly embraced the complete union of deity and humanity, with all of its inherent, physical limitations.

---

2. Michael Fabarez, *Preaching that Changes Lives* (Nashville: Thomas Nelson, 2002), 37–38.

3) Jesus willingly embraced the horrific death of crucifixion to provide a perfect atonement for human sin.
4) Jesus willingly embraced His exaltation over creation as a gift from His Father.

There are a number of other applications that Paul develops within the larger context of Phil 1:27–2:11. Paul argues that a humility modeled after Jesus will have the following benefits for the church: (a) Humility is an evidence of total dependence upon God, even in the face of persecution and suffering (1:27–30). (b) Humility is a requirement for unity in love and purpose within the church (2:1–2). (c) Humility is the antidote for rivalry and conceit within the church (2:3–4). (d) Humility is the attitude necessary to value others more than oneself (2:3–4). As we reflect upon these statements about humility, Jesus' demonstration of perfect humility is clearly the model for the interaction of believers within His church.

As you can see, all of these applications draw their significance from 2:5–11. Now, including all of this information in one sermon would be quite challenging. While exposition can be done on individual texts, and done well we must add, preaching through entire books allows the pastor-teacher to make the connections between individual texts and the larger context in which they are found. Over the long term, this approach is a great benefit to the church.

When the interpreter reaches this point, the process of exegesis, informed as it is by the principles of hermeneutics, is complete. The pastor-teacher has examined the substance of the text, discerned the structure of the text, and discovered the main idea of the text and its significance for his listeners. At this point, it is time to begin the process of using this material to craft an expository sermon. You will discover how to do this in section 2.

SECTION 2

CHAPTER 11

DEVELOPING THE MAIN IDEAS OF THE TEXT AND MESSAGE

C hapters 1–10 have taken us through the hermeneutical dimension of discovering how to build an engaging exposition of Scripture. To summarize, we have noted the following as essential components of steps 1 (studying) and 2 (structuring) of the hermeneutical process:

1. *Study the book as a whole*
   A. Consider the questions of date, authorship, recipients, and purpose (general matters of introduction).
   B. Develop an outline of the entire book (using study Bibles and commentaries).
   C. Examine the relationship of the passage under consideration in both its immediate and larger context.

2. *Establish the best textual base possible*
   A. Use the original languages if you can.
   B. Compare various versions and translations.

3. *Investigate the text linguistically (e.g., word by word within its context and semantic range)*
   A. Make a lexical (definitional) study of crucial words.

B. Research the passage for key words, phrases, and ideas.
C. Track the verbs.
D. Cross reference.

4. *Determine the genre of the discourse*
   A. What is the literary type (history, poetry, prophetic, apocalyptic)?
   B. What literary devices are used?
   C. Is there any indication of the life situation from which the material came?

5. *Analyze the structure of the passage*[1]
   A. Determine if the material constitutes a literary unity.
   B. Is there a logical sequence of ideas present?
   C. Isolate the basic themes or emphases.
   D. Outline the text you are studying. Use the outline as the framework for your teaching.

We can also highlight some of the basic interpretive rules we discovered, which must constantly guide us in the hermeneutical/homiletical construction process. First, the context rules when we interpret the text. Second, the text must be interpreted in light of all Scripture. Third, Scripture will never contradict itself. Fourth, Scripture should be interpreted literally (or according to its genre). Fifth, do not develop a doctrine from obscure or difficult passages. Sixth, discover the author's original intended meaning and honor that meaning. Seventh, check your conclusions by using reliable resources.

Now, at this point we want to introduce a diagram that provides an overview of where we have been and where we are. It should help you get a grasp of the "big picture" of sermon development.

---

1. A helpful resource for analyzing the structure of the text as it applies to the Old Testament is David Dorsey, *The Literary Structure of the Old Testament* (Grand Rapids: Baker, 1999).

As we have seen, the faithful interpreter and preacher of God's Word must bridge the gap or horizon between the cultural elements present in the text of Scripture and those in our own time. He must move from the hermeneutical to the homiletical. Some call this proposal to bridge this gap, "ethnohermeneutics," which recognizes three horizons in cross-cultural interpretation: (1) the culture of the Bible, (2) the culture of the interpreter, and (3) the culture of the receptor. Care must be exercised not to let the second and third horizons dictate the message of the first horizon. However, it would be utterly foolish to ignore the latter two.

Therefore, the following diagram helps visualize the essentials of our overall process, and it shows how we move from the ancient world of the biblical text to the modern world of the people we teach and instruct.

In our pyramidic diagram you can see a number of interesting points and parallels.

1. The hermeneutical and the homiletical beautifully balance one another.
2. Steps 2 and 6 complement each other, as do steps 3 and 5.
3. If the hermeneutical aspect of sermon development is done well, the homiletical component will naturally follow because the latter should flow from the former.
4. This method is simple and easily transferable to others we might teach and instruct to build biblically faithful expository sermons.[2]

---

2.   Our method is quite similar to that of Ramesh Richard, *Preparing Expository Sermon* (Grand Rapids: Baker, 1995, 2001). Certain aspects of our model draw significantly from his.

HOW TO STUDY AND PREACH THE BIBLE

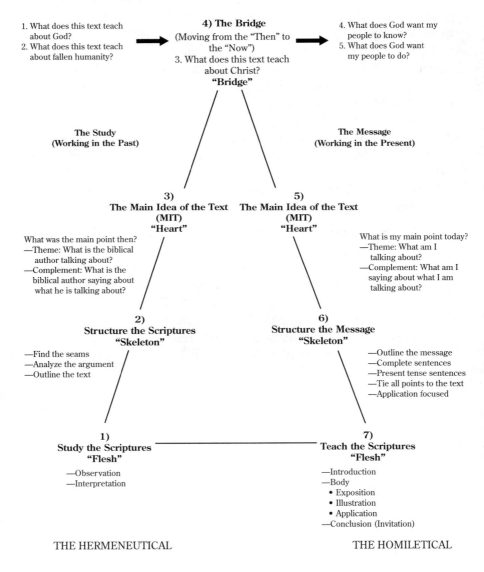

1. What does this text teach about God?
2. What does this text teach about fallen humanity?

4) The Bridge
(Moving from the "Then" to the "Now")
3. What does this text teach about Christ?
"Bridge"

4. What does God want my people to know?
5. What does God want my people to do?

The Study
(Working in the Past)

The Message
(Working in the Present)

3)
The Main Idea of the Text (MIT)
"Heart"

What was the main point then?
—Theme: What is the biblical author talking about?
—Complement: What is the biblical author saying about what he is talking about?

5)
The Main Idea of the Text (MIT)
"Heart"

What is my main point today?
—Theme: What am I talking about?
—Complement: What am I saying about what I am talking about?

2)
Structure the Scriptures
"Skeleton"

—Find the seams
—Analyze the argument
—Outline the text

6)
Structure the Message
"Skeleton"

—Outline the message
—Complete sentences
—Present tense sentences
—Tie all points to the text
—Application focused

1)
Study the Scriptures
"Flesh"

—Observation
—Interpretation

7)
Teach the Scriptures
"Flesh"

—Introduction
—Body
  • Exposition
  • Illustration
  • Application
—Conclusion (Invitation)

THE HERMENEUTICAL

THE HOMILETICAL

GETTING AT THE MAIN IDEA
OF THE TEXT (MIT)

The main idea of the text (MIT) was discussed at length in chapter ten in the hermeneutical section. Our discussion builds on the insights gleaned there. We have seen that the main idea of a text (step 3) naturally derives from our studying of the Scriptures (step 1) and our structuring of the Scriptures (step 2). Having prayed over the entire process, we have (1) tracked and identified the key verbs and parsed them; (2) looked for key words needing definition; (3) identified repetition of words and phrases; (4) located the seams in the text, which inform us as to the proper division of the passage; (5) noted the context; (6) searched for helpful and supporting Scripture; (7) written out any and all observations and applications uncovered in the discovery process; and (8) examined our study aids and commentaries for helpful insight, as well as a check and balance to our interpretation.

Now we move to the third important step in our study of the text: the MIT. This step is the text's heart. Every text will usually have several ideas that need to be studied and developed. Still, each text will also have a main idea that all other ideas support and amplify. Most students of hermeneutics and homiletics agree about this, even if they identify the main idea with different terminology such as the Big Idea, the Central Idea of the Text, or the Textual Idea. If our listeners leave with this main idea ringing in their ears and planted in their hearts, with the intent to act upon it, we will have succeeded in our holy assignment.

We believe three key questions can help us identify and clarify the MIT. First, what was the main point then (Idea)? Second, what was the biblical author talking about (Theme)? Third, what was the biblical author saying about what he was talking about (Complement)?

At the heart of a text, usually a paragraph, should be one cardinal thought: the MIT. This proposition is made up of two components: the *theme* and the *complement*. The main idea, as noted above, is sometimes called by other names: "textual idea," "central idea," "exclusive emphasis," or the "big idea."

The main idea is the single idea around which the details of the text are woven. Since we want to communicate one major point for the people to hear, understand, and obey, we seek to communicate the major idea of each Scripture text in contemporary terms. Charles

Simeon writes, "Reduce your text to a simple proposition . . . illustrating the main idea by the various terms in which it is contained."[3] The main idea of the text is the single unit of thought that binds together and gives meaning to all the particulars of a text. In some manner it should relate to your title. We will address how to relate the main idea of the text to the title later.

It should always be in the form of a full grammatical sentence, and be stated clearly and concisely. It places a laser beam focus on (1) what the author is talking about and (2) what the author is saying about what he is talking about.

A question naturally arises at this point. Where does one get the MIT? As we saw in the hermeneutical section, the answer is simple. The MIT is derived from your studying and structuring of the text. It is located right before you in your prior work in the text. In order to get the main idea of the text, put the content of the subjects, themes, main points, or summaries together. In arriving at the MIT, you are looking for accuracy and adequacy. The MIT should precisely reflect your particular text and must cover the assertions of the text. The theme of your text should be specific. Grammatical or content cues will tell you what is the controlling theme: What is the author talking about? That then leads to the supporting evidence gleaned from the complement: What is the author saying about the theme?

Now, here are some practical steps to consider in this stage of your work in the study.

1. Give a tentative title to the text. This title could well be the "theme" of the MIT.
2. If possible, write a personal translation or paraphrase of the text reflecting the flow or argument of the text.
3. Write out the main idea of the text. Put the theme and complement in full sentence form. The full statement does not need to be long, but it does need to be adequate. You will most likely refine it and even shorten it as you work with it.

Here you are culminating the study process as far as the text itself is concerned. If you desire to be an expositor of the Word of God, you will seek to impress on your people what the author stresses—the

---

3. Quoted in John R. W. Stott, *I Believe in Preaching* (London: Hodder & Stoughton, 1998), 226.

truth of this text. Remember, God is the ultimate author of the text. We want to honor what He put there. A good message should have a one sentence statement that summarizes the passage being taught. If you cannot come up with this sentence, then go back and do more work in the text until you find it. The task is not always easy, but if undertaken, it pays rich rewards. Here are three of those dividends: First, the preacher will avoid the often-heard criticism that expository sermons (and teaching) lack structure. Second, the discipline gives the preacher a better understanding of the truths he will share with his people. Third, it will assist listeners to understand the message.

The MIT must be discovered and defined. This discovery is essential and not optional in developing a biblically faithful message. Define the main idea precisely in your own mind. Unless it is clearly defined by a careful choice of words, the idea will remain vague to you and your audience. Strive to reflect what the biblical writer is saying. You want to see if what you are calling the main idea is actually what the writer is talking about. Give the main idea an accurate description so that the same words can be used in the message you will deliver. Unless we find the right words to identify the MIT, how will we ever teach that idea? Carefully locate the theological themes in the text. This locating will provide insight into its main idea. You can usually recognize the theological themes in the text by looking at the significant words you see there. Some words in Scripture bear enormous theological weight (e.g., justification, sanctification, reconciliation, repentance, calling, faith, election). Consider the plain and obvious meaning of the text for indications of the main idea. Look for a pivotal verse in the text that may contain the main theme.[4] Although every text does not have a pivotal verse, many texts will. It will be the one verse that seems to capture the idea of the entire section so that it summarizes its meaning.

THE BRIDGE FROM STUDY TO SERMON

At the completion of step 3 you are ready to move into a crucial and important phase of the homiletical process: "The Bridge" (step 4). In this step you transition from the study to the message, from the

---

4.   As we saw in chapter 10, Phil 2:5 serves that purpose for verses 1–11.

past world of the biblical period to the present world of the here and now. To ignore this dimension in the hermeneutical/homiletical process can be fatal to what happens when you stand up to proclaim the unsearchable riches of Christ. Basically, you are to fulfill the assignment of a divinely called translator. Your job is to translate the precious and eternal truth of Scripture so that a twenty-first-century audience can hear, understand, and respond to the biblical truth that has been made plain to them. Changing the truth is not an option. May God forgive those who play the fool in this area. Communicating the truth so that those who hear you speak genuinely grasp the message conveyed by the biblical revelation is what we are after.

At this step several things need to be taken into consideration and several important questions need to be raised to guide us through this step.

Considerations in Accomplishing Step 4

When you cross this bridge, you will have moved from studying the Scriptures—the hermeneutical exercise—toward teaching the Scriptures—the homiletical exercise. You will now begin to consider several new issues that will lay the foundation for the full development of your message.

1. Begin to focus on the introduction of the message and the issue that has been raised in the text and will be raised in the message.
2. Think about what must be included and/or excluded in the body of the teaching.
3. Give some thought to your conclusion and how you think you will wrap things up.
4. Consider the illustrations that will help accomplish the purpose of the message.
5. Most importantly, let the purpose of the teaching directly contribute to the form of the theme of the main idea of the message (MIM).

We fine-tune the purpose of the message (constructing the purpose bridge) by asking and answering two questions. On the basis of the main idea of this text, first, can I make an exegetical or theological case that my message's purpose is compatible with the purpose of the text? Second, can I make a pastoral case that my message's purpose is compatible with the needs of my audience? This last question is clearly secondary, but it should still be asked. You will be guilty of ministerial malpractice if you ignore the needs and conditions of your audience. You are both liberated and limited by the main idea of the text. You must identify the text's purpose and then craft it for the audience to whom you minister. This step now leads us to five crucial questions you should ask of every text. This questioning will solidify your purpose and guide you in sermon development. Hopefully, you will see that these five questions should follow the "Grand Redemptive Storyline" of **Creation (God) → Fall → Redemption → Sanctification** (leading to Consummation/Glorification).

Five Crucial Questions for Every Sermon to Raise and Answer

1. *What does this text teach about God and His character and ways?* This question is intentionally theological and focused on God. It is the first question you should always ask in sermon development. This question looks for the "vision of God" in the text. It probes the text to discover what it teaches about God's person, character, and attributes. It seeks to discover what we learn about God's purposes and ways. We are trying to learn more about the God who has made us and redeemed us, the God who tells us to call Him Father.

2. *What does this text teach about fallen humanity?* This question naturally follows the first one, and it should always follow it. It will keep us from being man-centered or anthropocentric in our preaching. Bryan Chappell has a wonderful word in this context. He speaks of the "Fallen Condition Focus" (FCF). He defines this concept as "the mutual human condition that contemporary believers share with those to or about whom the text was written that requires the grace of the passage for

God's people to glorify and enjoy him."[5] In other words, what does this text reveal and teach about human persons made in God's image who now bear the curse of sin and a depraved nature? Here is wisdom and balance. We are made in God's image. That is good. We are sinners by nature and choice. That is bad.

3. *How does this text point to Christ?* Since this question is central in the sermon construction process, we locate it "under the bridge" to support the entire structure. The Chicago Statement on Biblical Hermeneutics affirms "that the Person and work of Jesus Christ are the central focus of the entire Bible."[6] In short, Jesus is the hero of the Bible. The Old Testament anticipated Him, and the New Testament explains Him. This affirmation is not a novel idea. The church fathers were thoroughly Christocentric in their preaching. After all, they received it from the apostles, and they received it from Jesus. Jesus teaches us in Luke 24 that all of Scripture is about Him—all of it. In John 5:39, He says the Scriptures testify of Himself. Therefore, we dare not treat the Old Testament, as we noted earlier, as a Jewish rabbi would. To gain just a taste of what Christocentric hermeneutics and homiletics can do, listen to the insight of Tim Keller as he scans the redemptive story line of the Old Testament.[7]

4. *What does God want my people to know?* Every exposition of Scripture will have an element of conveying knowledge. There will be biblical and theological content. Biblical and theological illiteracy is rampant in our churches. It is a malady that afflicts far too many congregations. A faithful expositor will always

---

5. Bryan Chapell, *Christ-Centered Preaching: Redeeming the Expository Sermon,* 2nd ed. (Grand Rapids: Baker, 2005), 50.

6. For this quote, see Article III. For the full Chicago Statement on Biblical Inerrancy, see http://www.bible-researcher.com/chicago2.html. Retrieved July 12, 2010.

7. See the excursus at the end of question 5 in this section. Others who are also noted for their Christocentric approach to preaching include Alistair Begg, Matt Chandler, Bryan Chapell, Mark Driscoll, Sinclair Ferguson, Russ Moore, David Platt, John Piper, and Adrian Rogers. Of course no one excelled at this more than Charles Spurgeon.

strive to teach his people how to "grow in the grace and knowledge of our Lord and Savior Jesus Christ" (2 Pet 3:18).

5. *What does God want my people to do?* Doing follows knowing.
Having immersed my people in God's Word as to what it says
and means, I will now craft an action plan that paves a clearly
marked road for obedience. If we answer the knowledge
question but fail to follow up with an outlet for concrete and
specific action, our people will become confused and frustrated. They may not see the relevance and practical nature
of the Bible for how they should think and act today. Our goal
is to make disciples of Jesus who will think and act with a
Christian worldview. People who do not think as Jesus does
will not act as Jesus does, and people who do not act as Jesus
does are not really thinking as Jesus does.

EXCURSUS: IT'S ALL ABOUT JESUS (SLIGHTLY REVISED)

Jesus is the true and better *Adam,* who passed the test in the wilderness, not the garden, and whose obedience is imputed to us.

Jesus is the true and better *Abel,* who, though innocently slain by
wicked hands, has blood that now cries out, not for our condemna-
tion but for our acquittal.

Jesus is the better *Ark of Noah* who carries us safely thru the wrath
of God revealed from heaven and delivers us to a new earth.

Jesus is the true and better *Abraham,* who answered the call of God
to leave all that is comfortable and familiar and go out into the world
not knowing where he went to create a new people of God.

Jesus is the true and better *Isaac,* who was not just offered up by his
father on the mount but was truly sacrificed for us. When God said
to Abraham, "Now I know you love me because you did not withhold
your son, your only son whom you love from me" (cf. Gen 22:16–18),
now we can look at God taking his Son up the mountain of Calvary
and sacrificing him and say, "Now we know that you love us because
you did not withhold your Son, your only Son, whom you love, from
us."

Jesus is the true and better *Jacob,* who wrestled and took the blow of justice we deserved, so we, like Jacob, only receive the wounds of grace to wake us up and discipline us.

Jesus is the true and better *Joseph,* who at the right hand of the king forgives those who betrayed him and sold him, and uses his new power to save them.

Jesus is the true and better *Moses,* who stands in the gap between the people and the Lord and who mediates a new covenant.

Jesus is the true and better *Rock of Moses,* who struck with the rod of God's justice and now gives us living water in the desert.

Jesus is the true and better *Joshua,* who leads us into a land of eternal rest and heavenly blessing.

Jesus is the better *Ark of the Covenant,* who topples and disarms the idols of this world, going Himself into enemy territory and making an open spectacle of them all.

Jesus is the true and better *Job,* the truly innocent sufferer, who then intercedes for and saves his stupid friends.

Jesus is the true and better *David,* whose victory becomes his people's victory, though they never lifted a stone to accomplish it themselves.

Jesus is the true and better *Esther,* who did not just risk leaving an earthly palace but lost the ultimate and heavenly one, who did not just risk his life, but gave his life to save his people.

Jesus is the true and better *Daniel,* having been lowered into a lion's den of death, emerges early the next morning alive and vindicated by His God.

Jesus is the true and better *Jonah,* who was cast into the storm so that we safely could be brought in.

Jesus is the *real Passover Lamb,* innocent, perfect, helpless, slain, so the angel of death will pass over us. He is *the true temple, the true prophet, the true priest, the true king, the true sacrifice, the true lamb, the true light,* and *the true bread.*

The Bible really is not about you is it?—It really is all about Him.[8]

GETTING AT THE MAIN IDEA
OF THE MESSAGE (MIM)

The MIM is the heart and soul of your sermon. The MIM is derived from the MIT and channeled through the Purpose Bridge. It is then contemporized in the main idea of the message. The MIM takes you into the homiletical aspects of the sermon preparation process. This step is crucial to the success of your message. Stott notes, "For the sermon, as a living word from God to his people, should make its impact on them then and there. They will not remember the details. We should not expect them to do so. But they should remember the dominant thought, because all the sermon's details have been marshaled to help them grasp its message and feel its power."[9] In *On the Preparation and Delivery of Sermons,* we encounter a frequently quoted statement: "The subject [MIM] answers the question, what is the sermon about? . . . Whether a sermon has two points or ten points, it must have one point, it must be about something."[10] John Killinger adds, "The first thing in making a sermon, the *sine quo non,* is the idea. There can be no sermon that was not first preceded by an idea or a theme."[11] Finally, in a famous and much quoted statement, J. H. Jowett claims, "I have a conviction that no sermon is ready for preaching, not ready for writing out, until we can express its theme in a short, pregnant sentence as clear as crystal. I find the getting of that sentence is the hardest, the most exacting, and the most fruitful labour in my study."[12]

---

8.   Tim Keller, "It's All About Jesus" (*Theology and Quotes,* 12-4-06).

9.   Stott, *I Believe in Preaching,* 225.

10.   John A. Broadus, *On the Preparation and Delivery of Sermons,* 4th ed., rev. by Vernon L. Stanfield (San Francisco: Harper San Francisco, 1979), 38. We searched diligently in the earliest editions for this famous statement but could not locate it. Apparently, Broadus never said this.

11.   John Killinger, *Fundamentals of Preaching* (Philadelphia: Fortress, 1985), 44.

12.   J. H. Jowett, *The Preacher: His Life and Work* (New York: George H. Doran, 1912), 133.

The teaching process is thoroughly integrated. Our study (step 1) and structure (step 2) influence the main idea of the text (step 3). The MIT influences the purpose of the message (step 4). From the purpose of the message, we can now articulate the MIM (step 5).

Just as the text has a singular theme/complement, your teaching must have a singular theme/complement as well. For the MIM, you ask the key questions, of yourself rather than of the biblical author.

When we consider the Theme of the MIM, we ask this question: What am I talking about? Then when we consider its Complement, we ask this question: What am I saying about what I am talking about? Six guidelines guide us in honing in on the MIM.

1. Develop the MIM with your audience in mind.
2. State the MIM in the most memorable sentence possible.
3. State it positively, not negatively, if possible.
4. State it in the active voice, not the passive voice.
5. State it in words or phrases which are precise, concrete, and familiar to your listeners.
6. State it so that the truth is readily seen as relevant to your audience and their needs.

A good MIM has six characteristics.

1. It is derived from the main idea of the text. The MIT determines the MIM.
2. It is what the preacher will be talking about in his message.
3. It is a carefully worded statement.
4. It is geared to the audience.
5. It has a subject and a complement.
6. It is a complete sentence that is memorable.

Now let us voice a warning in closing this chapter. Identifying the MIT/MIM does not give one license or permission to ignore the supporting ideas of the text. The supporting ideas must be allowed to undergird the main idea. Allen Ross addresses this point well:

Too many so-called expositors simply make the one central idea the substance of their message. The narrative may be read or retold, but the sermon is essentially their central expository idea—it is explained, illustrated, and applied without further recourse to the text. This approach is not valid exegetical exposition. In exegetical exposition, the substance of the exposition must be clearly derived from the text so that the central idea unfolds in the analysis of the passage and so that all parts of the passage may be interpreted to show their contribution to the theological idea.[13]

Faithful exposition will honor the whole text, big ideas and little ideas. This kind of exposition will allow the whole as well as the parts to fulfill their divinely inspired assignment. Key points will support the main point, and minor points will support the key points. Text-driven preaching will be our guide and compass for every step of the way.

---

13. Allen P. Ross, *Creation and Blessing* (Grand Rapids: Baker, 1988), 47.

CHAPTER 12

THE WORK OF EXPOSITION: STRUCTURING THE MESSAGE

E ngaging exposition requires the preacher of God's Word to develop a comprehensive and structured method for moving from his study notes and research to the completed sermon. He must bring order and logic, that is, what Martin Lloyd-Jones called "logic on fire," to the work done in the study.[1] The goal is that the end product will have unity, cohesion, and form. It will be fit for passionate delivery to people who need to hear a word from God.

John Stott says, "the golden rule for sermon outlines is that each text must be allowed to supply its own structure."[2] We heartily agree.

---

1. D. Martin Lloyd-Jones was a tremendous preacher in Great Britain who emphasized passion, logic, and theology in the act of biblical preaching. Without it, he said, one was not fit to enter the pulpit. "What is preaching? Logic on fire! Eloquent reason! Are these contradictions? Of course not. Reason concerning this Truth ought to be mightily eloquent, as you see it in the case of the apostle Paul and others. It is theology on fire. And a theology which does not take fire, I maintain, is a defective theology; or at least the man's understanding of it is defective. Preaching is theology coming through a man who is on fire. A true understanding and experience of the Truth must lead to this. I say again that a man who can speak about these things dispassionately has no right whatsoever to be in a pulpit; and should never be allowed to enter one. What is the chief end of preaching? I like to think it is this. It is to give men and women a sense of God and His presence." *Preaching & Preachers* (Grand Rapids: Zondervan, 1971), 97.
2. John R. W. Stott, *Between Two Worlds: The Art of Preaching in the Twentieth Century* (Grand Rapids: Eerdmans, 1982), 229.

An effective teacher of the Word of God recognizes the wisdom of honoring the substance and structure of the text. What he says should be faithful to the text, as well as obvious from the text, both to himself and to those he instructs. Walter Kaiser reminds us, "The exegete must resist the temptation to impose a mold over the text by forcing that text to answer one of his favorite questions or to deal with one of the contemporary issues that our culture wants to have solved."[3] He then adds,

> It is hoped that God's men and women will be challenged to reread that very same Biblical text on their own soon after they have heard the message. Even if they cannot recall the outline (they probably will not—sorry!), the Word of Scripture will still speak to them because they have thought through its structure and shape in such a way as to have divinely met God in that text.[4]

As you proceed to expound the biblical text, a model or method will help guide you. We must remember that biblical exegesis is never an end in itself. We aim to take our work in the study and transfer it to those who listen to our preaching. As you move through this step, we suggest you follow 10 basic and related steps. Five will be addressed in this chapter, and five will be covered in the subsequent chapter. These steps will develop and be true to our short definition of expository preaching: "Christ-centered, text-driven, Spirit-led preaching that transforms lives." They will also be true to and develop our fuller description of biblical exposition:

> Expository preaching is text driven preaching that honors the truth of Scripture as it was given by the Holy Spirit. Its goal is to discover the God-inspired meaning through historical-gram-matical-theological investigation and interpretation. By means of engaging and compelling proclamation, the preacher explains, illustrates and applies the meaning of the biblical text in submission to and in the power of the Holy Spirit, preaching Christ for a verdict of changed lives.[5]

---

3. Walter Kaiser Jr., *Toward an Exegetical Theology* (Grand Rapids: Baker, 1981), 153.
4. Ibid., 160.
5. Definition developed by authors.

LET YOUR EXEGESIS DRIVE AND DETERMINE THE STRUCTURE OF YOUR MESSAGE

The benefit of our method is that you have already laid the groundwork for structuring your message (step 5) when you structured the Scriptures (step 2). In step 2, you analyzed the argument of the text, located the seams that reveal the divisions in the text, and outlined the text according to its natural and logical structure. Now you simply carry that work over so that it becomes the basis for how you will structure and outline your message.

This method allows you to have a "text-driven method" that will produce a "text-driven message." It will insure that your listeners receive more of God's Word than yours. Your goal is to get out of the way and let God speak in and through His Word. "Cut the text loose" on your audience and let God's Spirit do His work.[6]

We believe the faithful expositor will reject any method that would entice him to superimpose his preconceived agenda on the text. He will not use the text as a springboard to address particular issues that currently have his attention. The faithful expositor will make sure that his people hear the message of God who inspired the text and is in the text. To do anything less is to be derelict in one's pulpit ministry. Are there advantages in this expositional method? There are many. Don Carson highlighted six advantages:

1. It is the method least likely to stray from Scripture.
2. It teaches people how to read their Bible.
3. It gives confidence to the preacher and authorizes the message.
4. It meets the need for relevance without allowing the clamor for relevance to dictate the message.
5. It forces the preacher to handle the tough passages.

---

6. Ibid., 163. Kaiser painfully points out, "More recently, we have tended to specialize in emphasizing the introduction. In fact, we have usually overindulged ourselves in the art of introducing texts and messages. We have begun with references to the weekly news magazines, recent editorials, various opinion polls, and with quotes from prominent authors from the past. Meanwhile, much of our allotted time has been eaten up, and we still have not brought God's people near to the text. It is almost as if we were afraid to cut that text loose on God's people."

6. It enables the preacher to most systematically expound the whole counsel of God if sufficient chunks are handled.[7]

Unfortunately, in a therapeutic culture, where felt needs and how-to sermons are too often dominant and deemed essential (even by a number of evangelicals), text-driven preaching is viewed as simply inadequate for the day. The perspective of many was expressed well in an article entitled "What Is The Matter With Preaching?" The author writes,

> Every sermon should have for its main business the solving of some problem—a vital, important problem puzzling minds, burdening consciences, distracting lives . . . . And if any preacher is not doing this, even though he have at his disposal both erudition and oratory, he is not functioning at all. Many preachers, for example, indulge habitually in what they call expository sermons. They take a passage from Scripture and, proceeding on the assumption that the people attending church that morning are deeply concerned about what the passage means, they spend their half hour or more on historical exposition of the verse or chapter, ending with some appended practical application to the auditors. Could any procedure be more surely predestined to dullness and futility? Who seriously supposes that, as a matter of fact, one in a hundred of the congregation cares, to start with, what Moses, Isaiah, Paul or John meant in those special verses, or came to church deeply concerned about it? Nobody else who talks to the public so assumes that the vital interests of the people are located in the meaning of words spoken two thousand years ago. The advertisers of any goods, from a five foot shelf of classic books to the latest life insurance policy, plunge as directly as possible after the contemporary wants, felt needs, actual interests and concerns. . . . Preachers who pick out texts from the Bible then proceed to give their historic settings, their logical meaning in the context, their place in the theology of the writer, are grossly misusing the Bible. Let them not end but start with thinking of the audience's vital needs, and then let the whole sermon be organized around their endeavor to meet those needs. This is all good sense and psychology.

---

7. Don Carson, "Accept No Substitutes: 6 Reasons Not to Abandon Expository Preaching," *Leadership* (Summer 1996): 88.

Interestingly, this statement is not the musings of a contemporary pulpiteer. Its author is the theologically liberal Harry Emerson Fosdick, who penned these words in 1928.[8] Contemporary evangelicals need to be careful from whose homiletical stream they drink. This stream can be poison water.

HAVE AS MANY MAJOR POINTS AS THE TEXT NATURALLY DEMANDS

Our structuring of the text and locating its seams will naturally and helpfully impact the structuring of our message. Whether we refer to them as points, movements, or segments, we will honor the natural seams and divisions we discover in the text when we relocate them in the body of our message.

Sidney Greidanus reminds us that biblical preaching is a Bible-shaped word imparted in a Bible-like way. Further, "In expository preaching the biblical text is neither a conventional introduction to a sermon on a largely different theme, nor a convenient peg on which to hang a ragbag of miscellaneous thoughts, but a master which dictates and controls what is said."[9]

The faithful expositor is humbled, even haunted, by the realization that when he stands to preach, he stands to preach what has been given by the Holy Spirit of God. Why is he haunted? He understands that what is before his eyes is divinely inspired by God, and he trembles at the very thought of abusing, neglecting, or altering what God Himself wrote.

Although the Bible is best described as the Word of God written in the words of men, we must never forget it is ultimately the Word of God, whose intended meaning as deposited in the text should be honored. J. I. Packer captures this perspective well when he states, "The true idea of preaching is that the preacher should become a mouthpiece for his text, opening it up and applying it as a word from God

---

8.   Harry Emerson Fosdick, "What Is the Matter with Preaching?" *Harper's Magazine* (July 1928): 135.
9.   Sidney Greidanus, *The Modern Preacher and the Ancient Text* (Grand Rapids: Eerdmans, 1988), 10–11. The quote comes from Stott, *Between Two Worlds*, 126.

to his hearers, talking only in order 'that the text may speak itself and be heard, making each point from his text in such a manner that hearers may discern how God teacheth it from thence' (Westminster Directory, 1645)."[10]

MAKE SURE YOUR MAJOR POINTS AND SUB-POINTS CLEARLY AND NATURALLY FLOW OUT OF THE TEXT. BE ABLE TO SEE YOUR OUTLINE (OR MOVEMENTS) IN THE TEXT

Good outlining of the biblical text will be true to the text. It will naturally arise out of the text so that the preacher as well as his audience can clearly see it. It should not be so noticeable that it detracts from the message and draws attention to itself. This danger characterizes alliteration when the audience wonders more about the rhyming of the next point than they do the meaning of the biblical text.

If the biblical text naturally divides into three major sections, our sermon outline should reflect this division with three major points. If our first point has two sub-points clearly shown and discovered in the text, then the first point of our message should have two sub-points as well. An example might be helpful here. In Col 3:18–21 Paul addresses the structure and responsibilities of a Christian family. These four verses are a *Reader's Digest* version of Eph 5:22–6:4. It is easy to divide the text into four major sections because Paul clearly does.

Outlining the main points looks something like this:

   I.   Wives should be submissive to their husbands (Col 3:18).
   II. Husbands should love their wives (3:19).
   III. Children should obey their parents (3:20).
   IV. Fathers (Parents) should encourage their children (3:21).

This outline clearly reflects the text and honors the fact that the verbal forms in each verse are in the imperative. Drawing sub-points from this text is probably unnecessary. However, if you choose to outline a sub-point under any main point, it is best to sub-point under every main point. For example consider this basic, text-driven outline

---

10. J. I. Packer, *God Has Spoken* (Grand Rapids: Baker, 1965), 28.

of Psalm 110, a great Messianic text. When you read the text, you will see the text naturally divides into two stanzas, the sub-points naturally arise from the text, and the sub-points amplify the main point they support.

The Great King-Priest of Psalm 110[11]

Psalm 110

MIM: As the great, King-Priest, Messiah Jesus is worthy of our worship and full devotion.

I.	Messiah Jesus is our great King.	110:1–3
	1. He is enthroned by the Lord.	110:1
	2. He is empowered by the Lord.	110:2–3
II.	Messiah Jesus is our great High Priest.	110:4–7
	1. His priesthood is irrevocable.	110:4
	2. His power is invincible.	110:5–7

STATE YOUR POINTS IN COMPLETE SENTENCES THAT ARE PRESENT TENSE, APPLICATION ORIENTED, AND FOCUSED ON CONNECTING THEM TO THE SERMON TITLE, MIT, AND MIM

Both Ramesh Richard and Al Fasol have addressed the characteristics of good sermon outlining.[12] Using their helpful suggestions as a baseline, we would commend the following eight principles.

First, state your points in the present tense and in complete sentences that are application oriented. Depending on the content of the text,

---

11. Note that the name Jesus does not appear in these verses. However, in light of the whole canon and the prominence of this psalm in the New Testament (e.g., Hebrews 7), it is appropriate to use the name of our Lord in this outline. *The Believer's Study Bible* notes that Psalm 110:1 is quoted or alluded to more frequently in the New Testament than any other single verse from the Old Testament (Matt 22:44; 26:14; Mark 12:36; Luke 20:42–43; 22:69; Acts 2:34–35; 7:55; Rom 8:34; Eph 1:20–22; Col 3:1; Heb 1:3,13; 8:1; 10:12–13; 12:2; 1 Pet 3:22).

12. See Al Fasol, *Essentials for Biblical Preaching: An Introduction to Basic Sermon Preparation* (Grand Rapids: Baker, 1989), 65–66; Ramesh Richard, *Preparing Expository Sermons* (Grand Rapids: Baker, 1995, 2001), 184–85.

the application may challenge your audience in the areas of knowledge or action or in both. When you use the present tense, recognize you are preaching to this people on this occasion. Using a concise complete sentence helps insure you have accurately grasped the truth you are seeking to communicate.

Second, connect your points to the title of the sermon to show how they address the issue raised by the title. Good sermon titles are true to the text and relevant to the needs and interest of your audience. Gaining readers' attention can be achieved without being silly, trite, or ridiculous. Incorporating your main idea into the sermon title is often a good strategy.[13]

Third, make sure your points support the MIT and the MIM. This connection will help you honor the strategy of the author of Scripture.

Fourth, make sure that your points are parallel in structure. Kaiser notes,

> It is important to make sure that the main points are in a parallel structure . . . If one is in the imperative form or an interrogative, then it is best that the others also follow suit. Likewise, nouns should correspond with nouns, verbs with verbs, and prepositions with prepositions. Thus, if the first point begins with a preposition, so should each of the other main points. Like the main points, the sub-points must also be in parallel structure.[14]

Fifth, each point should be distinct, developing one particular aspect of the title or main idea. Specific wording rather than general wording is important. Zero in on exactly what you want to communicate.

Sixth, each point, while being true to the text above all else, should have approximately equal value and weight in the development, structure, and unfolding of the message.

Seventh, it goes without question that each point is rooted and grounded in the text. Provide the "biblical address" of each point and sub-point in your outline by showing the scriptural warrant for what you are saying.

---

13. The issue of sermon titles is addressed in chap. 19 on commonly asked questions.
14. Kaiser, *Toward an Exegetical Theology*, 158, 160.

Eighth, structure and build your outline in whatever form will best communicate the truth of the biblical text. You may choose to outline with a series of questions, indicatives, or imperatives. You may use the personal pronoun "we," or wisdom may on a particular occasion dictate the more direct pronoun "you." The key is to be *faithful to the text* and *relevant to the audience.*

MAKE YOUR SUB-POINTS CONNECT WITH THE MAJOR POINTS THAT THEY SUPPORT

Main points feed the title of a sermon which is related to the main idea, and sub-points feed the main points. Like the main points of your message, sub-points should also be biblically grounded and reflect the content and argument of the text. They will be subordinate to the main point, supporting, amplifying, clarifying, or even illustrating the particular main point that they are related to. In our view, main points should be designated by Roman numerals (I, II, III, IV), and sub-points with Arabic numbering (1, 2, 3). Outlining beyond this stage is too detailed and will almost always prove to be counter-productive.

To summarize at this point, what are the basic principles for effective sermon outlining?

1. Use concise, complete sentences—not single words or phrases.
2. Use, when possible, a key word or phrase to assure consistency and symmetry in your division statements.
3. Craft your statements so that they stand alone as universal principles of biblical truth. Your points should contain that which is true any place, any time, and under any circumstances.
4. Follow a logical progression of thought in the arrangement of the outline statements.
5. Use the present tense and contemporary language suitable for the particular audience you will address.
6. State your sermon points as sound theological principles that encourage faith and obedience in the hearer.

7. If additional development is needed under a particular point, work to make it simple.
8. Outline the sermon with your audience in mind.
9. Do not let the points stray from the main idea.
10. Alliteration is a good technique for some preachers but is not a requirement for effective preaching. If you are not good at it, then don't!

Why is sermon outlining helpful and important? Several quick and concluding observations:

1. It assists effective communication.
2. It is helpful for understanding.
3. The human mind seeks order and unity.
4. It helps us see how we have arrived where we plan to go.
5. It helps us gain a proper perspective on the text we are studying.
6. It helps us discover the pattern, order, and logic of the original author.
7. It helps us highlight the main points or thoughts in the text, as well as the sub-points, which explain and amplify those main points.

CHAPTER 13

THE WORD OF EXPOSITION: DEVELOPING THE MESSAGE

B uilding a sermon is similar to putting meat on a skeleton. It is adding the vital organs in order to bring the body alive. Of course, apart from the life-giving breath of the Holy Spirit, a beautiful body with all the necessary parts will be nothing more than a dead corpse. As we add content and substance to our structured outline, five additional steps, which build on the five we examined in chapter 12, should be followed. Through repetition, using all 10 steps will become a good habit and a fruitful method.

LOOK FOR THE THEOLOGICAL TRUTHS THE TEXT CLEARLY SUPPORTS AND DEVELOPS

The modern evangelical church faces a serious danger: the danger of being swallowed whole by shallow and sloppy theology. If we teach our people solid biblical theology rooted in biblical exposition, they will easily recognize extreme theological agendas from any direction and quickly set them aside.

It is our conviction that the development of biblical theology is prior to that of systematic theology. However, biblical theology must always proceed to systematic theology. The hesitancy on the part of some students of the Bible to follow through on this latter point is unwise and unacceptable. Allowing the priority of biblical/exegetical theology will result in a more faithful and honest interpretation, but it will also demand more tension in one's theological system. There is nothing wrong with this tension (see Rom 11:33–36).

Walt Kaiser reminds us that "the discipline of Biblical theology must be a twin of exegesis. Exegetical theology will remain incomplete and virtually barren in its results, as far as the church is concerned, without a proper input of "informing theology."[1] Doctrinal/theological preaching is noticeably absent in the modern pulpit. Theological and biblical illiteracy is the heavy price being paid. As the preacher exegetes his text and considers his audience, he should be sensitive to the theological truths contained in and supported by the text. He must endeavor to develop a strategy that will allow him to convey these truths in a clear, winsome, and relevant manner. Good preachers will teach theology. They will recover the high calling of the pastor/theologian. A faithful minister of the Word will bombard every text with a series of questions that many preachers of Holy Scripture never ask, questions that will inspire and equip a congregation to become competent systematic theologians themselves.

1. What does this text say about the Bible (and the doctrine of revelation)?
2. What does this text say about God (creation, angelology)?
3. What does this text say about humanity (sin, our fallenness)?
4. What does this text say about Jesus Christ (His person and work)?
5. What does this text say about the Holy Spirit?
6. What does this text say about salvation?
7. What does this text say about the church?
8. What does this text say about Last Things?

Now, we need to be honest and forthright at this point. It is impossible to preach without preaching some type of theology or doctrine. However, an anemic theology will only produce a "nursery church" full of immature spiritual babies. On the other hand, an unhealthy allegiance to a particular tradition of theology may give us a nice,

---

1. Walter Kaiser Jr., *Toward an Exegetical Theology* (Grand Rapids: Baker, 1981), 139.

tight, clean theological system, but it will also lead us to squeeze and twist certain texts of Scripture in order to force them into our theological mold, grid, or ghetto. We believe a better way is to let your exegesis drive your theology. Let your theological system be shaped by Scripture and not the reverse. You will most certainly have more tension and mystery, but you will be more true to the text of Holy Scripture. You will also embrace and cultivate a more healthy and balanced theology.

COVER AND FILL THE SKELETON OUTLINE WITH THE MEAT AND MARROW OF YOUR EXEGESIS

Now you put your hard work in reading and studying the text into your message. Having exegeted the text and read several translations, multiple commentaries, and other study aids, you build the strong Bible teaching component of your sermon. Tragically, you will need to leave some materials in the warehouse of your study, not placing them in the store window of your message. This setting aside is painful, but not everything you have learned will be necessary, even helpful, to the preaching and teaching of God's Word for your particular audience.

Strive to be a faithful and compelling Bible teacher and theologian. Explain the Bible to your parishioners. Teach the Bible to your church members. Model for them what good Bible study and teaching looks like. Unfold the grammar, highlight significant verb tenses, define important words, and show them how this text fits into the great redemptive story line of the Bible. Warren Wiersbe wisely notes, "For our preaching to be biblical, the message must be based on the Word of God, presented by a messenger who lives under the authority of that Word, organized in a manner that instructs the mind, moves the heart and captures the will, and interpreted and applied in a way that is true (intrinsic) to the text."[2]

---

2. Warren Wierbse, *Preaching and Teaching with Imagination: The Quest for Biblical Ministry* (Grand Rapids: Baker, 1994), 307.

Good exposition does not preach about the Bible. Good exposition preaches the Bible. It delights in the details and doctrines of Scripture. It teaches God's people to read and better understand the eternal and timeless truths of God's Word for themselves.

ADD TO YOUR EXPOSITORY CONTENT THE SUPPORTING ACCESSORIES OF INTRODUCTION, CONCLUSION, APPLICATION, AND ILLUSTRATIONS

Each of these components will be developed more fully, with individual chapters dedicated to each. Sermon construction has the goal of building a homiletical masterpiece. Reaching that goal means it must begin well (introduction) and end well (conclusion). It needs to show the relevance of biblical truth to real people in real life (application and illustration). Expository preaching is not simply a verse-by-verse exegesis or a running commentary. It is taking the eternal truth of the Bible and doing evangelism, ministering to human needs, calling believers to faith, motivating hearers to obedience, teaching theology, inspiring worship, building up the saints, and declaring the will and purposes of God. Cultivating an interesting introduction, crafting a compelling conclusion, making a clear application, and locating powerful illustrations involve hard work. However, they will yield great fruit when you stand up to preach the Word of God. Charles Spurgeon said, "You must endeavor, brethren, to make your people forget matters relating to this world by interweaving the whole of divine truth with the passing things of everyday, and this you will do by a judicious use of anecdotes and illustrations."[3]

AS YOU HONE THE FINISHED PRODUCT, MAKE SURE THE MESSAGE AS A WHOLE HAS BALANCE, SYMMETRY, AND COHESION

One of the non-negotiable dictums of good preaching is: "What you say is more important than how you say it, but how you say it has

---

3.   Charles Spurgeon, *Lectures to My Students* (Grand Rapids: Zondervan, 1972), 52.

never been more important." It is important that what you say, you say well. One aspect of preaching well is aiming for balance among the parts of the sermon. Basically, every sermon can be broken down as follows:

THE SERMON EVENT

Activity	% of Message	Time Allotment
Introduction		
Body		
1) Exposition	( )	
2) Illustration	( )	
3) Application	( )	
Conclusion (Invitation)		
Total	100%	?

Depending on the length of your message, you need to carefully and wisely consider how much time to allot for each part of the sermon. You only have so much time, and you want to strive for balance so that one component is not top heavy while another is all but neglected. Often, the application and conclusion are what get whacked. This excision results from poor planning as well as a lack of pulpit discipline to stay on point. Exposition should receive the bulk of your time and attention since you are called to teach the Bible, not entertain with a cute opening monologue or an endless string of stories. Thankfully, longer sermons are making a return. This practice is good as long as you have something to say and you say it well. Working off a 40-minute message with three or four main points to the exposition, a balanced and cohesive message would generally break down as follows:

THE SERMON EVENT

Activity	% of Message	Time Allotment
Introduction	10%	4 minutes
Body	75%	30 minutes
(1) Exposition	(50%)	(20 minutes)
(2) Illustration	(12.5)	(5 minutes)
(3) Application	(12.5)	(5 minutes)
Conclusion (Invitation)	15%	6 minutes
Total	100%	40 minutes

This breakdown should be sobering. With a very short introduction and conclusion, and with streamlined illustrations and applications, only half of the allotted time is given to explaining the Bible. Sadly, many fail to even do this! One thing is certain—there is no time to waste.

PRACTICE READING YOUR TEXT REPEATEDLY AND OUT LOUD, REMEMBERING THAT READING GOD'S WORD POORLY IS A SIN

This last principle should be unnecessary to state, but unfortunately experience dictates otherwise. Therefore, we address the issue in more detail. I (Danny) will never forget a preacher in a seminary chapel who read his text. He not only read it poorly, but he also read the wrong text. That reading of the biblical text may explain the poor preaching that followed as well as the complete absence of a biblical exposition from the text he intended to read.

The public reading of the Bible has become a lost practice. It needs to be recovered. Further, we must never forget what we are reading: the Word of God. It rightly demands respect and honor. As evangelicals who affirm the inerrancy and infallibility of the Bible, we do not worship the book, but we do love the book. We revere the book. When we read it aloud in corporate worship, we make sure that we read it well. With this in mind, here are some suggestions for the public reading of the Bible. These suggestions are drawn and adapted from Clay Schmit's *Public Reading of Scripture: A Handbook*.

TEN TIPS FOR READING SCRIPTURE IN PUBLIC WORSHIP

1. *Acknowledge that the public reading of the Scriptures is important.* Prepare and take the assignment seriously.
2. *See for yourself how interpretation and verbal nuances makes a difference.* Consider the words "Her name was Elizabeth." Say it aloud four times, each time emphasizing a different word. How does your emphasis change the meaning of that simple sentence?
3. *Make sure you understand the meaning of the passage.* This is a given for the preacher!
4. *Become comfortable with expressing a wide range of emotions.* Practice going overboard with gestures and vocal style. Read the same sentence in different ways to suggest different emotions.
5. *Read some children's books aloud.* "When you are reading to children or talking to children, you will often become *excessively expressive!* . . . Now back off about a quarter and you will probably have a good voice for reading Scripture in church worship."[4]
6. *Use that very effective communication device called the pause.* Note the difference in these readings of Luke 2:16:
   - They went with haste and found Mary and Joseph and the child lying in a manger.
   - They went with haste (pause) and found Mary and Joseph and the child lying in a manger.
   - They went with haste (pause) and found Mary and Joseph (pause) and the child (pause) lying in a manger.
7. *Look up from your reading only to reinforce the message.* Avoid the bobbing head effect. The eyes are the mirror of thought

---

4.   Adapted from Clayton Schmit, *Public Reading of Scripture: A Handbook* (Nashville: Abingdon, 2002). Schmit is a Lutheran minister and a professor at Fuller Seminary.

and imagination, so it is fine to look off into space as you are thinking of an image, say when the father looked up and saw the Prodigal Son at a great distance or the Psalmist says, "I lift up my eyes to the hills" (Ps 121:1 NIV). If you do this, look far off, not at individual people. A good time to look at worshipers would be while reading a sentence such as the one Jesus asked his storm-tossed disciples, "Where is your faith?" (Luke 8:25), or Paul's admonitions in Col 3:2 to "set your minds on what is above, not on what is on the earth."

8. *Read; do not act.* "People understand you are reading, so don't think you have to move your body or gesture a lot."[5] Simply stand tall so that your voice projects, use the mike, and read the text. However, try to read so that your facial gestures are evident, even if you have to hold the Bible above the lectern or you are addressing a large congregation. The bigger the crowd, the more dramatic your gestures should be.

9. *Prepare ahead of time by reading aloud.* Simply reading silently to yourself will not help you identify potential problems of pronunciation, pauses, and pacing. Several readings are wise. Listening to the text on audio is always a good idea.

10. *Be open to critique.* Ask for feedback. Seek to improve, and never be satisfied with the status quo.[6]

CONCLUSION

Why are we so strongly committed to an expositional model for preaching? The answer is really quite simple. The health and vitality of our churches is on the line. Amazingly, some of a more liberal church tradition see quite clearly what many evangelicals do not. William Willimon, former dean of the chapel at Duke University, said some years ago, "Today's conservatives sound like yesterday's liberals." Willimon sounds a prophetic warning to evangelicals that they might not be seduced by the sirens of modernity and follow the tragic path of insignificance that mainline denominations have trod. We should all listen carefully and heed his words:

---

5.   Ibid.
6.   Ibid.

I'm a mainline-liberal-Protestant-Methodist-type Christian. I know we are soft on Scripture. Norman Vincent Peale has exercised a more powerful effect on our Preaching than St. Paul . . . I know we play fast and loose with Scripture. But I've always had this fantasy that somewhere, like in Texas, there were preachers who preached it all, Genesis to Revelation without blinking an eye . . . I took great comfort in knowing that, even while I preach a pitifully compromised, "Pealed"-down gospel, that somewhere, good ole Bible-believing preachers were offering their congregations the unadulterated Word, straight up. Do you know how disillusioning it has been for me to realize that many of these self-proclaimed biblical preachers now sound more like liberal mainliners than liberal mainliners? At the very time those of us in the mainline, oldline, sidelined were repenting of our pop psychological pap and rediscovering the joy of disciplined biblical preaching, these "biblical preachers" were becoming "user friendly" and "inclusive," taking their homiletical cues from the "felt needs" of us "boomers" and "busters" rather than the excruciating demands of the Bible. I know why they do this . . . it all starts with American Christians wanting to be helpful to the present order, to be relevant (as the present order defines relevance). We so want to be invited to lunch at the White House or at least be interviewed on "Good Morning America." So we adjust our language to the demands of the market, begin with the world and its current infatuations rather than the Word and its peculiar judgments on our infatuations. If you listen to much of our preaching, you get the impression that Jesus was some sort of itinerant therapist who, for free, traveled about helping people feel better. Ever since Fosdick, we mainline liberals have been bad about this. Start with some human problem like depression; then rummage the Bible for a relevant answer. Last fall, as I was preparing in my office for the Sunday service, the telephone rang. "Who's preaching in Duke Chapel today?" Asked a nasal, Yankee-sounding voice. I cleared my throat and answered, "Reverend Doctor William Willimon." "Who's that?" asked the voice. "The Dean of the Chapel," I answered in a sonorous tone. "I hope he won't be preaching politics. I've had a rough week and I need to hear about God. My Baptist church is so eaten up with politics, I've got to hear a sermon!" When you have to come to a

Methodist for a biblical sermon, that's pitiful.[7]

Walt Kaiser would concur with Willimon. His words are just as pointed and should be equally convincing.

> It is no secret that Christ's Church is not at all in good health in many places of the world. She has been languishing because she has been fed, as the current line has it, "junk food"; all kinds of artificial preservatives and all sorts of unnatural substitutes have been served up to her. As a result, theological and Biblical malnutrition has afflicted the very generation that has taken such giant steps to make sure its physical health is not damaged by using foods or products that are carcinogenic or otherwise harmful to their bodies. Simultaneously, a worldwide spiritual famine resulting from the absence of any genuine publication of the Word of God continues to run wild and almost unabated in most quarters of the Church.[8]

Luther, in a different day to be sure, saw the church in a similar condition. However, he did not despair, for he saw, as we must see, the antidote that will cure the patient: the faithful proclamation of Holy Scripture. In his "A Treatise on Christian Liberty," he hits us right between the eyes with words we should heed:

> Let us then consider it certain and conclusively established that the soul can do without all things except the Word of God, and that where this is not there is no help for the soul in anything else whatever. But if it has the Word it is rich and lacks nothing, since this Word is the Word of life, of truth, of light, of peace, of righteousness, of salvation, of joy, of liberty, of wisdom, of power, of grace, of glory, and of every blessing beyond our power to estimate.[9]

Preaching the Word of God is for the glory of our Savior and the good of His saints. This preaching is an absolutely essential component for healthy churches in our day. It is an absolutely essential component for healthy churches in any day.

---

7. William Willimon, "Been There, Preached That," *Leadership Magazine* (Fall 1995).
8. Kaiser, *Toward an Exegetical Theology*, 7–8.
9. Martin Luther, "A Treatise on Christian Liberty," in *Three Treatises* (Philadelphia: Muhlenberg, 1943), 23. This great affirmation was also noted in the introduction, footnote 5. It is worth repeating.

CHAPTER 14

ILLUSTRATIONS: HELPING YOUR PEOPLE SEE BIBLE TRUTH IN ACTION

I llustrations are like the windows of a house. They allow you to look inside, see, and remember what you saw.[1] Illustrations are a crucial component of the sermon. As a rule, great preachers have always been great illustrators. They are wonderful storytellers gifted in painting word pictures that bring life and vitality to their exposition.

If we need biblical warrant for the use of illustrations, we need only to look to the preaching ministry of Jesus. His ability to tell a story, draw an analogy, and paint a picture with words is unparalleled. He was the master of illustration.

It is sobering for those of us who preach to remember that people will often forget our exegesis and points, but they will remember our illustrations, especially our stories. However, we should not be discouraged. As they recall our illustrations, they will once more be looking into the windows that will help them remember what was in the house (our exposition)!

Anthony Trollope (1815–82) said of his own day, "There is perhaps, no greater hardship at present inflicted on mankind in civilized and free countries than the necessity of listening to sermons."[2]

---

1. Charles Spurgeon also likened illustrations to windows in a house by saying they "brighten it with light." See Charles Spurgeon, *Lectures to My Students* (Grand Rapids: Zondervan, 1954), 349.
2. Quoted in *Journal of Biblical Counseling* (Winter, 1998): 44.

That comment hurts; however, wedding faithful exposition to clear and powerful illustrations provides a sure antidote for this homiletical illness.

THE IMPORTANCE OF ILLUSTRATIONS

Few things are more difficult than finding the right illustration, using it in the right way, and telling it at the right time. However, few things will yield greater fruit. Charles Spurgeon rightly noted, "You may build up laborious definitions and explanations and yet leave your hearers in the dark as to your meaning; but a thoroughly suitable metaphor [illustration] will wonderfully clear the sense."[3] Many people see preaching as dull, boring and irrelevant. The ideas are complex, theological jargon is unclear, and little if any specific direction is provided for commitment and action.[4] Jerry Vines and Jim Shaddix believe a good illustration can mean the difference between an average sermon and an outstanding sermon.[5] It may be the difference between a sermon that changes lives and one that does not.

Illustrations bring clarity to biblical truth and reveal how God's Word works and has worked in the lives of others.[6] They help us turn the ear into an eye so that our listeners see biblical truth more clearly. Illustrations make abstract truths concrete.

Humans are visual by nature, and we live in a visual age. Crafting "mental pictures" taps into this reality and engages the emotional aspect of human nature. Good illustrations move the emotions, stir the heart, and heighten our senses. We become more alert and sensitive to what is being said.

The fact that we emphasize the teaching of Bible stories to our children is instructive. They remember them. The aid to memorization

---

3.   Spurgeon, *Lectures to My Students,* 349.
4.   Bryan Chapell, *Christ-Centered Preaching,* 2nd ed. (Grand Rapids: Baker, 2005), 180. Chapell also has a work dedicated to illustrations entitled *Using Illustrations to Preach with Power,* rev. ed. (Wheaton: Crossway, 2001). We gladly commend it.
5.   Jerry Vines and Jim Shaddix, *Power in the Pulpit* (Chicago: Moody, 1999), 190.
6.   Chapell distinguishes what he calls "true illustrations from figures of speech, allusions, or examples" (*Christ-Centered Preaching,* 176). We appreciate his insight but do not make such a hard distinction in our treatment of illustrations.

makes these stories a valuable and powerful ally both for children and adults.

The great preachers who have preceded us were gifted in the art of illustration. Bryan Chapell brings this home when he writes,

> Had not the apostles punctuated their words with images of the full armor of God, the race course, living stones, olive trees, or walking in the light, we would strain to remember their instructions. Had not Jonathan Edwards dangled sinful spiders over a pit of flame, no one would know "Sinners in the Hands of an Angry God." If William Jennings Bryan had not decried, "You shall not crucify mankind upon a cross of gold," his political "sermon" would have been forgotten the next day. If Martin Luther King Jr. had not led us through a "dream" and onto a "mountaintop," would the march on Washington have been anything more than a ragged hike across a majestic mall?[7]

It is easy to see the importance illustrations play in engaging exposition. Effective preachers in every age of Christian history demonstrate this truth.

THE PURPOSE OF ILLUSTRATIONS

Good illustrations serve several important purposes. These purposes fall into both theological and practical categories. It is not surprising to find some overlap with sermon introduction and conclusions. In fact, illustrations are often the key to the effectiveness of both.

1. *Illustrations inform and instruct.* Our goal as gospel heralds is to teach our people the ways of God. The use of illustration recognizes that people more readily grab hold of pictures and images than they do propositions. However, the purpose of a picture or an image is to shed light on the proposition or principle that undergirds the picture.

2. *Illustrations explain and clarify.* Explanatory power resides in good illustrations that make the truths of the Bible apparent. Good

---

7.   Chapell, *Christ-Centered Preaching*, 182.

illustrations will evoke an "Aha" moment or provide a "Now I see" experience.

3. *Illustrations can help the preacher connect and identify with his people.* Good communicators learn how to touch the souls of their congregation and take hold of their hearts. This personal touch is a natural component of good illustrations. You and your people come together as you weigh the issues of real life that touch all of us.

4. *Illustrations are a tremendous aid to memorization and recall.* People remember stories. Remembering our stories or our striking and memorable statements will pave the road back to our exposition and aid in its recall.

5. *Illustrations help to capture and regain attention.* The average mind begins to wander after extensive and lengthy discourse. Good illustrations help refocus attention on the message. My friend Alistair Begg says if he has a really good illustration, he allows it to "float" along with the message until it is needed to recapture the attention of his congregation. Having listened to Alistair many times, we do not think he struggles to keep the attention of his audience. Still, his point about the usefulness of a powerful illustration is right on target.

6. *Illustrations motivate, persuade, and convince.* Illustrations are not meant merely to clarify; they are primarily meant to motivate. Scripture teaches us that we are to love the Lord our God with all our heart, soul, mind, and strength (Luke 10:27; Deut 6:5). Engaging exposition with good illustrations moves the whole person as the Holy Spirit through biblical truth impacts that person's total being.

7. *Illustrations allow for mental relaxation.* The mind naturally shifts gears when listening to a story. The need for intense concentration is lessened, and listeners are allowed to catch their "listening breath."

8. *Illustrations help our people see the immediate relevance of the biblical text for their lives.* The Bible is relevant. We do not have to make it relevant. However, making it relevant and showing it to be relevant are two different things. "Does God have a word for me today?" The answer is a resounding "yes." Good illustrations will make this answer abundantly clear.

9. *Illustrations personalize and particularize the general/universal truths revealed in the Bible.* When we structure and outline the biblical text, we want to capture that which is true any place, any time,

and under any circumstances. Illustrations allow us to take universal and eternal truth and show how it impacts and changes lives now. Illustrations reveal how God's truth changed the lives of others and how it can change our lives as we respond to the same truth in repentance and faith.

10. *Illustrations make biblical truth believable.* Sometimes the Bible seems otherworldly. However, God is in the business of changing lives and making things new today (2 Cor 5:17). Stories of real life transformations reveal the beauty of God's amazing grace found in King Jesus.

11. *Illustrations create interest.* The experience and stories of others fascinate people. A good illustration can capture the ear of a listener who had every intention of tuning you out and taking a nap.

12. *Illustrations explain biblical doctrine and personal duty in an understandable and compelling way.* Good preaching impacts the whole person. It recognizes that the mind, heart, will, and emotions are intertwined and interrelated. It understands that what impacts the heart and emotions can and should find its way to the mind and the will. It provides what I call a visual commentary on the inspired text. It allows us to see what God is doing.

SOURCES OF ILLUSTRATIONS

We can draw illustrations from a wide variety of sources and types. In particular, we will note 10.

1. *The best source for illustrations is the Bible.* Scripture is filled with exciting and memorable stories. Increasingly, we live in a biblically illiterate world. Therefore, we need to provide the book, chapter, and verse of where a biblical story is located as well as its context. Nothing is more valuable here than a "sanctified imagination." Making sure to make a distinction between what the Bible actually says and what one might reasonably conjecture, and telling a biblical story in a creative and faithful manner can show a congregation that the people in the Bible are a lot like us. They struggled with the same kinds of sins, and they were in desperate need of the same grace as we are.

2. *The experiences of others are an excellent source for illustrations.* However, we have a moral obligation to get their permission,

especially if we use their name. This dictum, by the way, is imperative when it comes to your wife and children. Failure at this point is
costly. It could be fatal.[8]

3. *Personal experiences are also a very valuable source for illustration.* Here, we must follow several guidelines. We must honestly
avoid even a hint of embellishment and be willing to share both our
successes and our failures. If you are always the hero of your stories, your people will not be able to relate to you. Further, you are
a fraud. Use wisdom and discretion in using personal illustrations.
Admit your sins, failures, and shortcomings, but do not air out your
dirty laundry or go into details that are inappropriate. Again, utilize
a valuable rule of thumb: "when in doubt, don't!" At the very least,
run the illustration by trusted confidants for their opinion. If you do
not say it, you will not have to apologize for it later.

4. *Human interest stories make for good illustrations.* This category includes biography. In recent years, I (Danny) have become
fond of using the writings and lives of great missionaries to illustrate
the biblical text. For example, I utilized the life of William Carey in
a sermon on Matt 28:16–20. I drew from the life of Jim Elliot in an
exposition of Psalm 96. The response and feedback far exceeded
my expectations. People find the stories and experiences of other
people interesting. Take full advantage of them.[9]

5. *Current events are a helpful source for illustrations.* Our people
are naturally interested in things that happen around them. The
daily news, weekly magazines, and informational blogs provide
massive resources. I believe wise pastors will spend time with their
people to learn what concerns and interests them. Most likely, their
people are concerned about many of the things that concern their
classmates, fellow employees, and neighbors. When major events
happen on a local, national, or international level, use these to show
how God speaks to them at the most fundamental levels. Your people
will appreciate your making these connections.

---

8. For a humorous video that makes this point, go to YouTube and type in "Before
    he speaks." Preacher, beware!
9. The wedding of a great saint of God to a biblical text can be seen in Daniel
    L. Akin, *Five Who Changed the World* (Wake Forest: Southeastern Baptist
    Theological Seminary, 2008).

6. *Historical events that are significant and colorful are an excellent source.* For years Paul Harvey demonstrated the value of using historical events as illustrations in his radio series "The Rest of the Story." He also demonstrated the importance of being a good storyteller. Most engaging expositors are students of history, recognizing it provides an abundance of illustrative material.

7. *Good literature is a valuable resource for illustrations.* This literature can include poetry, songs, and short stories. Great hymns of the faith, which are rich in theology, serve the dual role of providing an illustration and teaching doctrine. The background to the composition of a hymn can also provide a powerful illustration.[10]

8. *The world of science and nature that reveals the marvelous creativity of our great God is often an excellent resource.* Scripture repeatedly points to creation as testifying to the greatness of God (Job 38–39; Ps 19:1–6; Rom 1:20). Avoid technical jargon and unfold the wonders of creation so that all can see and understand the point you are making.

9. *Figures of speech or pithy statements that are striking and memorable are excellent sources for good illustrations.* All of us can recall jingles, catchy phrases, and colorful metaphors that stay with us. They lodge in our brains and are nearly impossible to vanquish. Be wise and discerning in this area, but recognize that these statements have tremendous potential for effective communication.[11]

10. *Finally, there is humor.* Humor can be one of the most effective forms of illustration. It can also be one of the most dangerous. The retention value of humor is exceedingly high. People remember funny stories that make them laugh. However, wisdom in what to say and how to say it is at a premium in this area. Humor should add to and not detract from your sermon. It should be appropriate to the subject matter of your message. The use of humor should be

---

10. See for example *Handbook to the Baptist Hymnal* (Nashville: Convention Press, 1992); Cliff Barrows, *Crusaders Hymns and Hymn Stories* (Chicago: Hope, 1967); Robert Morgan, *Then Sings My Soul: 150 of the World's Greatest Hymn Stories* (Nashville: Thomas Nelson, 2003); Robert Morgan, *Then Sings My Soul, Book 2: 150 of the World's Greatest Hymn Stories* (Nashville: Thomas Nelson, 2004).

11. Someone who excels in this area is Andy Stanley. See his *Communicating for a Change: Seven Keys to Irresistible Communication* (Sisters, OR: Multnomah, 2006).

natural to your personality. We should not use humor simply to be cute or funny. Some preachers believe humor is never appropriate in preaching. However, we believe this God-given gift can have a sanctified use. Just remember that God called you to be a preacher, not a comedian.[12]

CHARACTERISTICS FOR GOOD ILLUSTRATIONS

Several elements characterize good illustrations. Regardless of their nature and origin, good illustrations will always have the following components.

1. *They will make more clear and understandable the truth you are sharing.* If you have to illustrate your illustrations to make your point, you will fail.

2. *They tug at the heartstrings and help persuade your people to make a decision for Christ.* This decision may be one for salvation, recommitment, or service, but a good illustration will show them the way and wisdom of following Jesus in discipleship.

3. *They connect with your people.* They enable your people to feel as if you are talking directly to them. Once a man told me my message made him think I had been hiding under his bed. A good connection was obviously made.

4. *They are colorful and compelling, capturing the heart and imagination of the listener.*

5. *They address real people with real-life problems and solutions.* In other words, good illustrations live where people live. They reach out and touch someone.

6. *They are sensitive to and appropriate for the particular audience you are addressing.* This is crucial. Sharing something that is inappropriate due to age, gender, or race, can be devastating to a sermon's effectiveness. It can also be sinful.

7. *They are believable.* Honesty and integrity are at a premium in our day and time and are always at a premium when we stand to proclaim the Word of God. Never exaggerate or embellish. Tell the truth

---

12.   Also consult the chapters on introduction and conclusion in this volume for more on sources and types of material that also apply to illustrations.

and nothing but the truth, so help you God. If you do not, do not be surprised when your sins find you out.[13]

GUIDELINES FOR USING ILLUSTRATIONS

Having read dozens of books on sermon preparation and delivery over the years, we have compiled a list of guidelines or parameters for the use of illustrations. The following list is simple but extensive. Please take note of the insights of wise expositors who have gone before us and understand our sacred calling.

1. *Avoid using too many illustrations.* Your primary task is to expound the Scriptures, not to tell stories.
2. *Use, but do not abuse, personal illustrations.* Your sermon is about Jesus, not about you.
3. *Seek variety.* Routines can create ruts. Avoid getting into one.
4. *Represent the truth.* Be honest, tell the truth, and make it credible. Avoid misrepresenting the truth.
5. *Avoid using illustrations in bad taste.* Always follow the rule of speaking with modesty and decency.
6. *Never use counseling situations without prior permission.* It violates confidences and can slap you with a lawsuit.
7. *Master the art of using illustrations.* Learn to do it well.
8. *Avoid announcing the illustration.* If you have to announce it, you probably have a poor illustration.
9. *Make sure it has life!* Visualize the story in your mind. Get into it and tell it from the inside out.
10. *Avoid overusing a particular illustration (especially in the same church).*
11. *Avoid using illustrations as mere decorations or fillers to take up time.* You should be better prepared and more serious about your assignment.
12. *Be sure the illustration works well!* If it does not, then do not use it.

---

13. See Vines and Shaddix, *Power in the Pulpit*, 190–95; Chapell, *Christ-Centered Preaching*, 200–204. Their discussions on the characteristics of sermon illustrations are very helpful.

13. *Be vivid.* Learn how to tell a story well. Some are gifted at telling stories; others have to work at it.

14. *Develop a sense of humor that is natural to you.*

15. *Practice the dramatic.* It is no sin to study from and learn from actors who excel at this art.

16. *Avoid using canned, trite, commonplace and overused illustrations.* Throw away those illustration books you bought. You do not need them.

17. *Avoid using an illustration simply to play on people's emotions.* Pull on but do not trample on their feelings. Playing on people's emotions is another component of ministerial malpractice.

18. *Keep the occasion and congregation in mind.* What works in one place may not fit in another (especially in a different country or culture).

19. *Avoid making fun of anyone other than yourself.* Ridiculing others is homiletical suicide and will destroy credibility with your audience.

20. *Always give credit for borrowed illustrations.* It is a shame we even need to make this point.

Chuck Swindoll provides some concluding wisdom that captures the essence of this chapter well:

> If you think that the gathering of biblical facts and standing up with a Bible in your hand will automatically equip you to communicate well, you are deeply mistaken. You must work at being interesting. Boredom is a gross violation. Being dull is a grave offense. Irrelevance is a disgrace to the Gospel. Too often these three crimes go unpunished and we preachers are the criminals.[14]

Preachers need not be convicted as spiritual criminals, guilty of the crimes of boredom, dullness, and irrelevance. Powerful and pointed illustrations will help spare you of homiletical jail time.

---

14. Quoted in Rick Warren, "Flavoring Your Sermon's Impact," *Ministry Toolbox*, Issue #327 (9-5-07).

CHAPTER 15

APPLICATION:
HOW DOES IT WORK?

I n Jas 1:22, the half brother of Jesus writes, "But be doers of the word and not hearers only, deceiving yourselves." Why? "A doer who acts–this person will be blessed in what he does" (Jas 1:25).

Engaging exposition that is faithful to Scripture will not only explain the text; it will, of biblical and theological necessity, apply the text. Unfortunately, this area displays some homiletical confusion so that the church has suffered. On the one hand, topical and felt needs preaching gives significant attention to application, but it fails to expound the text and provide the necessary biblical and theological grounding for the application. On the other hand, some expositors of the Bible provide a running commentary on the text, but neglect to show the relevance of the text for the eagerly listening audience who is desperate for a word from God that will educate the mind, motivate the heart, and activate the will. Howard Hendricks and William Hendricks say, "Application is the most neglected yet the most needed stage in the process. Too much Bible study begins and ends in the wrong place: It begins with interpretation, and it also ends there."[1] They then shock our hermeneutical and homiletical sensibilities with a startling image, "Observation plus interpretation

---

1. Howard Hendricks and William Hendricks, *Living by the Book* (Chicago: Moody, 1991, 2007), 289. They provide a simple, three-step process for faithful Bible study: (1) Observation: what do I see? (2) Interpretation: what does it mean? (3) Application: how does it work?

without application equals abortion. That is, every time you observe and interpret but fail to apply, you perform an abortion on the Scripture in terms of their purpose. The Bible was not written to satisfy your curiosity, it was written to transform your life."[2] Walt Kaiser also recognizes that application can be banished to the sidelines:

> A gap of crisis proportions exists between the steps generally outlined in most seminary or Biblical training classes in exegesis and the hard realities most pastors face every week as they prepare their sermons. Nowhere in the total curriculum of theological studies has the student been more deserted and left to his own devices than in bridging the yawning chasm between understanding the content of Scripture as it was given in the past and proclaiming it with such relevance in the present as to produce faith, life, and bona fide works. Both ends of this bridge have at various times received detailed and even exhaustive treatments: (1) the historical, grammatical, cultural, and critical analysis of the text forms one end of the spectrum; and (2) the practical, devotional, homiletical, and pastoral theology (along with various techniques of delivery, organization, and persuasion) reflected in collections of sermonic outlines for all occasions forms the other. But who has mapped out the route between these two points?[3]

This chapter will provide a map that crosses the bridge from exposition to application and will demonstrate its essential nature in a healthy and holistic homiletical strategy. The place to begin is with a good, solid definition and description.

WHAT IS TEXT-DRIVEN APPLICATION?

Application in expository or text-driven preaching can be defined as "the process whereby the expositor takes a biblical truth of the text and applies it to the lives of his audience, proclaiming why it is relevant for their lives, and passionately encouraging them to make necessary changes in their lives in a manner congruent with the

---

2. Ibid., 290.
3. Walter Kaiser Jr., *Toward an Exegetical Theology* (Grand Rapids: Baker, 1981), 18.

original intent of the author."[4] To this excellent definition, we would add that the application should be God-centered and Christ-focused, fitting into the "grand redemptive storyline of the Bible" and the pattern of "Creation → Fall → Redemption → Consummation." What characterizes this kind of preaching?

First, text-driven application is grounded in biblical truth gained through historical, grammatical, literary, and theological analyses of the biblical text. Application necessarily flows from our exegesis and exposition. The order is not optional. It is essential. Practical application must find its foundation in biblical exposition.

Second, text-driven application must be based on the author's intended meaning found in the text. Authorial intent determines and dictates application. Because we believe the ultimate author of Scripture is the Holy Spirit of God, we dare not trifle or manipulate the plain sense of Scripture to fit any preconceived agenda with respect to how we want to apply the text in our sermon. That approach is homiletical malpractice worthy of pastoral disbarment.

Third, text-driven application should demonstrate the relevance and practical nature of biblical truth for the listeners in their present life context. The Bible does not need to be made relevant. It is relevant now and forever as revealed, eternal truth. However, the preacher has the responsibility to unfold and make clear the Bible's relevance.

Fourth, text-driven application must include practical illustrations, examples, and suggestions, as we saw in chapter 14, so that the audience can adopt and model their lives after the biblical truth being taught. The best place to begin is with biblical examples. In particular, the Old Testament contains a reservoir of resources. One should then proceed to contemporary examples, taking into careful consideration the specific context in which one ministers the word. In this sense a cross-cultural contextualization in good preaching must not be ignored, especially when we find ourselves in an increasingly missiological context, even in America. David Hesselgrave is extremely helpful at this point:

---

4.   Hershael York and Scott Blue, "Is Application Necessary in the Expository Sermon?" *SBJT* 3.2 (Summer 1999): 73–74. Blue's dissertation is entitled "Application in the Expository Sermon: A Case for Its Necessary Inclusion" (PhD diss., Southern Baptist Theological Seminary, 2001). It is an outstanding work.

Contextualization can be defined as the attempt to communicate the message of the person, works, Word and will of God in a way that is faithful to God's revelation, especially as it is put forth in the teachings of the Holy Scripture, and that *is meaningful to respondents in their respective cultural and existential contexts.* Contextualization is both verbal and nonverbal and has to do with the theologizing, Bible translation, *interpretation and application*, incarnational life-style, evangelism, Christian instruction, church planting and growth, church organization, worship style—indeed with all those activities involved in carrying out the Great Commission (italics ours).[5]

Fifth, text-driven application must persuade and exhort listeners to respond in obedient faith to the truths of Holy Scripture. York and Blue state, "Sermon application must persuade listeners that they should conform their lives to the biblical truths presented and encourages them to do so, warning them of the negative consequences of failure in this regard."[6] Jay Adams adds that preachers should "make scriptural truths so pertinent to members of their congregations that they not only understand how those truths should effect changes in their lives but also feel obligated and perhaps eager to implement those changes."[7]

WHY IS TEXT-DRIVEN APPLICATION NECESSARY?

Application in preaching helps us answer two important questions based upon the exposition of God's Word: (1) So what? and (2) Now what? In other words, how does the Bible speak to me today, and

---

5. David Hesselgrave, "Contextualization that is Authentic and Relevant, "*International Journal of Frontier Missions* 12 (July–August, 1995): 115. Also writing in a missiological context, Stan Guthrie adds, "The message must be tailored or contextualized in such a way as to remain faithful to the biblical text while understandable in and relevant to the receptor's context." Stan Guthrie, *Missions in the Third Millennium: 21 Key Trends for the 21st Century*, rev. and exp. (UK and Waynesboro, GA: Paternoster, 2000), 129.
6. York and Blue, "Is Application Necessary in the Expository Sermon?", 73.
7. Jay Adams, *Truth Applied: Application in Preaching* (Ministry Resources Library, 1990), 17.

what do I do about it? So important is this two-fold component of preaching that the father of modern exposition, John Broadus, said, "The application in a sermon is not merely an appendage to the discussion or a subordinate part of it, but is the main thing to be done. . . . Spurgeon, says 'Where the application begins, there the sermon begins.' . . . Daniel Webster once said, and repeated it with emphasis, 'When a man preaches to me, I want him to make it a personal matter, a personal matter, a personal matter!' And it is our solemn duty thus to address all men, whether they wish it or not."[8]

Text-driven application is necessary because it requires a decision on the part of the listener. Further, if done well, it provides a specific action plan that allows the Spirit of God to take biblical truth and make it a part of who we are and are becoming in Christ (Rom 8:28–29). Text-driven application is necessary then for at least five reasons.

First, it is one of the main purposes for God's revelation. God wants us to know Him, love Him, and obey Him. The act of proclaiming biblical truth is incomplete without the call to obey. Second, it brings balance to the information element in preaching. Knowing precedes doing, but knowing must lead to doing. Anything else will come up short of the intended goal of biblical exposition. Third, it focuses Scripture on the genuine needs of the congregation. Sin brings separation, sorrow, pain and death. Ours is a hurting world. Application speaks to those needs and provides the healing balm of divine truth. Fourth, it makes biblical principles specific to real-life situations. Addressing the whole person with the whole truth of Scripture is what good application does. Fifth, it provides the necessary bridge between the world of the Bible and the world in which we live. Application shows us that our problems ultimately are the same as those of the ancients. Sin is our problem, and Christ is the answer. Some things remain the same across the centuries.

Wayne McDill provides helpful insight concerning the "right use" and necessity of text-driven application:

> Application is more than just taking the sermon truth and attacking the congregation with it. Application presents the implications

---

8.   John Broadus, *A Treatise on the Preparation and Delivery of Sermons* (New York: A. C. Armstrong and Son, 1894), 230.

of biblical truth for the contemporary audience. It is a call for action, for putting the principles of Scripture to work in our lives. It deals with attitudes, behavior, speech, lifestyle, and personal identity. It appeals to conscience, to values, to conviction, to commitment to Christ.[9]

John Calvin, the great Reformation theologian, also saw the essential and necessary nature of text-driven application. He said it would impact how and what we teach to the congregation in our charge and under our watchful care:

> What advantage would there be if we were to stay here a day and I were to expound half a book without considering you or your profit and edification? . . . We must take into consideration those persons to whom the teaching is addressed . . . For this reason let us note well that they who have this charge to teach, when they speak to a people, are to decide which teaching will be good and profitable so that they will be able to disseminate it faithfully and with discretion to the usefulness of everyone individually.[10]

HOW DO WE DO TEXT-DRIVEN APPLICATION?

Timothy Warren is most certainly correct, "[Preaching] is not complete until God's people think and act differently for having heard the Word expounded."[11] Text-driven preaching has as its goal the formation of a community of believers who think and live differently as a result of their confrontation with the Word of God. Nothing less than changed lives will satisfy the faithful expositor. Pastor Rick Warren expresses this point well:

> I'll say it over and over: The purpose of preaching is obedience. Every preacher in the New Testament—including Jesus—emphasized conduct, behavioral change, and obedience. You only really believe the parts of the Bible that you obey. People say, "I

---

9. Wayne McDill, *The 12 Essential Skills for Great Preaching* (Nashville: B&H, 1994), 187.
10. Quoted in Peter Adam, *Speaking God's Word* (Downers Grove: IVP, 1999), 132–33.
11. Timothy Warren, "A Paradigm for Preaching," *BibSac* (Oct–Dec 1991):143.

believe in tithing." But do they tithe? No? Then they don't believe in it.

That is why you should always preach for response, aiming for people to act on what is said. John did this: "The world and its desires pass away but the man who does the will of God lives forever" (1 John 2:17 NIV). And in 1 John 2:3 (NIV), "We know that we have come to know him if we obey his commands."[12]

As we prepare to set forth our method, several observations should guide our process. Let us again draw on the insights of Pastor Warren. He notes nine.

1. All behavior is based on a belief.
2. Behind every sin is a lie I believe.
3. Change always starts in the mind.
4. To help people change, we must change their beliefs first.
5. Trying to change people's behavior without changing their belief is a waste of time.
6. The biblical term for "changing your mind" is "repentance."
7. You do not change people's minds, the applied Word of God does.
8. Changing the way I act is the fruit of repentance.
9. The deepest kind of preaching is preaching for repentance.[13]

Faithful expositors are not only responsible to explain and expound the meaning of the text; they are also responsible to apply the text for the purpose of a life-changing verdict from the audience. We are called to be doers of the Word and not just listeners of the Word. Therefore, we must instruct and inspire our people to apply Holy Scripture to their everyday lives. How, then, do we do it?

First, your application should be Christocentric. No one has said this better than Dennis Johnson:

> ... preaching must be *Christ centered*, must interpret biblical texts in their *redemptive-historical contexts*, must aim for *change*, must proclaim the *doctrinal center* of the Reformation (grace alone,

---

12. Rick Warren, "Preaching Tips That Will Change Lives," *Ministry Tool Box*, Issue #246 (2-15-06).
13. Ibid.

faith alone, Christ alone, God's glory alone) with passion and personal application, and must speak in a language that connects with the *unchurched* in our culture, shattering their stereotypes of Christianity and bringing them face to face with Christ, who meets sinners' real needs—felt and unfelt.[14]

Drawing upon the insights of Timothy Keller, a pastor in New York City, Johnson adds, "What both the unbeliever and the believer need to hear in preaching is the gospel, with its implications for a life lived in confident gratitude in response to amazing grace."[15]

This observation is crucial and must drive all aspects of biblical proclamation. Jesus is the hero of the whole Bible. He is the Savior in that He delivers us from the penalty of sin (justification), the power of sin (sanctification), and ultimately the presence of sin (glorification). Text-driven application is particularly interested in sanctification. Our people must understand that although they are saved by Jesus, they mature into Christlikeness through Jesus.

Mark Driscoll, a pastor in Seattle, calls this emphasis on Jesus as the hero the "Christological Question" in preaching.

"How Is Jesus The Hero-Savior?" He notes, "The Bible is one story in which Jesus is the hero. Therefore to properly teach and preach the Bible we have to continually lift him up as the hero. Any sermon in which the focus is not the person and work of Jesus will lack spiritual authority and power because the Holy Spirit will not bless the teaching of any hero other than Jesus. . . . There is an ongoing debate as to the purpose of the sermon and whether it should focus on converting the lost or maturing the saved. The apparent conflict between the preaching for seekers and preaching for believers is resolved simply by noting that both need to repent of sin and trust in Jesus to live a new life empowered by the Spirit."[16]

---

14. Dennis Johnson, *Him We Proclaim: Preaching Christ from All the Scriptures* (Phillipsburg: P&R, 2007), 54.
15. Ibid., 55.
16. Mark Driscoll and Gerry Breshears, *Vintage Church* (Wheaton: Crossway, 2008), 101–2.

Second, weave your application into the outline or movements of your sermon. In other words let the outline of your message be the application points of your sermon. State them in complete sentences that are clear and concise, in the present tense, and in harmony with the plain meaning of the text of Scripture.

We should recognize that some applications of a text will more readily apply to the mind (belief) and other applications will more readily apply to the will (behavior). Some will actually speak to both. The key is that the application must be faithful to the meaning of the text.

Third, aim for specific action on the part of your people. Fuzzy thinking is deadly to any aspect of a sermon, especially in the portions dealing with the application of the biblical text. Using the imagery of the Bible, we must remember that we are preaching to sheep (Ps 23; John 10). Sheep need very specific and particular guidance and direction. We must not assume that they will understand on their own. This weakness is one of the deadly ones of the so-called "New Homiletic." We cannot hope our people will "fill in the blanks" of sermon application. Practical steps that are challenging but obtainable by God's grace and Christ's strength are our goal. We cannot beat them over the head with "oughts" without also providing "hows." Challenge your men to be leaders in the church and home, to be godly husbands and fathers, but make sure you show them how.

Fourth, tie application to illustrations and provide some practical examples of Scripture at work. Again, the text must drive this union. Some examples will appeal to the mind and be deeply theological. Others will move the heart and will and give attention to the practical. Warren says, "If you want your people to share their faith with others, then tell stories about people in your church who are already doing that. If you want your people to care for the sick, tell stories about people in your church who care for the sick. If you want your people to be friendly to visitors tell stories about people who were friendly to visitors."[17]

Fifth, state your application in the form of a universal principle. Look for that which is true anywhere, anytime, and under any circumstances. Also, remember the ultimate principle: the solution to

---

17. Rick Warren, "Put Application In Your Messages," *Ministry Tool Box*, Issue #317 (6-27-07).

any problem is a person, and his name is Jesus. As you state your universal principle, be in line with the needs, interests, questions, and problems of today. This awareness is the key to relevance. The chart below visualizes what we mean:

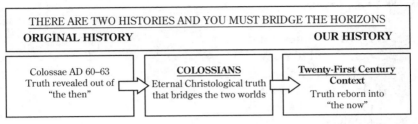

Diagram 15.1

Your principles must be in harmony with the general tenor and totality of Scripture. The analogy of faith is crucial here: "Scripture will not contradict Scripture." As you state these principles, be specific enough to indicate a course of action. Always ask any text these 13 questions :

1. Is there an example for me to follow?
2. Is there a sin to avoid or confess?
3. Is there a promise to claim?
4. Is there a prayer to repeat?
5. Is there a command to obey?
6. Is there a condition to meet?
7. Is there a verse to memorize?
8. Is there an error to avoid?
9. Is there a challenge to face?
10. Is there a principle to apply?
11. Is there a habit to change, either to start or to stop?
12. Is there an attitude to correct?
13. Is there a truth to believe?

Sixth, saturate your mind in terms of the many relationships of life. Examine the text with relations to education, social life, business, church, values, thought life, worldview, marriage, family, and sex in view. Release your mind to run freely, and explore the various possible relationships the text speaks to. Be realistic. Think concretely, not abstractly. Work to see the text vicariously through the eyes of those you shepherd. Hans Finzel in *Unlocking the Scriptures* highlights four broad categories with specific considerations under each:

A. WITH GOD

1. A truth to understand
2. A command to obey
3. A prayer to express
4. A challenge to heed
5. A promise to claim
6. A fellowship to enjoy

B. WITH YOURSELF

1. A thought or word to examine
2. An action to take
3. An example to follow
4. An error to avoid
5. An attitude to change or guard against
6. A priority to change
7. A goal to strive for
8. A personal value or standard to hold up
9. A sin to forsake

C. WITH OTHERS

1. A witness to share
2. An encouragement to extend
3. A service to do
4. A forgiveness to ask
5. A fellowship to nurture
6. An exhortation to give
7. A burden to bear
8. A kindness to express
9. A hospitality to extend

10. An attitude to change or guard against
11. A sin to forsake

D. WITH SATAN

1. A person to resist
2. A device to recognize
3. A temptation to resist
4. A sin to avoid and confess
5. A piece of spiritual armor to wear[18]

Seventh, remember the meaning of the text is always one but the applications are many. Jerry Vines and David Allen have rightly argued, following E. D. Hirsch, that a distinction must be made between "meaning" and "significance" (what we would call application). They note, "When the biblical exegete comes to a text of Scripture, he can proceed on the premise that there is a determinate meaning there. His job is to discover this meaning through exegesis. Having done this, there remains the further task of applying this meaning to modern man . . . We propose then that a text has one primary meaning with multiple significances or applications of that meaning."[19]

Eighth, consciously put into practice the application(s) gleaned from the exegesis of the text. Never forget that you have not applied the text until you have appropriated and put into practice what you have learned. Indeed, the application and practice of the text will serve as a commentary on your understanding of the biblical truth. It will be extremely difficult for you to apply to others what you have not first applied to yourself. Granted, no one can apply everything, but you should diligently and intentionally be working to apply something.

---

18. Hans Finzel, *Unlocking the Scriptures: Three Steps to Personal Bible Study* (Portland: Victor, 2003), 64. Another excellent resource in this regard is Daniel Overdorf, *Applying the Sermon: How to Balance Biblical Integrity and Cultural Relevance* (Grand Rapids: Kregel, 2009), especially 123–30.
19. Jerry Vines and David Allen, "Hermeneutics, Exegesis and Proclamation," *CTR* 1.2 (Spring 1987): 315–16. Vines and Allen's insight does not negate the intriguing possibility of a fuller meaning or what is called *Sensus Plenoir.* For an excellent treatment of the issue, note again Douglas Moo, "The Problem of *Sensus Plenior,*" in D. A. Carson and John Woodbridge, eds., *Hermeneutics, Authority, and Canon* (Grand Rapids: Baker, 1995), 179–211.

What are you trusting God for right now? In what ways are you looking to Jesus and appropriating His grace? What is your action plan to experience change in what you think and how you live? You should ask yourself these questions before you present them to your audience. Howard Hendricks and William Hendricks provide a helpful comparison between where we have been/are and where we hope to be/move:[20]

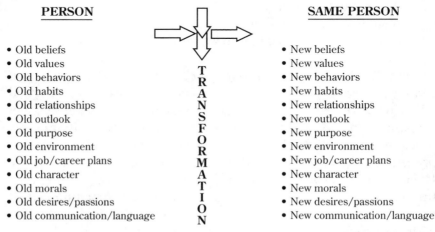

PERSON	**SAME PERSON**
• Old beliefs	• New beliefs
• Old values	• New values
• Old behaviors	• New behaviors
• Old habits	• New habits
• Old relationships	• New relationships
• Old outlook	• New outlook
• Old purpose	• New purpose
• Old environment	• New environment
• Old job/career plans	• New job/career plans
• Old character	• New character
• Old morals	• New morals
• Old desires/passions	• New desires/passions
• Old communication/language	• New communication/language

T R A N S F O R M A T I O N

Diagram 15.2

Ninth, beware of the challenges and problems that the application of biblical texts involves. Howard Hendricks and William Hendricks warn us of what they call "substitutes for application."[21] A summary and a quick survey of the five substitutes they mention will be beneficial for our study.

1. We substitute interpretation for application.

It is easy to settle for knowledge rather than change. That resignation is tragic because as the Hendrickses' say, "according to the

---

20. Howard Hendricks and William Hendricks, *Living by the Book* (Chicago: Moody, 1991, 2007), 291–97.
21. Ibid. I follow their analysis very closely in this section and quote directly at some length.

Bible, to know and not to do is not to know at all."[22] Jesus said, "Why do you call me 'Lord, Lord,' and do not do what I say?" (Luke 6:46 NIV). The implication is clear: either stop calling me, "Lord," or start doing what I tell you. You cannot have one without the other. James 4:17 reminds us, "Anyone, then, who knows the good he ought to do and doesn't do it, sins" (NIV).

2. We substitute superficial obedience for substantive change in life.

Here, we apply biblical truth to areas where we are already applying it, not to new areas. The result is no noticeable and genuine change in our lives. A blind spot remains so that the truth never affects that part of our life needing change.

3. We substitute rationalization for repentance.

The Hendrickses' note "Most of us have a built-in early-warning system against spiritual change. The moment truth gets too close, too convicting, an alarm goes off, and we start to defend ourselves. Our favorite strategy is to rationalize sin instead of repenting of it."[23]

4. We substitute an emotional experience for a volitional decision.

There is nothing wrong with responding emotionally to spiritual truth. However, if that response is our only one, then our spirituality is nothing more than an empty shell with nothing inside. We are aiming for a volitional response to God's truth. We are aiming for substantive, life-changing decisions based on what the Scriptures say.

---

22. Ibid., 292.
23. Ibid., 293.

5. We substitute communication for transformation.

"We talk the talk, but we don't walk the walk."[24] We think that if we can speak eloquently or convincingly about a point of Scripture, we are on safe ground. However, God is not fooled. He knows our hearts. He knows our actions. First Samuel 16:7 says, "The Lord does look at the things man looks at. Man . . . looks at [and listens to] the outward appearance, but the Lord looks at [and listens to] the heart."

Tenth, be on guard against "the heresy of application." Here we make an application that, though true, does not come from the text we are expounding. Haddon Robinson calls this kind of application "a good truth applied in the wrong way."[25] Exposition and application must be true to the text before us.

CONCLUSION

The *Westminster Directory for Public Worship* reads, "The preacher is not to rest in general doctrine, although never so much cleared and confirmed, but is to bring it home to special use by application to his hearers."[26] To do this effectively, we must know the Scriptures and the culture of our people, the world of the Bible and the world in which we find ourselves. Eric Alexander says it well:

> We are thus to be contemporary in our application. For that reason, it is important that we know the world and the pattern of thinking in the world in which we live. For that reason too it is important that we know the world in which our congregation lives. Evangelicals have traditionally been strongest in knowing the Scripture, and weakest in knowing the world. Others have mostly been stronger in knowing the world and weakest in

---

24. Ibid., 295.
25. Ed Rowell with Haddon Robinson, "The Hersey of Application," *Leadership* 18.4 (Fall 1997): 21. This article contains a detailed and excellent treatment of this issue.
26. Quoted in Eric Alexander, *What Is Biblical Preaching?* (Phillipsburg: P&R, 2008), 29.

knowing the Scripture. But there is no reason why these two things should be mutually exclusive.[27]

Of course, to do this well we must ask the Holy Spirit of God first to apply the biblical truth to the heart of the man of God. Hear Alexander once more,

> Now of course we will recognize and acknowledge that it is the Holy Spirit who is the true applier of the Word. That is a vital, central, basic truth for all our thinking. It is the Holy Spirit who takes the Word of God and uses it as the sword that pierces to the dividing asunder of soul and spirit. But that does not excuse us from the labor of asking, "How ought I to apply these truths to my own conscience and then to the conscience of this people?"[28]

The great puritan John Owen would add, "A man preacheth that sermon only well unto others, which preacheth itself in His own soul. If the word does not dwell with power in us, it will not pass with power from us."[29] Let our Lord apply his Word first to your heart. Then you will be well prepared for Him to use you to apply that same Word to others.

---

27. Ibid., 30.
28. Ibid., 29.
29. Ibid., 28.

CHAPTER 16

THE INTRODUCTION:
HOW TO BEGIN WELL

S ermon introductions and conclusions have been compared to the takeoff and landing of an airplane. The analogy is appropriate. Almost all airplane crashes occur when the plane is either taking off or coming in for landing. The same is usually true for the successful delivery of most sermons. Quintilian said, "a faulty exordium [introduction] is like a face seamed with scars, and he who runs his ship ashore while leaving port is certainly the least efficient of pilots."[1] Paraphrasing Quintilian's words, Bryan Chapell writes that "'a flawed introduction is like a scarred face'—you want to turn from it."[2]

Every time anyone stands to speak they will of necessity have a beginning or an introduction. They will start somewhere and in some manner. The introduction may be done well or poorly, but it will be done. We believe that for a sermon to begin well, it must have a clear and compelling introduction. The great homiletican John Broadus believed in the importance of a good introduction. He wrote,

---

1. Quintilian, *Institutio Oratoria*, trans. H. E. Butler, Loeb Classical Library (Cambridge, MA: Harvard Univ. Press, 1920; repr. 1969).
2. Bryan Chapell, *Christ-Centered Preaching: Redeeming the Expository Sermon*, 2nd ed. (Grand Rapids: Baker Academic, 2005), 239.

"Ill begun is apt to be wholly ruined."[3] We could not agree more. We believe the introduction may be the most important part of the sermon, especially when you take into consideration the entertainment culture in which most of us will preach. Basically, you have five to seven minutes to win the people's attention or lose their interest. Chapell again writes, "today's communication researchers say that audiences generally decide within the first thirty seconds whether they are interested in what a speaker will say. This modern reality underscores the importance of gaining attention in the opening moments of a sermon . . . ."[4]

Probably, more sermons fail in the introduction than anywhere else. You may have a thoroughbred of a sermon, but if it falters coming out of the starting gate, you will most likely fall short of your goal in bringing home a winner for your people. God is certainly capable of overcoming our shortcomings at this point, but as in all parts of the sermon process, He deserves our best. What then do we need to do in order to have a good introduction? Let us begin by analyzing its importance in more detail.

THE IMPORTANCE OF THE INTRODUCTION

The importance of the introduction is self-evident. It includes the first words that your audience hears coming out of your mouth. It is the first impression you make. If you start poorly, you will struggle to regain their attention and receive a hearing. John Stott says, "A good introduction serves two purposes. First, it arouses interest, stimulates curiosity, and whets the appetite for more. Secondly, it genuinely introduces the theme by leading the hearers into it."[5] You must make the case that you deserve a hearing. The burden is on the preacher to make the argument that what he has to say is important. Of course, we know that what we say is important. We know it has eternal consequences and that the souls of men and women are at stake. Nevertheless, we must convince the people who come to

---

3. John A. Broadus, *A Treatise on the Preparation and Delivery of Sermons*, 20th ed. (New York: A. C. Armstrong & Son, 1894), 250.
4. Chapell, *Christ-Centered Preaching*, 239.
5. John R. W. Stott, *Between Two Worlds: The Art of Preaching in the Twentieth Century* (Grand Rapids: Eerdmans, 1982), 244.

hear us that our words have import. We dare not assume they come convinced.

An introduction also sets the tone for your message. The tone must match the theme. A message on the doctrine of hell and eternal judgment, which begins with a joke or a funny story, is doomed from the start. Your introduction will determine whether you gain or lose credibility for your message. It will determine whether they will lend you their ear, open their mind, and expose their heart.

Finally, the introduction is the preface to the body of your sermon and your exposition of the Word of God. A good introduction is something of a map. It guides the audience into the message to show them both where we are and where we are going. To guide them well takes careful thinking and precise planning. A good introduction will not happen by accident.

THE PURPOSE OF THE INTRODUCTION

G. Campbell Morgan stated, "Someone has said that the introduction to a sermon may be likened to the prelude to a poem, the preface of a book, the portitico to a building, or the preamble to the statement of a case in court. The prelude introduces us to a poem, suggesting its methods and meaning or message. The preface to a book also does that. . . . An introduction then, must introduce."[6]

Morgan's point is simple, direct, and correct. An introduction must introduce. In fact, it does introduce, for good or bad. What then, should be the goals or purposes we wish to accomplish in an introduction? We will quickly examine seven.

First, a good introduction will capture the audience's interest. It will seize their attention and, at the same time, hopefully build good will between the preacher and his audience. We live in a culture saturated with entertainment. The media is fast and hard-hitting, dynamic and highly visual. The challenge to speak and to speak well has never been greater. How we start is crucial. We cannot afford to fail here.

The ethos of the preacher becomes a critically important issue. Pastors and priests are held in suspicion and even derision in our world today. Many neither trust nor respect pastors and priests.

---

6.   G. Campbell Morgan, *Preaching* (New York: Fleming H. Revell, 1937), 81.

Goodwill between a pastor and his people begins long before he steps up to preach the life-changing Word of God. However, how he begins a sermon is also significant in this context. A pastor is a shepherd. He cares for and feeds his sheep. He protects and ministers to his sheep. He exposes his life for their benefit and works to let them know he is on their side, that he wants them to excel for God's glory. An encouraging word in the introduction will go far in gaining interest and building goodwill.

Second, a good introduction helps create the audience's anticipation for the body of the message. The introduction should move the audience to want to hear what you have to say. They should anticipate that the issue raised in the introduction will find resolution in the message. If you raise a compelling question with significant interest, your people should anticipate that the question will receive an answer and that the answer will come from the Word of God. "What does the Bible say about _____?" "Let's examine the Word of God and see God's perspective on _____." A good introduction raises a question or addresses a subject your people are interested in, and it sets the table for the Scriptures to provide the answer.

Third, a good introduction demonstrates and emphasizes the importance of what the Bible has to say about the subject at hand. People need to hear a word from God. They need to hear that God speaks to the real issues of life and eternity. Therefore, in the introduction, make it crystal clear that we are going to move to see what God says. The opinion of the preacher is not important. Human experts are not the ones we need to consult. God's Word alone is infallible and inerrant, authoritative and sufficient. We want to know His mind on the subject, and a good introduction will reveal this.

Fourth, a good introduction will show the Bible's relevance. It will also answer every listener's unspoken question, "Why should I listen to what you have to say?" Once more we want to make the point: The Bible does not need to be made relevant. It is relevant now and forever. However, a preacher needs to demonstrate and make plain its relevance from the beginning of his message. The Bible is an ancient book. Some people in your congregation may be skeptical as to its ability to address the difficulties of life that they are experiencing. A good introduction will help bridge the ancient and modern worlds. It will demonstrate that humans have been sinners in need of a Savior since the Fall. Humans have always been sinners in need of reconciliation with God, others, and themselves. Humans have always been sinners in need of a relationship with God. Hard thinking will help the preacher discover the "common ground" that the people of the Bible and the modern world share. God had a word for the people of Bible times, and God has that same word for us in spite of different time periods and contexts. Again, demonstrating this relevance this will require some hard thinking, but it will be fruitful and productive thinking.

Fifth, a good introduction helps to show the preacher's intended course or plan of discussion. In this way, the audience can more easily follow the course of the message and not get lost on the journey. This principle is simple: tell them where you are going (although preaching a parable may be an exception). Chart for them the trip they are about to take. You have raised their interest; now help them see how you plan to answer their questions and address their concerns.

Sixth, a good introduction raises an appropriate need. We believe appropriate needs are genuine needs. These needs will be defined biblically and recognized as present in everyday life.

Seventh, a good introduction moves your listeners into the body of the message and the exposition of the biblical text. Here a good transition is essential. Clarity and conciseness should characterize the transitional statement, which provides the shift from the introduction to the body of the message. Tell them where you are going, and then take them there.

CHARACTERISTICS OF A GOOD INTRODUCTION

A solid and engaging introduction will have several important elements. Some of these are fairly fixed and specific. Others have some flexibility and may be adjusted a bit from sermon to sermon. We note eight for careful consideration.

1. *A good introduction quickly engages the audience.* It enables the audience to connect and has high interaction value. It draws the congregation into the message.
2. *A good introduction is usually short.* It will be five to seven minutes in length although there may be an occasional exception to this rule. Many sermons falter before they ever

get started because the introduction is too long. Remember that your aim is to get them into the Word of God. They need to hear from God, not you. Some preachers we know begin by just launching immediately into the text. This approach is much preferred over the long, drawn-out introduction that rivals the body of the message in terms of time allotment.

3. *Good introductions vary from message to message.* Do not get predictable. Do not get into a rut by introducing your sermon the same way week after week.

4. *A good introduction quickly turns to the needs of the audience with the promise that God has a word for them.* Inform your people that we are going to get a "God's eye" perspective on this issue, this problem, or this need.

5. *A good introduction is appropriate to the sermon, the audience, and the occasion.* It takes into consideration the *content* of the Scriptures to be studied and the *context* of the specific preaching occasion. We will address special occasions in particular in a later chapter. Suffice it to say that an inappropriate introduction can thrust a dagger into the heart of any sermon.

6. *A good introduction introduces the MIT and the MIM, though it may be best to do so in reverse order.* Of course, the two are intimately related and connected as we have previously seen. The MIM flows naturally and clearly from the MIT. Often the MIM and the MIT may simply converge into one single concept that gives vital information and direction to your message.

7. *A good introduction provides a clear and natural transition to the Scriptures you will expound in the body of the message.* It helps your people see (and hear) that you are shifting gears and taking the sermon in a new direction. They should sense the change taking place with little effort and hopefully with no confusion.

8. *A good introduction has both a good opening sentence and a good closing sentence.* We suggest that you consider scripting your introduction word for word, keeping in mind that you do so for the ear not the eye. You should at least script your opening and closing sentence in your introduction. Doing so

will add confidence as you begin; it will also force you to carefully prepare a crucial component of your sermon.

ELEMENTS TO BE AVOIDED IN AN INTRODUCTION

There are a number of "no-no's" to avoid so that you construct a good introduction. The body of your sermon may be a homiletical masterpiece, but a poor introduction may prevent it from even receiving a hearing. Therefore, mark the following and avoid them at all cost.

1. *Do not waste time with trivial drivel in the initial stage of the introduction.* Do not mumble, stumble, meander, or loiter about. You are there to represent God and preach the Word. Proceed with what you are there to do.
2. *Do not promise more than the sermon can deliver.* Avoid absolute kinds of statements like, "this may be the most important sermon you will ever hear." This statement is foolish and will hurt your credibility.
3. *Do not apologize.* Do not tell them "I've been sick," "this was a busy week and I did not have time to prepare" (they will probably find this out soon enough), "I'm pressed for time this morning," or "I have a cold and a sore throat." Now there is one clear exception. If you have sinned in some way and wronged your people, then confess your sin and ask for their forgiveness. When you confess from your heart sincerely and genuinely, they will be ready to listen.
4. *Do not use humor just to be funny.* Do not tell a joke totally unrelated to your message just because you want to start your message with a laugh. Use humor wisely, judiciously, and appropriately. It should have a connection with your sermon.
5. *Do not be trite or cute.* It comes across as insincere and uncaring.
6. *Do not be misleading.* This approach will rob you of authenticity and compromise your integrity. Trust between you and your people will evaporate.

7. *Do not refer to the last time you preached, either last week or earlier in the day.* You are here at this time for this congregation. There may be legitimate times to set this principle aside, but do so rarely, not as a regular habit.

8. *Do not refer to the last time you preached this sermon.* (See principle #7 on previous page.)

9. *Do not use materials unrelated to the message.* A brief pre-introduction (30 seconds to 2 minutes) to the actual introduction of the message may occasionally be justified (e.g., praying for a specific need, an important announcement that is relevant to the entire congregation, a word of greeting if you happen to be a guest speaker).

10. *Never approach the place where you will preach with hesitation or the appearance that you are unprepared.* Make sure you have a word from God for your people because you have been with the Lord. You should approach the pulpit with excitement and anticipation. Your people should sense that you have something for them and that you can hardly wait to share it. If you are not excited about preaching, you have no reason to expect that they will be excited either.

SOURCES FOR DEVELOPING A GOOD INTRODUCTION

With the coming of the Internet and search engines, unlimited and "ready at hand" sources are now available for developing introductions and conclusions and for finding illustrations. However, we will highlight some specific categories and areas to research as you gather the necessary materials for a good introduction to your message.

1. Current statistics or data that highlight a contemporary problem you will address in the message.

2. Historical illustrations that acquaint listeners with the main idea of the message. Be concise, but provide enough detailed information to make the illustration work.

3. Appropriate humor that fits your personality and the occasion.

4. Current events (human-interest articles) that relate to the message.
5. A careful and creative reading of the biblical text from which the message comes.
6. Real-life stories.
7. Biographical illustrations (we have found this especially powerful).
8. Striking quotations or statements.
9. Rhetorical, thought-provoking questions directed to the audience.
10. Personal experiences of the preacher (used tactfully and honestly).
11. References to well-known books, songs, or poetry.
12. Life-related problems for which biblical solutions will be demonstrated.
13. Questions or confusion over a biblical teaching to which the preacher will bring correction and clarity.
14. Highly interesting personal correspondence.
15. Appropriate prayer.
16. Fictional stories (be clear that this is what it is).
17. Modern-day parables (if you are good at doing this).
18. Personal testimony of yourself or another (you may need permission from another).
19. Hymns related to the message.
20. Asking the audience for their response to a hypothetical situation or a compelling question.

PREPARING A GOOD INTRODUCTION

Haddon Robinson says, "I believe it is absolutely essential that a minister have his introduction clearly in mind when he stands to speak. While other parts of the sermon may be outlined [we still believe it is wise to write out a full sermon manuscript], the introduction ought to be written out. It is in the introduction that the preacher establishes contact with the people in the pew . . . If there is ever a time that the mind will go blank, it is in the first moment or two you get on your feet."[7] What are some careful and simple steps we can follow that will enable us to craft interesting, engaging, and attractive introductions? We suggest these steps:

1. *Pray over and through your introduction.* Commit this aspect of sermon development to God, seeking the assistance and the guidance of the Holy Spirit. As a faithful Christian herald, there should be a theocentric/Christocentric component to the introduction regardless of the text, its genre, or the theme you will develop. Help your people see that God has a word about the subject you will address and that Christ will be the key to its resolution.

2. *Keep before your mind's eye (and ear) the truth that this is one of the most important parts of the sermon, if not the most important part.* God deserves, and the sermon demands, excellence at this point.

3. *Write the introduction out word for word.* Script it for the ear, asking the question, "How does this sound?" Your goal should aim to get your audience's attention and grab their interest. You want to show them why they want to hear what you have to say. You want them to see the wisdom of giving you their undivided attention for the next 30 to 40 minutes.

4. *Write the introduction, as a general rule, toward the end of your sermon preparation.* Your exegesis and exposition of the text should shape and guide your introduction, not the reverse; however, there can always be an exception to this rule. If the Lord brings the right introduction to your mind, then write it down and do so immediately! Do not let it pass just because it does not come in sequence with your normal pattern of sermon preparation.

5. *Remember the value and impact of a powerful illustration, pointed and specific information, and a compelling question.* Keep in mind that the delight is often in the details. Work at being a creative and interesting story-teller.

6. *Keep your introduction brief.* Far too many sermons falter at this point. An introduction should never be longer than the

---

7.   Haddon Robinson, source unknown. His fine treatment of the introduction can be found in *Biblical Preaching*, 2nd ed. (Grand Rapids: Baker, 2001), 165–75.

body of your message. It should not be longer than any one of your main points or movements. In a 30- to 40-minute message, a five- to seven-minute introduction is about right.

7. *Memorize your introduction.* Know exactly and precisely what you want to say and how you want to say it. Know it so well you can naturally and freely deliver it.

8. *Build in a smooth and logical transition to the Scripture text and the body of your sermon.* Scripting your transition is a wise strategy to consider.

CONCLUSION

Haddon Robinson cites a wise Russian proverb when it comes to a sermon's introduction: "It is the same with men as with donkeys: whoever would hold them fast must get a very good grip on their ears!"[8] The proverb is right. When we stand to proclaim "the unsearchable riches of Christ" or as the HCSB translates it, "the incalculable riches of the Messiah" (Eph 3:8), it is imperative that we get a good grip on our audience's ears from the beginning. It is essential that we begin well.

Proverbs 25:11 reminds us that, "A word aptly (NKJV, "fitly") spoken is like apples of gold in settings of silver" (NIV). In other words, the right word spoken at the right time and in the right way is a beautiful and valuable thing. We believe this dynamic is true anytime we speak. It is especially true when we introduce the Word of God to people who need to hear from the Lord.[9]

---

8.   Robinson, *Biblical Preaching*, 166.
9.   "You must remember that you come to the pulpit having spent hours in the study pouring over the passage on which you are to preach. You have been thinking over your subject for days, or weeks, perhaps even for years. But your people have probably not thought about it at all. Indeed, they may not even know what it is going to be before you stand up to speak. (Pray that they will know after you have finished.) The chasm separating their thoughts from biblical ideas may be vast. In the introduction you must enter their world and persuade them to go with you into the world of biblical truth, and specifically the truth that is the burden of the sermon." (William L. Hogan, "It Is My Pleasure to Introduce . . . ," *The Expositor* 1.3 (August 1987): 1.

CHAPTER 17

THE CONCLUSION: HOW TO LAND THE PLANE SAFELY

A s we noted in the previous chapter, a number of teachers of preaching have likened the conclusion of a message to the landing of an airplane. It requires planning, skill, and timing. Using this analogy, Haddon Robinson writes, "An experienced pilot knows that landing an airplane demands special concentration, so an able preacher understands that conclusions require thoughtful preparation. Like a skilled pilot, you should know where your sermon will land."[1] The point we are making is crystal clear: as a plane can be destroyed by a crash landing, a wonderful sermon can be destroyed by a poor conclusion. In fact, Stephen and David Olford believe, "More sermons are ruined by a poor conclusion than for any other reason."[2] Our experience and observation has shown that this is often true. Therefore, if the introduction is the most important part of the sermon, the conclusion runs a close second in our judgment.[3]

---

1. Haddon Robinson, *Biblical Preaching*, 2nd ed. (Grand Rapids: Baker, 2001), 175.
2. Stephen and David Olford, *Anointed Expository Preaching* (Nashville: B&H, 1998), 78.
3. Interestingly, Walter Kaiser would go even further. He says, "I would urge God's ministers and teachers of the Word in every type of ministry inside and outside of the Church to severely limit their work on the introduction and to devote that time and those energies on preparation to an expanded

A good preacher will not shortchange this vital component of his message because of time constraints, fatigue, or laziness. He will take to heart the wise words of E. K. Bailey, "A great sermon not only starts well, it ends well."[4]

One aspect of the conclusion is the invitation. The former leads (at least it should) naturally to the latter. Because of the importance of the invitation, we will devote a whole chapter to its consideration. At this point let us move to thinking about the various facets of the conclusion, and how to put together an excellent one for the glory of God and the good of our people.

THE IMPORTANCE OF THE CONCLUSION

The conclusion of a sermon can make or break the message. It can bring the message home or leave it lost in the wilderness. It can put before your people a challenge they cannot ignore, or it can leave them unmoved, uninspired, or wondering what the point was their pastor was trying to make. G. Campbell Morgan says a good conclusion, "storms the citadel of the will."[5] It grabs their heart, informs their minds, and challenges their will. It forces them to enter into a time of decision. From a practical perspective, we can note several reasons for the importance of the conclusion.

First, it is the last words that your audience will hear. If the conclusion is done well, your listeners most likely will leave with these words ringing in their ears. If poorly done, they may not even recall your excellent exposition of the text. A poor conclusion can inflict sermonic amnesia on a congregation.

---

and clearly-thought-out conclusion." *Toward an Exegetical Theology* (Grand Rapids: Baker, 1981), 103.

4. E. K. Bailey, "Smoothing Out the Landing," *Leadership* (Fall 1997): 39. Tony Merida would add, "The conclusion is generally the least prepared part of the Sunday sermon. So much time is devoted to constructing an effective outline, developing strong functional elements, and adding a wonderful introduction, that the conclusion is often given little thought. The conclusion, though, is very important. Sometimes it is the most remembered portion of the sermon." *Faithful Preaching* (Nashville: B&H, 2009), 117.

5. G. Campbell Morgan, *Preaching* (New York: Fleming H. Revell, 1937), 89.

Second, the conclusion is the best time to drive home the main idea of the message. A number of students of preaching have argued for the value of "recapitulation," which at this point quickly, simply, and clearly recalls for your audience the biblical truth you have shared. Bryan Chapell says this summation is "like hammer strokes."[6] You are driving home what you want them to take home from the message.

Third, the conclusion is your final opportunity to motivate your people to respond and obey the Word of God. Appealing to the total person (here is the value of a powerful story), you have your final chance to move them to action. Broadus says, "Whatever truth a sermon may present to the mind, it should not end without aiming to bring about some practical result, some corresponding determination of the will, state of the affections, or course of action. If this be true, many of the remarks we hear in the conclusion of sermons are inappropriate."[7]

THE PURPOSE OF THE CONCLUSION

A conclusion is basically the climax of the sermon. It is the final act of a redemptive drama or discourse. Everything in the message has been moving toward this moment of truth, this time of divine decision-making. Several important elements encapsulate the purpose of the conclusion. We highlight seven.

First, the conclusion should conclude and bring the message to a timely and appropriate end. Do not just stop; conclude your sermon with prudence and wisdom. You do not want to slam on the brakes, catching everyone off guard (although a sudden and surprising ending leading into the invitation can sometimes be quite effective). You also do not want to torture with a long, drawn-out conclusion that seems as though it will never end. Either extreme will be counterproductive and harm your message.

Second, the conclusion should restate the major idea and points of your message. Tell them what you have told them. Be simple and

---

6.   Bryan Chapell, *Christ-Centered Preaching: Redeeming the Expository Sermon,* 2nd ed. (Grand Rapids: Baker Academic, 2005), 255.
7.   John Broadus, *A Treatise on the Preparation and Delivery of Sermons* (New York: A. C. Armstrong and Son, 1894), 280.

concise. This summary usually can be accomplished in less than a minute or two.

Third, the conclusion is where you make your final appeal to encourage your people to action. Exhortation for a response, even pleading for it, should characterize your closing words. Appealing for such a response is at the heart of our assignment as ministers of reconciliation (2 Cor 5:18–21).

Fourth, the conclusion should engage the mind, elevate the emotions, and excite the will. You want to address the whole person as you confront them with truth that demands action. As in all aspects of the sermon, we must avoid any trace of manipulation. Our motivation for what we say and how we say it is critical at this point. We present the truth and call for a response. The Holy Spirit is responsible for the results.

Fifth, the purpose of the conclusion is to ask for a verdict. It is a call to respond. We are not delivering a lecture. We are not merely teaching a Bible lesson. We are confronting men and women, boys and girls, with the life-changing truths of God's Word. A faithful expositor will also be a faithful evangelist (2 Tim 4:5). You are not primarily interested in making smarter saints. Your passion is to make faithful disciples of Jesus who love and obey God.

Sixth, a good conclusion is tied to the introduction and helps answer the question, "So what?" It demonstrates the relevance and applicability of the Scripture to the lives of our listeners here and now. It shows how the message addresses them today in their real-life circumstances.

Seventh, a good conclusion intends to encourage and challenge, as well as comfort and guide. Bringing the whole thrust of your message to a head, you point the way forward with words that encourage the heart and challenge the will, that comfort the soul and give guidance to the mind. To the whole person, the whole message now speaks words of life and truth, words that ring with eternal significance and promises that find their resolution in a Savior whose name is Jesus.

CHARACTERISTICS OF A GOOD CONCLUSION

A number of traits will be present in a good, well-planned conclusion. Inspiration and instruction will be the dual tracks on which this train will make its way to the station. Carefully prepared, the preacher will know exactly where he wants to go and how he wants to get there. He will not fail to bring his people with him. What then characterizes a good conclusion?

1. *You work to finish strongly by reaching something of a crescendo.* Emotionally, there is no letdown. This is the climax.
2. *Your conclusion has cohesion; everything comes together as you wrap things up.* It is marked by a sense of resolution that indicates you have made the argument and nothing more needs be said on this occasion.
3. *You reflect and restate the main points and ideas of your message in the form of a summation.* The repetition of certain key words or phrases is invaluable as you summarize the sermon.[8]
4. *A good conclusion fits the message in tone and tenor.* If the message is on judgment, then the tone should be serious, even somber. If the message was one of encouragement, then be encouraging as you close.
5. *A good conclusion is clear and transparent in its thought and expressions.* Your listeners understand where they are and how they arrived at this point of the message. They see the truth of the Word of God and understand what is now expected of them.
6. *A good conclusion, like a good introduction, should be brief.* A length of three to five minutes is best. Do not circle the airport several times before coming in for the landing. Get the plane on the ground and to the gate with no delays!
7. *Be open to the value of the element of surprise.* Godly wisdom and a sanctified imagination are essential when providing this type of ending.
8. *Strive for good timing.* There is no formula for finding good timing, only years of experience in preaching. You will know when you hit it, and you will know when you miss it too.

---

8. Merida has some helpful thoughts on using summation in your conclusion (*Faithful Preaching*, 117–18). Vines and Shaddix actually use the term summation when talking about the conclusion. Their fine discussion is found on pages 207–10 in *Power in the Pulpit* (Chicago: Moody, 1999).

Brevity, crispness, and a fixed target will assist you in this area.

9. *Be personal in application.* The use of "you" will be most forceful, although using "we" will include you with your audience and help you in identifying with them and they with you.

10. *Make your application and appeals to individuals, to real and specific people who need to make real, specific, and personal responses.* Think concretely in a twenty-first century context that fits the people you are addressing.

11. *A good conclusion naturally flows out of the body of your message as the clear teaching of the biblical text.* It connects directly and without any question to the inspired Scriptures.

12. *A good conclusion has the note, even the feel, of preparedness.* It is not willy-nilly or haphazard. Your people sense, "This is where our pastor intended to take us all along." Broadus was quite direct at this point: "Let us lay down the rule, then, that the conclusion should be carefully prepared."[9]

ELEMENTS TO AVOID IN A CONCLUSION

Like a good introduction, there are a number of no-no's to guard against when preparing and delivering the conclusion. These homiletical snares can grab a superb message by the throat and render it both useless and helpless in achieving its intended goal.

1. *Never announce your conclusion.* When you have reached your well-planned and carefully crafted conclusion, your audience should know it. You do not have to tell them.

2. *Never announce the conclusion and then not conclude.* If the first is a mistake, the latter can be fatal. When you announce your conclusion, your people will begin to shut down. If you announce your conclusion and then fail to conclude the sermon, your people will become frustrated and even irritated.

3. *Do not introduce new material in your conclusion.* This is the time to wrap up not start up.

---

9.   Broadus, *A Treatise*, 278.

4. *Never go long.* Your conclusion should be clear, crisp, and concise. It must never be longer than the body of your sermon or even your major points.[10]

5. *Avoid poor conclusions with unhelpful phrases like, "I know the hour is late" or "I realize I am out of time."* Never look at your watch, or at least if you do, do so in such a way that no one realizes you are doing it.

6. *Do not stop before you are finished.* If you have prepared the message well, your conclusion will have both a "good fit" and a "good feel" to it.

7. *Avoid monotony in the way you conclude your sermons each week, both in your style and rate of speed and in the tone you use.* Variety is important, even essential, in each of these areas. In other words, avoid using the traditional approach of summarizing the three points and reciting a poem. Be creative and think through each aspect of your conclusion.

8. *Do not give the conclusion before you conclude unless doing so is strategically important to your message.* The conclusion comes at the end for a reason.

9. *Avoid energy drain or power loss at the end of your message.* Build toward a strong conclusion. This area is one in which African-American preachers excel. You have been building toward this moment. An emotional letdown at this point can spell disaster for your sermon.

10. *Never have multiple conclusions.* We refer to this error as the "unpardonable sin of preaching." Multiple conclusions will kill a message. When it is time to finish, finish well! Summarizing how we bring our sermon to an appropriate conclusion, Broadus admonishes us with words of wisdom and common sense: "The last sentence, of whatever it may consist, ought to be appropriate and impressive, but its style ought not to be elaborate or ambitious. It is a very solemn moment. Do not be thinking of your reputation, good brother, but of your responsibility, and of your hearer's salvation."[11]

---

10. Broadus says, "The length of the conclusion, like that of the introduction, is dependent on circumstances, and no rule can be laid down. But there is great danger of making it too long" (*A Treatise,* 286).

11. Ibid., 288.

SOURCES FOR DEVELOPING A GOOD CONCLUSION

When you are looking for good illustrative material for the conclusion of a sermon, the sources you would consult for the introduction apply here as well. Therefore, we would direct our readers to the previous chapter for a listing of helpful resources. At this point, let us add that the Bible itself is still the best source, especially for providing a story to illustrate the biblical truth of a didactic text. A psalm or a proverb may also illustrate the concluding points.

In this context we note that there are a variety of ways to conclude a sermon, some of which we have alluded to previously. You may conclude (1) with a summary of the main point(s); (2) by making specific and pointed application(s); (3) by making a passionate, heartfelt appeal to love, obey, serve, give, pray, witness, or worship; (4) by contrasting the main thrust of your message with an opposing viewpoint or perspective; and (5) by raising and answering potential objections to your message that may be on the minds of your audience. In these ways we can craft and deliver an effective conclusion.

PREPARING A GOOD CONCLUSION

Ramesh Richard says, "Faulty conclusions are notoriously discouraging."[12] Hershael York and Bert Decker are even more adamant in their concern, "We will go so far as to say that the *greatest error* most otherwise good preachers make is in their conclusion—or lack thereof."[13] Taking to heart what these excellent practitioners of preaching say about the conclusion, what guidelines can help us in safely and effectively bringing our message home? Here we summarize and bring together some of our previous observations.

1. As with all parts of the sermon, pray. Ask the Holy Spirit to direct you as you put your conclusion together. Be careful to

---

12. Ramesh Richard, *Preparing Expository Sermons* (Grand Rapids: Baker, 2001), 127.
13. Hershael York and Bert Decker, *Preaching with Bold Assurance* (Nashville: B&H, 2003), 185.

exalt Christ and avoid mere moralisms that gut the power of the gospel.

2. Let the body of your message dictate how you craft your conclusion. You do not start with a great conclusion and then search for a sermon and a text. The conclusion should flow clearly and naturally from your exposition of God's Word. Plan your conclusion carefully after your expository work.

3. Remember that the conclusion is a crucial component of your sermon. It must not be prepared in haste or with minimal attention.

4. Think in terms of how your conclusion can easily move from the body of the message and next into the Christ-centered invitation.

5. Briefly summarize your major idea.

6. Highlight your points of application.

7. Keep it brief. Three to five minutes sets wise parameters.

8. Remember the value of a powerful and memorable story.

9. Challenge your audience to act, decide, and respond.

10. Ask and answer the question, "What do I want my people to leave with and do in response to this message?"

11. Work at developing a clear, concise statement that captures the essence of your sermon.

12. Script the conclusion, at least as it pertains to its over-arching structure, so that you will end your message exactly as you want.

Our friend E. K. Bailey is now with the Lord, but he understood well the necessity of ending well. He would affirm, without hesitation, these 12 principles; yet, he would encourage us to always have an ear for the voice of the Holy Spirit as we bring the message to a close:

As I approach the end of the sermon, I'm watching and reading the congregation. I've been here before, many times, but I know that God may want to do a new thing today. So I watch my people and listen for the Spirit, even as I'm speaking. In the African-American tradition, when a preacher strikes a chord with the congregation, he'll not only get a verbal response, but the body language of the congregation changes. The Spirit may then lead me to develop a thought, because that's where the Spirit is dealing in the hearts of people. But other times I've sensed, it's time to shut it down and land.[14]

CONCLUSION

John Broadus says it well, "Preachers seldom neglect to prepare some introduction to a sermon, but very often neglect the conclusion; and yet the latter is even more important than the former."[15] It is difficult to overstate the crucial nature of the conclusion. It includes your last words, and last words should be lasting words. A conclusion brings things to an end with the goal of making a lasting impression on your listeners. You do not want to let them off the hook. Like men and women in a jurors' box, they have heard the final argument and must render a verdict. They cannot escape. They must decide. What should we do at this critical moment that is of eternal weight and significance? The invitation provides the natural opportunity for a decision to be made and confirmed. It is to that important component of the sermon that we now turn.

---

14. Bailey, "Smoothing Out the Landing," 39.
15. Broadus, *A Treatise*, 277.

CHAPTER 18

GIVING AN INVITATION: SOUL WINNING FROM THE PULPIT

I n 2 Cor 5:11 Paul writes, "Knowing, therefore, the terror of the Lord, we persuade men . . ." Then in verse 20 he adds, "Now then, we are ambassadors for Christ, as though God were pleading through us: we implore you on Christ's behalf, be reconciled to God" (NKJV). Again in 6:1–2, he exhorts, "We then, as workers together with Him, also plead with you not to receive the grace of God in vain. For He says: 'In an acceptable time I have heard you, And in the day of salvation I have helped you.' / Behold, now is the accepted time; behold, now is the day of salvation" (NKJV).

Scripture is clear that it is right for us to invite men and women, boys and girls, to repent of sin, trust Christ, believe the gospel, be reconciled to God, and receive the free and gracious gift of salvation. However, a question must be asked and answered: How does this translate to what is commonly called the public invitation?[1] For many this "tradition" attached to the end of a message is a given, and to question its legitimacy is to expose oneself to the charge of being non-evangelistic at best and possibly heretical.[2] On the other

---

1. For a historical study of the public invitation see David Bennett, *The Altar Call: Its Origins and Present Usage* (Lanham: Univer. Press of America, Inc., 2000).
2. Those who defend the public invitation include Roy Fish, *Giving a Good Invitation* (Nashville: Broadman, 1974); Leighton Ford, "How to Give an Honest Invitation," *Leadership* 5 (1984): 105–8; and "The Place of Decision,"

hand, some are greatly troubled by what they designate as "the altar call," "walking the aisle," or "coming forward to receive Jesus." They see the invitational system to be without biblical justification, often manipulative, and potentially misleading when it comes to what constitutes salvation. Because of the danger of abuse, the invitation has come under severe and sustained attack.[3]

Marv Knox raises the interesting question, "Will the traditional . . . invitation—a trip down the church aisle during a hymn at the end of a worship service—go the way of the funeral-home fan?"[4] Whether it will or not, it is our conviction that it should not. Yes, it is open to abuse and manipulation, but then so is marriage! That something is abused and misapplied is no argument for its complete rejection. A better approach is to begin by asking two crucial questions: (1) Is there biblical warrant for publicly inviting people to respond to the gospel and receive Christ? (2) If there is biblical justification, how do we extend a public invitation with integrity?

Choose Ye This Day (Minneapolis: World Wide, 1989); William (Billy) Franklin Graham, *The Challenge* (Garden City: Doubleday, 1969); Ken Keathley, "Rescuing the Perishing: A Defense of Giving Invitations," *Journal for Baptist Theology and Ministry* 1.1 (Spring 2003): 4–16; R. T. Kendall, *Stand Up and Be Counted: Calling for Public Confession of Faith* (Grand Rapids: Zondervan, 1984); Greg Laurie, "Whatever Happened to the Clear Invitation? How to Make the Call to Christ Compelling," *Leadership* 16 (1995): 52–56; R. Alan Street, *The Effective Invitation: A Practical Guide for the Pastor* (Grand Rapids: Kregel, 1984); Jerry Vines and Jim Shaddix, *Power in the Pulpit: How to Prepare and Deliver Expository Sermons* (Chicago: Moody, 1999); Faris Whitesell, *Sixty-Five Ways to Give Evangelistic Invitations*, 3rd ed. (Grand Rapids: Zondervan, 1945).

3.   Those who are skeptical toward or reject outright the public invitational system include Jim Ehrhard, *The Danger of the Invitation System* (Parville, MO: Christian Communicators Worldwide, 1999); J. Elliff, "Closing with Christ," *Viewpoint* (Jan–Mar 1999): 11–13; David Engelsma, *Hyper-Calvinism and the Call of the Gospel* (Grand Rapids: Reformed Free Publishing Association, 1994); Erroll Hulse, *The Great Invitation: Examining the Use of the Invitation System in Evangelism* (Hertfordshire: Evangelical Press, 1986); D. Martin Lloyd-Jones, *Preaching and Preachers* (Grand Rapids: Zondervan, 1972); Iain Murray, *The Invitation System* (London: The Banner of Truth Trust, 1967).

4.   Marv Knox, "Will Altar Call Go the Way of Funeral-Home Fans?" *Baptist Standard* (5-6-98): 15.

Now, it must be honestly acknowledged that the public invitation is a modern invention, at least in its present form.[5] It appears to have developed gradually with roots in the eighteenth century and gained momentum in the nineteenth century, when it was popularized by Charles Finney and his "new measures." In the modern era, no one has had greater influence on the public invitational approach than Billy Graham. His model of giving a "come forward" invitation at the end of a message has doubtless been repeated thousands of times in both evangelistic rallies and local church meetings. However, the pressing issue that must first be addressed is the biblical basis for inviting persons to respond to the gospel invitation and to biblical truth. Can a biblical argument be made? We believe it can, at least in principle, if not in precept.

A BIBLICAL UNDERSTANDING AND DEFENSE OF PUBLIC INVITATIONS

In both the Old and New Testament we find prophets and preachers challenging their hearers to make an open, public, and clear decision for the Lord. Note the following examples from the Old Testament.

- When Moses confronted the people for their idolatry, he commanded, "Whoever is on the LORD's side—come to me!" (Exod 33:26 NKJV).
- In his last days of leading the Hebrews, Moses concluded his sermon by calling on the congregation to choose: "I have set before you life and death, blessing and cursing; therefore choose life . . ." (Deut 30:19 NKJV).
- Joshua called on Israel to publicly decide between the Lord and false idols when he said, "Choose for yourselves this day whom you will serve . . ." (Josh 24:15 NKJV).

---

5.   For a fine overview of the development of the public invitational system, see Jason Rodgers, "The Development and Use of the Public Invitation System" (Th.M. thesis, The Southern Baptist Theological Seminary, 2002), 4–19.

- Elijah challenged the people of Israel by asking, "How long will you falter between two opinions? If the LORD is God, follow Him; but if Baal, follow him" (1 Kgs 18:21 NKJV).

As Keathley well notes, "The very nature of the prophetic message demands a clear and public decision."[6]

The New Testament also contains invitations to respond publicly to the proclamation of the Word of God.

- John the Baptist called upon his listeners to "repent" and to "bear fruits worthy of repentance" (Matt 3:2,8 NKJV).[7]
- Jesus called those who were following him to, "Come to me, all you who labor and are heavy laden, and I will give you rest" (Matt 11:28 NKJV).
- On the Day of Pentecost, Peter called the people to, "Repent, and let everyone of you be baptized in the name of Jesus Christ for the remission of sins . . ." (Acts 2:38). Verses 40–41 are even more vital to our investigation because there we see that Peter "with many other words . . . testified and exhorted them, saying 'Be saved from this perverse generation.'" What was the result? "Then those who gladly received his word were baptized; and that day about three thousand souls were added to them" (NKJV).
- In fact, there was both an expectation and actual response (an immediate response) to Peter's preaching. The public response to the message was that they "get in the water" and be baptized. Regardless of how one understands or even approves of the use of the public invitational system, an individual's public declaration for Christ is always baptism in the New Testament. There can be no substitute for this act of public confession and obedience (e.g., Matt 28:18–20).

---

6. Keathley, "Rescuing the Perishing," 6. Keathley also highlights these four examples in his excellent article. Note also the public response of the Ninevites to the preaching of Jonah in Jonah 3:5–9.
7. John, Jesus, and Peter each began their public preaching ministries with a call to repent (Matt 3:2; 4:17; Acts 2:38). Authentic gospel proclamation will always contain a command to repent of sin.

- In 2 Corinthians 5, Paul says we persuade men (v. 11), and as Christ's ambassadors God pleads through us and we implore men to be reconciled with God (v. 20). A public component of this assignment is certainly implied.
- The final book and chapter of the Bible concludes with an invitation, "And the Spirit and the bride say, "Come. . . . And let him who thirsts come. Whoever desires, let him take the water of life freely" (Rev 22:17).

We conclude that though Scripture may not depict the use of the invitation in the exact manner in which it takes place today, numerous examples in both Testaments indicate that persons are called and even challenged to declare their allegiance to God publicly. The call for the lost to repent of sin, believe the gospel, trust Christ, and publicly profess Him, culminating in believer's baptism, should characterize the faithful proclamation of the Word of God.

PROBLEMS AND CONCERNS WITH THE MODERN INVITATIONAL SYSTEM

Criticisms of the public invitation almost always make a beeline to the "altar call" where one "walks the aisle" and "comes to the front" of the auditorium at the urging of the preacher. Jim Eliff represents the criticism of many when he says, "There is no biblical precedent or command regarding a public altar call." He quickly adds, "it must be said that I espouse a *verbal* call to Christ in a most serious way and believe that the spoken invitation to come to Christ is a part of all gospel preaching. We 'compel' them to come in. But there is nothing sacrosanct about getting people to occupy a certain piece of geography at the front of the building."[8] Elliff goes on to critique "the sinner's prayer" and inviting Christ into one's life. What is his conclusion? The sinner's prayer "is not found anywhere but in the back of booklets" and inviting Christ into one's heart or life "hangs on nothing biblical (though John 1:12 and Rev 3:20 are used, out of context, for its basis)."[9]

---

8.   Elliff, "Closing with Christ," 11.
9.   Ibid., 12.

Keathley has done an excellent job in cataloging and responding to the more common objections to the public invitation. With his permission, we closely follow his argument at this point, adding our own thoughts as well. The analysis includes both historical and theological arguments.[10]

Historical Arguments

Charge: *The practice of giving invitations was invented (or at least popularized) by Charles Finney.*

Engelsma refers to the altar call as "that johnny-come-lately innovation of Finney."[11] That Finney held aberrant views concerning salvation calls into question the validity of the invitational system.

Reply: *This example is one of guilt by association and begs the question as to whether or not the public invitation has scriptural support.*

Keathley points out that the Separate Baptists of the Sandy Creek tradition were giving public invitations 30 years before Finney was even born. An eyewitness described the manner in which the "ranting Anabaptists" would conduct services during the great revivals in the Carolinas in the 1760s:

> At the close of the sermon, the minister would come down from the pulpit and while singing a suitable hymn would go around among the brethren shaking hands. The hymn being sung, he would then extend an invitation to such persons as felt themselves poor guilty sinners, and were anxiously inquiring the way of salvation, to come forward and kneel near the stand, or if they preferred, they could kneel at their seats, proffering to unite with them in prayer for their conversion.[12]

That Separate Baptists gave altar calls is important. Many were converted while hearing George Whitefield preach during the Great Awakening of the mid-eighteenth century. Further, as we have seen,

---

10. Keathley, "Rescue the Perishing," 7–15.
11. Engelsma, *Hyper-Calvinism and the Call*, 63.
12. William L. Lumpkin, *Baptist Foundations in the South* (Nashville: Broadman, 1961), 56.

there is biblical support for inviting people to publicly declare their faith for Christ.

Charge: *Historically, the results of invitations are dismal and produce many false converts.*

Opponents of the invitation point to the often disappointing results of many evangelistic meetings and church services. The invitation is said to be a distraction that short-circuits the very process that it is meant to facilitate.

Reply: *This accusation is by far the most serious one. Some of the critiques are certainly valid.*

For many preachers, the problem is not that an invitation is being given, but that poor and unclear preaching precedes it. Their preaching lacks clarity about the desperate sinfulness of man, the necessity of repentance and faith, and the atoning work of the Lord Jesus Christ. Many who are saved later in life have testified that they went forward earlier and wrongly identified salvation with walking the aisle and the handshake of the preacher.[13] The practice of the invitation is not itself at fault. Rather, the anemic theology and poor presentation of the gospel by the one giving it are the problems. Replacing biblical words like repentance and faith with a phrase like "getting connected with God" is not helpful. As Keathley rightly notes, "When salvation is replaced with therapy, the result will be false converts whether an altar call is given or not."[14] In addition, some invitations are unclear in their presentation and leave listeners confused and unsure as to what they are being asked to do.

Without a doubt, the evangelistic methods used by some preachers are shameful. Others are simply sloppy and poorly given. Again, Keathley notes, "When Christ is preached in the power of the Holy Spirit, manipulative methods are not necessary. Those who use such

---

13. This tragic reality is an all-too-common occurrence that demands an honest admission of failure on the part of many preachers and a change in how they give the invitation. Close to half of all incoming seminary students admit to having been "baptized" more than once due to a prior confession of faith that they later deemed inauthentic. The fault and correction of this situation falls squarely on the shoulders of pastors.
14. Keathley, "Rescue the Perishing," 7.

techniques are revealing their lack of confidence in the power of the gospel."[15]

Theological Arguments

Charge: *There is no "well meant offer" of the gospel to all.*

Hyper-Calvinists such as David Engelsma reject the view that the gospel is genuinely offered to everyone who hears it. They do not believe that God loves all people and desires their salvation. Therefore, a public invitation to all to come to Christ is a gross theological error. Engelsma claims that Paul,

> did not believe, nor did he ever preach, that God loved all men, was gracious to all men, and desired the salvation of all men, that is he did not believe, teach, or give the well-meant offer of the Gospel. . . . Paul did not regard the preaching of the gospel as an *offer* of salvation to everyone, directed to everyone in a universal love of God and providing everyone with a chance to be saved.[16]

Reply: *Evangelicals recognize that God's offer of salvation to all is real.*

Second Corinthians 5:19 teaches "that God was in Christ reconciling the world to Himself" (NKJV). To this world we are called to be ambassadors, pleading with and imploring for men to be reconciled to God. To this verse, we easily add John 3:16, which is a well meant-offer of the gospel to all.

Charge: *Pleading with men to come to Christ is disgraceful and even idolatrous.*

According to Engelsma, preachers are called to proclaim the gospel, not to persuade men to receive it. He likens those who urge men to come to Christ as similar to the prophets of Baal. He says giving invitations is tantamount to idolatry because it focuses on the sinner rather than the sovereign work of grace.[17]

---

15. Ibid.
16. Engelsma, *Hyper-Calvinism and the Call*, 70.
17. Ibid., 87.

Reply: *Besides being offensive, this characterization is patently false.*

We would agree that salvation is completely a work of God and that the gospel is a Christ-centered doctrine. However, we also believe that God uses intermediate means to accomplish His work. Clearly, God is the one who calls men to salvation, but He uses the gospel preacher to issue the summons (Rom 10:14–17). There is a place for earnest, brokenhearted, passionate preaching. The invitation is a natural expression of the sincere, godly desire for people to come to Christ, which finds its motivation in the truth that lost people matter to God (e.g., Jonah 4).

Charge: *Occupying a certain piece of geography does not save people.*

Reply: *This argument is a straw man, plain and simple.*

No authentic gospel preacher believes that a person is saved by the act of going forward and walking the aisle. As Keathley again notes, "Gospel preachers make clear that salvation is not in any public act or repeating any prayer. Salvation is [in] Jesus Christ. We publicly invite people to come to him. No method of giving an invitation is sacrosanct and sensitivity to the particular situation in which the minister finds himself is in order. What must be upheld is the principle of calling the hearers to a decision and expecting the Spirit of God to do his work."[18]

CHARACTERISTICS OF A GOOD INVITATION

We acknowledge that the public invitation, like many spiritual and religious practices, is open to abuse and manipulation. However, the solution is not to kill it but redeem it. We need to extend it in a manner that is biblical, authentic, and Christ-honoring, all to the glory of God. Key concepts in doing it in this manner are *motivation* and *information*. In that context, we note 11 components of a good and responsible invitation.

> 1. *Good invitations are given with integrity.* The key to avoiding manipulation is to examine your motives. Why are you

---

18. Keathley, "Rescue the Perishing," 13.

inviting people to trust Christ and believe God? Are you attempting to get them to come forward to stroke your ego and tally numbers, or are you seeking to urge them to believe the gospel and trusting God's Spirit to do the work that only He can do in their hearts?

2. *Good invitations are gospel-centered.* Biblical heralds are heralds of the good news of who Jesus is and what Jesus has done to reconcile sinners to God. The Bible is faithfully proclaimed, Christ and his cross are beautifully exalted, and the lost are urged to trust Jesus and Jesus alone for salvation. Because the gospel is multi-faceted, our invitations should be as well. There is absolutely no reason to fall into a rut saying the same thing the same way every time. Let the text drive and guide your invitation.

3. *Good invitations are clear in what we are asking our listeners to do.* We must be clear that the call to come forward, to raise your hand, or to sign a card does not save. We are saved when we trust in Christ and believe the gospel. Coming forward or even praying the sinner's prayer is, however, an opportunity to fortify one's decision for Christ that has been made in the heart. Billy Graham notes, "There's something about coming forward publicly out from the crowd, saying, 'I receive Christ.' It settles it in your heart."[19]

4. *Good invitations are sensitive to the makeup of the congregation.* A faithful pastor, or evangelist for that matter, will not manipulate the emotions of those susceptible to such tactics and tricks. We have children particularly in mind.

5. *Good invitations avoid using Christian jargon and "the language of Zion" without a clear and precise explanation of what those terms mean.* Non-believers are less churched and less

---

19. Graham, *The Challenge*, 33. I (Danny) would note that I have no memory of praying the sinner's prayer nor did I equate coming forward as an act of salvation. I was about 10 years old when I was converted. On the other hand, I led all four of my sons in praying the sinner's prayer in a private setting at home. Each one is convinced that this was the time of their conversion. They are now all adults. I also went forward publicly and immediately when I sensed God's call to be a gospel minister. I have never doubted what transpired that Monday evening at a revival service in Sells, Arizona, on the Papago Indian Reservation.

theologically informed than at any other time in our history. Even our church members are far too often theologically ignorant of the great truths embedded in a biblical vocabulary. Our goal is always to communicate the gospel and all its implications well. Otherwise, we will only confuse, frustrate, and alienate those we are trying to reach.

6. *Good invitations recognize faithful biblical preaching, which is guided by a Christocentric hermeneutic, and plays a key role in calling people to trust and follow Christ.* Herbert Arrowsmith is correct, "Exposition is the best evangelism. It is still true that the Spirit of God takes the Word of God to make a child of God."[20]

7. *Good invitations are characterized by clear instructions and explanations.* Leighton Ford writes, "People need to know what responding to your invitation means and what it does not mean."[21] Your people should well understand to whom the call is directed, what they should do, and why they should do it. Are they to respond to the call of salvation? Baptism? Church membership? Vocational service? Consecration of life? Repentance from sin and a pattern of disobedience?

8. *Good invitations will provide competent, well-trained counselors who have both a good location and the time to do their job right.*

9. *Good invitations will be warm and personal, but also urgent and direct.* They will be extended in a time frame that is balanced and establishes a high level of trust in the preacher who is calling them to respond to the gospel. Our people should always believe we have their best interest at heart.

10. *Good invitations have a sense of expectancy grounded in the promise of God that his Word will not return void but will accomplish what he desires (Isa 55:11).* Roy Fish shares an insightful story in this context: "On one occasion, a young student of Spurgeon came to the great preacher complaining that he wasn't seeing conversions through his preaching. Spurgeon inquired, 'Surely you don't expect conversions

20. Herbert Arrowsmith, *One Race* (Henry and Mooneyham, n.d.), 15.
21. Ford, "How to Give an Honest Invitation," 106.

every time you preach, do you?' The young man replied, 'Well, I suppose not.' Spurgeon then said, 'That's precisely why you are not having them.'"[22]

DIFFERENT APPROACHES IN GIVING THE INVITATION

The public invitation reminds people that the gospel requires—yes it demands—a response. It helps clarify in their minds what they are doing and why they are doing it. It allows the preacher and counselor to talk to them about their decision and answer their questions. With these basic foundational principles, what are some different approaches to giving an invitation? What are the advantages and disadvantages of each? We highlight six.

1. A verbal appeal to trust Christ and embrace the gospel that has been clearly explained.

Advantages: (a) It avoids the danger of manipulation that can accompany a call to come forward. (b) It is personal in that it directs the listener to do business with God.

Disadvantages: (a) There is no immediate opportunity to publicly acknowledge one's faith in Christ. (b) It can leave the one responding to the gospel with unanswered questions that may need an immediate answer. However, this disadvantage can be overcome by adding to the verbal appeal one of the next two options.

---

22. Fish, *Giving a Great Invitation*, 221. Vines and Shaddix list seven characteristics of a good invitation (*Power in the Pulpit*, 215–18). Among these they note that it must: be *cohesive* with the sermon that precedes it, be characterized by simplicity and clarity, be functional, involve some decisive element, be non-manipulative and non-threatening, be personal to every listener, and incorporate an evangelistic twist.

2. An invitation to come forward at the end of the sermon in response to the biblical message and gospel appeal.

Advantages:(a) It is an easier way to get with someone immediately. (b) It is a more effective way to get with someone one-on-one. (c) It can encourage others who have prayed for them and are interested in their decision. (d) It allows for public celebration. (e) It can provide personal confirmation to the one responding to the preached word.

Disadvantages: (a) It is open to coercion and manipulation. (b) It can be misunderstood even when properly communicated. (c) One may equate the call to come forward with the genuine invitation to believe the gospel.

3. An invitation to come to a side room or counseling room for further inquiry and information.

Advantages: (a) There is less pressure, certainly of a public nature. (b) The danger of abuse is minimized. (c) It helps those who are shy. (d) It provides private one-on-one time that is neither rushed nor distracted by a congregation.

Disadvantages: (a) The church misses the immediate celebration of the salvation. (b) Not all churches have proper facilities.

4. "Raise your hand if you've trusted Christ."

The advantages and disadvantages of this method are similar to #2 noted above.

5. Invite people to "trust Christ now" and come forward afterward for information on how to grow.

Advantages: It keeps separate trusting Christ and coming forward.

Disadvantages: Follow up can be difficult, if not impossible, if they fail to come forward later.

6. Commitment card.

Advantages: (a) It is great for follow-up. (b) It is the most non-threatening of all. (c) It provides a record of all who made a decision and wish to have it noted. (d) It can be used in a wide variety of settings.

Disadvantages: (a) It too is open to misunderstanding or at least a lack of full understanding. (b) There are the pragmatics of getting the cards after the service has ended.

These methods are not exhaustive. They are certainly not infallible. Acting with proper motivation and integrity is essential. Being contextually sensitive is crucial. How you extend the gospel invitation is not the most important issue. That you do it is![23]

CONCLUSION

In addressing the definition of evangelism, J. I. Packer says, "The message begins with information and ends with an invitation."[24] David Larsen adds, "The gospel is an invitation to which sinners are to R.S.V.P. A response is called for."[25] The manner in which one is called to respond may vary. Responding to the greatest message the world has ever known or will ever know is imperative. The public invitation provides an outlet and an opportunity for the outward expression of the inward work of the Holy Spirit of God. Clothed with integrity and delivered with clarity, heralds of the gospel may rightly plead with sinners to be reconciled with God. They may challenge them to respond publicly. Because of the promises of God, we can expect and believe they will.

---

23. Vines and Shaddix also note six possible models for the invitation. They include: (1) verbal appeal, (2) physical relocation, (3) post-meeting ministry, (4) written record, (5) physical gesture, and (6) multiple approaches (*Power in the Pulpit*, 212–15).

24. J. I. Packer, *Evangelism and the Sovereignty of God* (Downers Grove: IVP, 1961), 92.

25. David L. Larsen, *The Evangelistic Mandate: Recovering the Centrality of Gospel Preaching* (Wheaton: Crossway, 1992), 102.

CHAPTER 19

PREACHING ON
SPECIAL OCCASIONS

Those who teach and preach the Word of God can expect to be invited to speak on numerous occasions at special events unrelated to their weekly expositions. These special events may include weddings, funerals, banquets (Valentine's Day, Leadership, Sunday school/Bible Teaching Appreciation, Stewardship, Student Recognition), conferences (Bible, Marriage and Family, Prophecy, Cults, Doctrinal), revivals, and community events (local clubs, baccalaureates, graduations). Additional special days during the church year also may need recognition and attention in your sermons. These days could include Christmas, Easter, Mother's Day, Father's Day, Sanctity of Life Sunday, and Thanksgiving. Some would also consider New Year's Day, fourth of July, and Memorial Day worthy of a special emphasis and message.[1] The faithful expositor must approach his Sunday-by-Sunday schedule with wisdom and prudence. He will be hard pressed to recognize all the special occasions, otherwise he may spend half of his time or more preaching on them. On the other hand, we would consider it foolish to ignore them altogether. These times are often excellent ones to invite lost, unbelieving family and friends to church. The minds of your people are focused on these special days in the calendar as well, so do not

---

1. Stephen Rummage provides an excellent overview of planning for special days in *Planning Your Preaching* (Grand Rapids: Kregel, 2002), 117–36.

ignore them. Use them for the advantage of proclaiming the gospel of Jesus Christ! Regardless of location or occasion, our goal is to confront our audience with a word from God and point them to a Savior who saves.

PRINCIPLES TO FOLLOW FOR SPECIAL OCCASIONS

There are some basic principles we would suggest for any special occasion. Spiritual sensitivity needs to be at its highest level, especially for opportunities that are not in a specific Christian context. Compromise of biblical truth is not an option, but doing one's best to extend Christ-honoring grace and goodwill should be at the front and center of our agenda. What then should we consider as we prepare and then deliver our message?

1. *Biblical exposition is always appropriate.* Indeed, it should be the norm and not the exception. God's Word has a word for any occasion and every situation. It is truth, and people need truth, even if they may not want it. Preachers may often discover that the scheduled text for exposition holds legitimate application for the special occasion at hand.

2. *Biblical exposition of a short text or familiar passage is a wise course of action. Most likely, you will be the only person with a Bible.* This even includes occasions like a graduation ceremony at a Christian school. The audience is not going to have before them a Bible by which they can follow your explanation of the text. Therefore, a short text, one with one to three verses, or a popular text (e.g., "The Good Samaritan") is a smart way to go. Give them something they can hear, digest and take home.

3. *Brevity in your preaching is normally expected, and the wise decision in most of these situations is to meet this expectation.* It will almost never get you in trouble, and it will foster goodwill and enhance the odds for a return invitation. Fifteen to twenty minutes is about the right length for your sermon, though we recognize on some occasions you can preach much longer, even an hour, with no one becoming upset. Of course, we (and they) are counting on your being interesting

and engaging. Remember that it is a sin to make the Bible boring!

4. *The power of a good story or powerful illustration will never be more important.* As noted earlier, illustrations are windows into the house of your message which allow your audience to see what is in there. As we all know, this part of your message is the one that they are most likely to remember. Therefore, make this illustration a key component of your address on these special occasions.

5. *Principled exposition that is reflected in the life of Jesus or a biblical character is usually a fine strategy to consider.* Leadership principles drawn from the life of Jesus, Paul, David, or the Proverbs, for example, can be very effective. Sometimes exploring negative or anti-examples will powerfully make the point. Think about the squandered privileges of Cain, Jephthah, Saul, or Judas. Work hard to strike a balance in your message so that it is appropriate to the occasion but also lifts up the Lord Jesus. You may find this task is sometimes quite challenging, but it may also be spiritually fruitful as people see the significance of Jesus both for now and eternity.

6. *We should always be focused on the application of our message when we preach, but this is especially crucial when speaking at special occasions.* Lost people need to see the power of biblical truth and its relevance to everyday life.

7. *The use of humor, if appropriate to the occasion, can be extremely valuable in pressing your message upon your hearers.* Of course, you have to use humor well. Most persons have a sense of humor unique to their personality. Therefore, just be you, and allow yourself to be humorous in a way that fits who you are.

8. *Never betray the trust of those who have invited you to speak.* Follow their instructions as to the time and the address. Going beyond the specified time is rude and irresponsible. It is probably sinful. Not honoring the particular instructions and expectations concerning your message is dishonest and arrogant. Their expectations may require you to turn down some invitations because you are asked to compromise your convictions or expected to be silent when you know you must

speak. Integrity demands honesty and transparency, even if it means saying "no" to a lucrative speaking opportunity and a generous honorarium. Do the right thing in the right way, and God will honor you.

9. *Finally, always speak of Jesus and His gospel.* You will need to be sensitive to the context and creative in your presentation. Nevertheless, you are a gospel herald, and so herald the gospel.

WEDDINGS AND FUNERALS

The two special occasions for which you will most often be called upon to speak are weddings and funerals. These occasions are divinely ordained moments for sharing the gospel with persons who never attend church, read the Bible, or receive a gospel witness. A funeral in particular is a time when persons are likely to be more sensitive and open to the gospel. The issues of life, death, and eternity are in the air. These realities are inescapable, and they take center stage during a funeral. What follows are some specific and practical helps as you preside and speak at these important occasions. Each of the nine principles previously noted will apply here as well.

Weddings

A wedding is a time of joy and celebration. Your service should reflect this spirit. Make sure to walk carefully through each facet of the service with the prospective bride and groom. Let them know that you are open to their wishes and suggestions, but that you reserve absolute veto power over everything. That includes bridal attire, the words spoken by all, and the music. Tell them that whatever is Christ-honoring and extols the beauty of Christian marriage will be allowed. Anything that does not will not be allowed. Hold your ground here no matter what pressure you receive.

What does a wedding service look like? What are appropriate words to be spoken and shared? Of course, there can be significant variety as long as the guidelines noted above are honored. Let us provide a basic pattern or outline as well as the words that might be spoken, for consideration. This outline will provide a baseline for developing each particular wedding ceremony.[2]

The Wedding of Groom's full name
and
Bride's full name
(A General Outline)

PRELUDE

LIGHTING OF CANDLES/SEATING OF MOTHERS

A song may be sung at this point. This is also a place to consider the sharing of the gospel, though having it proclaimed in the actual ceremony is an excellent location as well.

PROCESSIONAL

OPENING WORDS/GREETING BY THE MINISTER

Dearly beloved (family and friends), we are gathered together here in the presence of God and in the fellowship of this Christian Community to join this man, <u>Groom's full name</u>, and this woman, <u>Bride's full name</u>, in Christian marriage. Christian marriage is a divine covenant of faith and trust between a man and a woman. It is established within their shared commitment in the covenant of faith in the Lord Jesus Christ. It requires of both man and woman openness of life and thought, freedom from doubt and suspicion, and commitment to speak the truth in love, as they grow up into Christ, who is the head of the Church and is to be the head of their home. This covenant is not to be entered into lightly, but reverently, discreetly, and wisely in the fear of God.

---

2. Guidelines and outlines for weddings and funerals can be found in various pastor's manuals and guidebooks. Two classics in the field are W. A. Criswell, *Criswell's Guidebook for Pastors* (Nashville: Broadman Press, 1980) and J. R. Hobbs, *The Pastor's Manual* (Nashville: Broadman, 1962).

In Eph 5:21–33 God speaks to the marriage relationship, addressing both the wife and the husband. Paul writes:

And be subject to one another in the fear of Christ. Wives, be subject to your own husbands, as to the Lord. For the husband is the head of the wife, as Christ also is the head of the church, He Himself being the Savior of the body. But as the church is subject to Christ, so also the wives ought to be to their husbands in everything. Husbands, love your wives, just as Christ also loved the church and gave Himself up for her. That He might sanctify her, having cleansed her by the washing of water with the word. That He might present to Himself the church in all her glory, having no spot or wrinkle or any such thing; but that she would be holy and blameless. So husbands ought also to love their own wives as their own bodies. He who loves his own wife loves himself. For no one ever hated his own flesh, but nourishes and cherishes it, just as Christ also does the church. Because we are members of His body. For this reason a man shall leave his father and mother and shall be joined to his wife, and the two shall become one flesh. This mystery is great; but I am speaking with reference to Christ and the church. Nevertheless let each individual among you also love his own wife even as himself; and the wife must see to it that she respects her husband (NASB).
(Gospel may be shared at this point)

Prayer

GIVING OF THE BRIDE

Minister: "Who gives this bride to be married to this groom? The one giving the bride responds.

(Congregational Hymn/Duet/Solo may be sung)

Minister: Marriage is about loving another, giving to another, serving another. It is about placing your mate before and ahead of yourself. It is about having the mind of Christ in this tender and precious relationship. Paul addresses this in Phil 2:1–5. Listen to these important words.

Therefore if there is any encouragement in Christ, if there is any consolation of love, if there is any fellowship of the Spirit, if any affection and compassion, make my joy complete by being of the same mind, maintaining the same love, united in spirit, intent on one purpose. Do nothing from selfishness or empty conceit, but with humility of mind regard one another as more important than yourself; do not merely look out for your own personal interests, but also for the interests of others. Have this attitude in yourselves which was also in Christ Jesus.

EXCHANGE OF VOWS

Minister: <u>Groom's First name,</u> will you have <u>Bride's First name</u> to be your wedded wife, to live together in the covenant of faith, hope, and love according to the plan of God for your lives together in Jesus Christ? Will you love her sacrificially as Christ loves the Church and gave Himself for her? Will you listen to her inmost thoughts, be considerate and tender in your care of her, stand by her faithfully in sickness and in health, and preferring her above all others, accept full responsibility for her every necessity as long as you both shall live?

Groom: "I will."

<u>Bride's First name</u> will you have <u>Groom's First name</u> to be your wedded husband, to live together in the covenant of faith, hope, and love according to the plan of God for your lives together in Jesus Christ? Will you submit to him as the Church submits to Christ? Will you listen to his inmost thoughts, be considerate and tender in your care of him and stand by him faithfully in sickness and in health, and preferring him above all others, accept full responsibility for his every necessity as long as you both shall live?

Bride: "I will."

EXCHANGE OF RINGS AND COMMITMENTS

Minister: First John 4:8 teaches that love is a reflection of the very heart and character of God. It is also an essential companion of a blessed and joyful marriage. God did not leave it to chance or human imagination as to what real love looks like. He inspired the apostle

Paul to beautifully describe it in the "love chapter" in 1 Corinthians 13.

1 Corinthians 13

If I speak with the tongues of men and of angels, but do not have love, I have become a noisy gong or a clanging cymbal. If I have the gift of prophecy, and know all mysteries and all knowledge; and if I have all faith, so as to remove mountains, but do not have love, I am nothing. And if I give all my possessions to feed the poor, and if I surrender my body to be burned, but do not have love, it profits me nothing. Love is patient, love is kind and is not jealous; love does not brag and is not arrogant, does not act unbecomingly; it does not seek its own, is not provoked, does not take into account a wrong suffered, does not rejoice in unrighteousness, but rejoices with the truth; bears all things, believes all things, hopes all things, endures all things. Love never fails; but if there are gifts of prophecy, they will be done away; if there are tongues, they will cease; if there is knowledge, it will be done away. For we know in part and we prophesy in part; but when the perfect comes, the partial will be done away. When I was a child, I used to speak as a child, think as a child, reason as a child; when I became a man, I did away with childish things. For now we see in a mirror dimly, but then face to face; now I know in part, but then I shall know fully just as I also have been fully known. But now abide faith, hope, love, these three; but the greatest of these is love.

Minister: <u>Groom</u> do you possess a pledge of your love and affection to give to your bride, a sign and seal of this holy covenant?

Groom: "I do."

"I, <u>Groom's First name</u>, take you <u>Bride's First name</u>, to be my wedded wife, to have and to hold from this day forward, for richer, for poorer, for better, for worse, to protect, and to cleave unto you and to you only, as long as we both shall live. With this ring I thee wed, all my love, I give to you, all my worldly goods with you I share, in the name of the Father, and the Son, and the Holy Spirit, blessed forever more, Amen."

Minister: <u>Bride</u> do you possess a pledge of your love and affection to give your husband, a sign and seal of this holy covenant?

Bride: "I do."

Invested with the same significance as the ring you have just received, a circle of precious gold, indicating the purity of your love and the pricelessness of your devotion, place this ring on the wedding finger of your husband and repeat after me:

"I, <u>Bride's First name</u>, take you <u>Groom's First name</u>, to be my wedded husband, to have and to hold, from this day forward, for richer, for poorer, for better, for worse, to protect, and to cleave unto you and to you only, as long as we both shall live. With this ring I thee wed, all the love of my heart I commit to you, in the name of the Father, the Son, and the Holy Spirit. Amen."

Prayer

KNEELER (optional) As the couple kneels and/or prays, a song is often sung. "The Lord's Prayer" is a classic and is often chosen for this moment.

LIGHTING OF THE UNITY CANDLE

PRONOUNCEMENT

In as much as you <u>Groom's First name</u> and you <u>Bride's First name</u> have pledged yourselves to each other in Christian marriage, and have witnessed the same before God and these witnesses, and have pledged your love and faithfulness each to the other, and have declared the same by joining hands, and by giving and receiving a ring: I am delighted to pronounce you husband and wife. Those whom God hath joined together, let no man put asunder. Amen. <u>Groom's First name</u>, you may kiss your bride.

RECESSIONAL

The Covenantal Nature of Marriage

Because we believe in the sacredness of marriage, we take pre-marital counseling very seriously. Danny requires that each couple whom he counsels and marries sign a pre-marital wedding covenant as a pledge and recognition of the awesome nature and permanence of Christian marriage. That covenant follows for your reading and consideration.

PRE-MARITAL WEDDING COVENANT

The decision to marry is the second most important decision one will ever make in a lifetime. The first is the decision whether or not you will personally commit your life to Jesus Christ as Savior and Lord. Keeping this in mind, we commit to God, our minister, and each other to:

1. Seek God's will for our lives personally and together by following biblical principles for Christian living and marriage.
2. Not engage in pre-marital sex, or in any other inappropriate sexual behavior.
3. Be sure to do everything possible to build a Christian marriage and home. This means that both of us confess that we have a personal relationship with Jesus Christ, and that we desire growth for that relationship over the entire course of our lives by being obedient to His Word.
4. Read and listen to all pre-marital material provided by our minister.
5. Be active in a Bible-believing church, beginning now and during our marriage.
6. Buy and read *His Needs, Her Needs* by Willard Harley; *The Act of Marriage* by Tim LaHaye; *God on Sex* by Danny Akin; and *A Promise Kept* by Robertson McQuilkin.
7. Total openness and honesty with our minister and with each other, both now and after our wedding.

8. Postpone or cancel the marriage if, at any time between now and the wedding, either one of us comes to believe this marriage is not right.

9. Never allow the word "divorce" to enter the realm of our relationship. We are in this together for the duration of our lives. Divorce is not an option for us.

10. Inform our minister and seek competent Christian counsel should we encounter any difficulty in our marriage.

With the above commitments made, we believe God will be honored, and the prospects for a meaningful and happy marriage will be enhanced. With God's help, we will seek to honor God with our lives and marriage all the days of our lives.

Funerals

In conducting a funeral, you must balance sensitivity with authority. Gracious leadership, both with the family and the funeral director, is essential, especially with the family. John Bisagno is absolutely correct when he writes.

> When the time and place have been determined for the memorial service, contact the funeral director to be certain you are in agreement about every detail of the service and subsequent burial. Advanced planning will save confusion and resultant embarrassment.[3]

The family will be in varying stages of grief and shock. Gently, but firmly, guide them to plan out a service that will honor God and be appropriate. Of course, there may be occasions when you are called in just to preach at the funeral of a deceased person, with no control over the other aspects of the service. Be kind and loving, strong and comforting. Then, open your Bible and preach the gospel.

Avoid at all costs dishonest or uninformed eulogizing at any funeral, especially for someone you did not know well or know at all. Stick to what you do know: the gospel and the Word of God.

---

3. John Bisagno, *Letters to Timothy: A Handbook for Pastors* (Nashville: B&H, 2001), 98.

W. A. Criswell was "spot on" when it comes to this assignment and opportunity:

> The pastor should accept the funeral hour as God's open door for him to speak to the people about the fundamental, basic verities of life, death, earth, heaven, time, and eternity. To waste the hour in drivel with cheap eulogy and empty ostentation is to sin against the presence of the Holy Spirit. Speak the message of God. They will hear it as never before when they are seated in the service before you.[4]

The order of service should be basic and simple under most circumstances. What follows is a suggested outline for the memorial service.

PATTERN FOR A FUNERAL SERVICE

The family is seated as others stand in respect.
Scripture reading and prayer
Song (solo or congregational)
Eulogy
Prayer
Song (solo or congregational)
Message by the Minister
Gospel invitation
Benediction

There will usually be a short graveside service. The reading of Scripture with brief comments, and then closing in prayer, is always appropriate. Psalm 23; John 14:1–6; 1 Cor 15:50–58; and 1 Thess 4:13–18 are wonderful texts to read as the body is being prepared to be lowered in the grave.

---

4.   Criswell, *Criswell's Guidebook for Pastors*, 297.

SERMONS FOR THE FUNERAL SERVICE[5]

Below are some suggested texts and outlines that may be of help as you pray through your funeral message. Remember you will probably be the only one with a Bible, so keep that in mind as you choose a text, read the text, and expound the text. Clarity and conciseness will be at a premium.

"The Good Shepherd of Psalm 23"

I.	The Good Shepherd provides for us what we need.	23:1–3
II.	The Good Shepherd protects us where we are.	23:4–5
III.	The Good Shepherd promises us what we will have.	23:6

"Precious Promises of a Great God" (Rom 8:28–39)

I.	We have the promise of His power.	8:28
II.	We have the promise of His purpose.	8:29–30
III.	We have the promise of His provisions.	8:31–34
IV.	We have the promise of His presence.	8:35–39

"The Grace of God for When We Hurt" (Rom 8:28–39)

I.	God assures us.	8:28
II.	God changes us.	8:29–30
III.	God supports us.	8:31–33
IV.	God hears us.	8:34 also 8:26–27
V.	God loves us.	8:35–39

"The New Things of Heaven" (Rev 21:1–8)

For the child of God who dies there is a:

I.	New Creation	21:1—curse reversed; creation restored; creature redeemed
II.	New City	21:2—a people/a place

---

5. Ibid., 301–28, has a number of sermons, poems, and songs for the funeral message that are of great value and worthy of consideration.

III. New Commitment   21:3
IV. New Condition   21:4
 V. New Confidence   21:5
VI. New Covenant   21:6–7

Special occasions are special opportunities that come only rarely. Do not miss the moment or squander the privilege of magnifying Jesus and ministering to unbelievers. The gospel is right for the situation. Preach it, and preach it well.

20 COMMON QUESTIONS AND ANSWERS IN DEVELOPING BIBLICAL MESSAGES

1. HOW MUCH TIME DO YOU SPEND IN STUDY FOR YOUR MESSAGES?

As pastors become more efficient in their work in the study, they will discover that they can do more in less time. You will spend more time in sermon preparation in the earlier part of your ministry as you develop your method and become more familiar with the tools of the trade. Through repetition and practice, your method will be refined and improved. When I (Danny) first began preaching at the age of 21, I would spend somewhere between 15 and 20 hours on each message. Fortunately, I was only preparing one message per week. Today, after more than 30 years in ministry, I can now do in 7 to 10 hours what used to require 15 to 20. After all of these years in preparing messages, I would never step into the pulpit to proclaim the Word of God without a minimum of 7 to 10 hours of study on that message. The bottom line is this: take the time that is necessary to prepare messages that will feed the flock of God placed under your care. Adrian Rogers once told me that there is no more valuable commodity in ministry than time. He admonished me to train students to learn the sermon craft well, and to discover ways to maximize the limited amount of time they have for carrying out all the duties of the pastor.

2. HOW MANY COMMENTARIES DO YOU USE, AND WHICH ONES ARE YOUR FAVORITES?

Never use less than five to seven commentaries. We were startled several years ago to discover that many men believe that two or three are adequate for sermon preparation. We could hardly imagine using so few. We are aware of our own limitations and shortcomings. I am finite and sinful, and too often can miss the wonderful truths revealed in God's Word. Good commentaries are like inviting friends to sit down with you and talk about the Bible. Through their writings we have access to their insights. A wide variety of commentaries is essential. We always utilize exegetical, expositional, homiletical, and devotional commentaries. We are especially fond of the *Expositor's Bible Commentaries*, the *New American Commentaries*, the *New International Commentaries on the Old and New Testament*, the *Pillar New Testament Commentaries*, the *NIV Application Commentaries*, and the *Tyndale Series*. We have also benefited greatly from John MacArthur's commentaries, as well as the *Preach the Word Series,* authored and edited by Kent Hughes. I (Danny) also enjoy reading Warren Wiersbe because he speaks in the language of common people. All of this commentary work is no substitute for personal work in the Hebrew, Greek, and English text. If time allows, I try to work through at least 7 to 10 commentaries as I prepare each message. We would prefer to read 15 to 20, but time limitations are simply a reality of life.

3. WHAT TRANSLATIONS OF THE BIBLE DO YOU READ IN SERMON PREPARATION? FROM WHICH TRANSLATION DO YOU PREACH?

We read through as many different translations as we can during our sermon preparation. We especially appreciate the *English Standard Version*, the *New American Standard Version*, the *New International Version*, the *New King James Version*, the *King James Version*, the *Holman Christian Standard Bible*, and the *New Living Translation*.

We also read the paraphrase *The Message* by Eugene Peterson, though we would never preach from a paraphrase. We would limit our choices for preaching to the *King James Version,* the *New King James Version*, the *English Standard Version*, the *New American Standard Version,* or the *Holman Christian Standard Bible* (my current choice). Each of these is a very accurate translation, and would be a good text for your people to read through and study as they sit under your ministry. We also like the following Study Bibles: the *ESV Study Bible*, the *NIV Study Bible*, the *MacArthur Study Bible,* the *Believer's Study Bible,* and the *HCSB Study Bible*. We help our people understand the distinction between a translation and a study Bible. They must also understand that study notes, though valuable, are not infallible and inerrant. Help them understand that these valuable study aids are the result of godly, but flawed, persons. Over the years we have recognized that there is significant confusion in this area.

4. WHAT DO YOU THINK ABOUT THE USE OF MOVIE AND TELEVISION CLIPS FROM THE SECULAR WORLD IN YOUR SERMON PREPARATION?

This question raises the whole issue of the use of technology in sermon delivery. We need to note that the Bible does not speak directly to this issue one way or the other. We think there can be a "sanctified use" of technology. Visual aids can be very powerful in driving home truth. However, discretion and wisdom are imperative. We believe a good rule of thumb by which to operate is this: when in doubt, don't! We should not use any type of technology that even remotely runs the risk of distracting from or potentially denigrating biblical truth. One could do more damage than good by the use of an inappropriate movie or television clip.

5. HOW MUCH SHOULD ONE DEPEND ON NOTES, IF AT ALL?

This question is a hotly debated one. We were all taught to preach without notes. It was said that this approach is a superior method because it allows for spontaneity and the leading of the Spirit. Adrian Rogers, with a different perspective, said, "The weakest ink is still stronger than the sharpest mind." There is truth in both perspectives. We believe that a faithful expositor should follow the method that works best for him. Some men are outstanding in preaching without notes, and tend to falter when they use them. Others are far more effective with a brief outline, and still others are more effective with a full manuscript. Of course, dangers can occur in using notes. One may stumble in terms of eye contact. Pastors may also be so tied to their notes that they are not open and sensitive to the Spirit's leading in the delivery of the message. Therefore, use what is best for you, recognizing the strengths and the weaknesses of your particular method.

6. WHAT ARE SOME KEY POINTS FOR PREACHING NARRATIVE TEXT?

This question is an excellent one that requires a careful and more in-depth response than we can give here. As previously shared, the biblical text should determine both the substance and the structure of the message. A narrative text should be preached as a narrative text. Explain the story within the larger story of the grand redemptive story line of the Bible. Recognize that theology is more implicit than explicit in biblical narrative. Recognize that the ultimate hero is not a human person but our sovereign God. Narrative text, when rightly proclaimed, will be theocentric and not anthropocentric. Take advantage of this particular genre, recognizing that people easily recall stories. Let the biblical theology of the Bible provide parameters for your interpretation and exposition. Let the grand redemptive story line provide the over-arching umbrella under which you expound each particular narrative. Recognize how a particular narrative text, especially in the Old Testament, anticipates its ultimate resolution in Messiah Jesus.

7. HOW DO YOU INCORPORATE THE GRAND REDEMPTIVE STORY IN EACH INDIVIDUAL MESSAGE?

The grand redemptive story line of Scripture can be laid out as Creation → Fall → Redemption → Consummation. When pastors expound a biblical text, they should examine how that particular text falls into one of these categories. Determine what God initially intended (Creation), how the fall affected that, how Christ redeems, and what we can look forward to in the New Creation. The grand redemptive story line provides an umbrella under which we interpret and proclaim the biblical text. It will bring a healthy biblical, theological focus to our preaching, helping us see how God has been working throughout history and moving all things to a wonderful consummation.

8. WHAT IS THE PROPER LENGTH OF A SERMON IN TERMS OF TIME?

This answer will vary from preacher to preacher. We have observed a remarkable transformation in recent years in this area. Many homileticians were saying that because of the "attention span" of modern and post-modern culture, sermons need to be kept in the range of 20 to 25 minutes. However, a whole host of new expositors are preaching an hour or longer. Matt Chandler, Mark Driscoll, and David Platt come to mind. One also should recall that both John MacArthur and Rick Warren, preachers coming from different perspectives to be sure, have been preaching right at an hour for the whole of their ministries. We believe we need to give at least 35 to 40 minutes for the proclamation of the Word of God. A 20-minute sermon week after week is going to do little to feed the flock of God. Of course, a key issue here is one's ability to communicate and maintain audience interest. If the pastor's sermons are dull and boring, 20 minutes can seem like an hour to church members. On the other hand, if the pastor has developed the skills to be an engaging expositor, then a sermon of an hour will pass by quickly for those listening. Remember this dictum one more time: what we say is more important than how we say it, but how we say it has never been more important.

9. HOW DO YOU BALANCE SERMON PLANNING WITH CONGREGATIONAL CONCERNS AND NEEDS THAT INEVITABLY ARISE?

This task is easier to answer than many think. You respond to serious congregational concerns and needs when they arise. If there is a national tragedy, like 9/11, pastors would be irresponsible to continue their verse by verse exposition through a particular book of the Bible that does not speak to that situation. One can be a faithful expositor and still deviate at particular times to address needs and issues pertaining to the congregation. This deviating is not a betrayal of one's responsibility as a faithful expositor. Now having said that, we believe that when you do address particular concerns and needs, you need to do so expositionally. Find Scripture that truthfully and genuinely speaks to the needs of the day and let the text loose!

10. IS IT YOUR EXPERIENCE THAT MANY WHO CLAIM TO PREACH EXPOSITIONALLY ACTUALLY DO NOT?

Tragically, the answer is "yes." Many believe that they are expositors but betray their confession by their practice. They believe that opening the Bible, reading a text, and then making some passing remarks about it qualifies them as a biblical expositor. However, how one treats the text in terms of substance and structure is the issue. If pastors are not honoring the authorial intent of the text, then they are not being faithful to the biblical text. One must always ask the question, "What did this text mean to the original audience?" We must expound the text in that regard if we are to be faithful expositors. For those who are failing in this area, we need to find ways to encourage them and instruct them, even as we pray for them.

11. WHAT IS THE BEST WAY TO TEACH THE HISTORICAL BACKGROUND IN AN ENGAGING AND RELEVANT MANNER?

The key is through personalization and use of details. Do your best to step into that context personally. Find colorful and interesting personalities, events, and places that can cause that world to come alive to your audience. Further, work hard to draw parallels that demonstrate that though we are separated by thousands of years, we are still very much the same. We are all sinners in need of a Savior. Very little has changed with respect to human nature, needs, and conduct. Help your folks see that people in the ancient world were asking the same kind of questions and dealing with the same kinds of issues that we do in a twenty-first-century context.

12. CAN WE LEGITIMATELY ALLEGORIZE A TEXT TODAY FOLLOWING THE PRECEDENT OF PAUL IN GALATIANS 4:21–31?

We believe the answer is "no." We do not believe that we should engage in an allegorizing hermeneutic or homiletic. Paul clearly tips us off as to what he is doing in Galatians 4, and he only did it once. He did so under the inspiration of the Holy Spirit. If pastors followed his pattern, they would have to go to great lengths to make it clear that what they are doing is allegory. It was not how the author intended the text to be understood, and we are doing so primarily, if not exclusively, for illustrative purposes. We are convinced that we are on much safer grounds with using typology. The author of Hebrews develops this type of hermeneutic. Typology is usually located in the Old Testament, though there may be occasions where we find it in the New Testament as well. Taking advantage of the grand redemptive story line under which we operate can provide a helpful guide and safe parameters for engaging the interpretive process in this kind of a way. We are always asking of each and every text, "How does this text point to Christ?" A balanced and careful typology will often be a valuable hermeneutical tool.

13. AS ONE BEGINS THEIR PREACHING MINISTRY, WHICH BOOK OF THE BIBLE WOULD YOU RECOMMEND PREACHING THROUGH FIRST?

We think beginning with the Gospel of Mark or the letter to the Philippians would be a good choice. I would also take advantage of books in the Old Testament like Genesis, Psalms, and Jonah. We would not jump immediately into Leviticus, Esther, or Revelation. We would consider the needs of the congregation. A particular book of the Bible may address some specific issues. If your people need to put action to their faith, then the book of James would be a great place to begin. If your people are having a difficult time understanding that salvation is by grace through faith alone, apart from any works, then Galatians would be a great choice. We would seek to be working on a regular basis through one of the gospels because our people need to continually hear about the person and work of the Lord Jesus. The bottom line is your people need a balanced diet in terms of biblical teaching.

14. HOW DOES ONE EXPOSIT BOOK LIKE LEVITICUS OR DEUTERONOMY WITH RELEVANCE TO A CONTEMPORARY COMMUNITY OF FAITH?

Carefully! Now, all of God's Word is relevant as we have repeatedly made clear. Books like Leviticus and Deuteronomy address important issues in a much different context, but if we are asking the right questions of the text, we will find that their relevance will appear. What does this text teach me about God? What does this text teach me about man? We are looking for that which is true anywhere, any place, anytime, and under any circumstances. How does this text point to Christ? These questions should guide us in the interpretation and proclamation of any text of Scripture. Asking these questions will cause Leviticus, Deuteronomy, and any other difficult book in the Bible to come alive with relevance for your people.

15. HOW DO YOU OUTLINE, AND WHAT ARE YOUR THOUGHTS ON ALLITERATION?

We outline the text in such a way as to honor the substance and structure of the text. We seek to draw from a biblical text as many points as naturally arise. Different genres of biblical literature will significantly influence the manner in which one outlines. We prefer to outline in complete sentences, using the present tense, oriented toward application. We recognize that sometimes an application will be knowledge focused, sometimes it will be action focused, and sometimes it will be both. The key is to draw out, accurately, the truth embedded in the text. I also work hard to be theocentric and christocentric in my outline. We want to develop the God'a vision in the text that testifies to Christ's glory. We want our people to see that the Bible proclaims to us a big God. When it comes to alliteration, our thoughts have changed over the years. I (Danny) used to work very hard to alliterate each message. I no longer do that. If I can develop an alliterative outline that naturally arises from the text, is not forced, and clearly conveys the message of the text, then I will use it. However, forced alliteration or bad alliteration can be homiletical suicide. Some men are just not very good at writing with alliteration and therefore they should not do it. Other men use this tool quite well, though they must guard against being driven by a desire to alliterate everything. The key is to outline the truth of Scripture in a way that your people can readily comprehend and understand it.

16. WHO ARE YOUR FAVORITE PREACHERS?

My (Danny) favorite preacher initially was my home pastor. He was the one I listened to the most. As a young boy, Billy Graham was (and continues to be) a hero. As I began preparing for the ministry at the age of twenty, suddenly my world was greatly expanded in this area. I immediately was introduced and blessed by the preaching ministries of W. A. Criswell, Paige Patterson, Adrian Rogers, Jerry Vines, Stephen Olford, John MacArthur, and Chuck Swindoll. In recent years I have come to greatly appreciate and enjoy the preaching ministries of David Jeremiah, John Piper, Mark Dever, Alistair Begg, David Platt, Matt Chandler, and Mark Driscoll. I always enjoy hearing two of my best friends preach on any occasion: James Merritt and Al Mohler. Now, one will immediately recognize that these men are very different in terms of their style. Yet, each is a faithful expositor of the Word of God. I do not seek to copy any of them, but I do seek to learn from all of them. Adrian Rogers used to say, "I milk a lot of cows but I churn my own butter." Dr. Rogers meant that he read and listened widely in preparing his own messages for his congregation. We think that advice is wonderful.

17. WHAT ARE YOUR THOUGHTS ON CONGREGATION/PEER REVIEW AND CRITIQUE OF YOUR SERMONS?

We think this idea is great, and we wish more pastors would do it. We can improve through review and critique. In this age with audio and video capabilities at our fingertips, a pastor has no excuse not to continue to improve his preaching through feedback from those who desire to see him excel for the glory of God. We can all become better at what we do. All of us have blind spots. We may develop annoying habits. We may think that we are communicating the Word of God clearly, when in actuality our people feel as though they are in a fog each time we speak. This particular discipline requires humility and openness to receiving criticism. However, we can think of nothing that would be more valuable to the man of God who wants to be an effective expositor of Holy Scripture.

18. DO YOU SEE VALUE IN AUDIO/VIDEO FEEDBACK?

Yes. Though it is a painful and humiliating process, each pastor will be well served to listen to and watch himself on a regular basis. We promise you, this experience will be no ego trip unless you are the king of narcissism. You will be your harshest critic. You will hear yourself say things and see yourself do things that will embarrass you. Good! Now that you know what those things are, get busy correcting them.

19. HOW DO YOU DEVELOP GOOD TITLES?

Developing a good title is something of an art that some men are more adept at than others. We do believe that giving a title to your message is important. We also believe that the MIT and the MIM should be imbedded in the title of your message. We would encourage all faithful expositors to stay away from cute and sensational titles. The titles need to reflect what you are going to teach from the Bible. I (Danny) remember several years ago an independent Baptist who preached a sermon entitled, "Seven Reasons Why Elvis Presley Did Not Go To Hell." Now, that is an interesting title. However, I think one will find it difficult to find that title reflected in any biblical text. Let your title be true to the text, and then explain to your people how that text is going to speak to their lives today.

20. HOW DO YOU DEVELOP GOOD TRANSITIONS?

The immediate answer is that practice helps toward learning how to develop good transitions. This area is one that young preachers in particular often struggle with. Poor transitions can also be a death nail to your sermon, as they will cause it to be disjointed, sound rough, and lose energy. It is like an eight-cylinder car hitting on six. You will be skipping and jumping, and your people will feel uneasy. We would suggest developing a number of easy transitional phrases that help your people see that you are moving from one thought to another. Don't underestimate the importance of this area in your preaching. Though transitional statements will comprise very little of the totality of your message, they can either make or break your message in terms of an engaging and compelling delivery.

SECTION 3

CHAPTER 21

WHAT'S THE BIG DEAL
ABOUT DELIVERY?

I t is Friday afternoon. You have spent the week studying a passage of Scripture, delving into the language of the text, and answering questions about its word meanings, its history, its grammar, and its theology. You have crafted a sermon that conveys the main idea of the passage, with a clearly defined theme and a structure that honors the text. Your message has a compelling introduction, an understandable explanation, well-chosen illustrations, practical application that is right on target, and a conclusion designed to call your listeners to faith and obedience. You have prepared careful notes so that you can see the overall design of your sermon clearly. Your message is done, right?

Maybe not. A crucial part of the sermon is still to come. Until a sermon is delivered before an audience, it may be a plan or a set of notes, but it is not really a sermon. The truth is, no matter how careful you were in your exegesis and interpretation and no matter how skillfully you put together your message, your sermon will be evaluated on the basis of how you deliver it. A sermon is an oral and an aural event. By that we mean the message only comes to completion when it is spoken and heard. That is why the delivery dimension is such a big deal in preaching.[1]

---

1. All three of us believe we can learn much about preaching from the African-American pulpit when it comes to delivery. A well-respected teacher and

A TALE OF TWO PREACHERS

Imagine listening to two preachers preaching exactly the same sermon. Every word that the two men speak is precisely identical. The only difference is in their delivery styles.

"Preacher A" reads his message in a monotonous, expressionless voice, standing behind the pulpit with his eyes down the entire time. He never moves or gestures. He has no facial expression other than a blank stare. His energy level is low. He stumbles over his words regularly and seems ill at ease from start to finish. Even if you were able to remain awake through the entire message, you would probably find the experience to be somewhat painful to endure.

Now, imagine "Preacher B" delivering exactly the same sermon, word for word; but his delivery is much different. He speaks with energy and conviction. He gestures to emphasize important points and ideas. His facial expressions are animated throughout the message. He moves closer to you when he is making applications. He even acts out some parts of his illustrations. His voice is supple and expressive, emphasizing words with his pitch and volume. He speeds up and slows down his words, depending on his content. He pauses dramatically from time to time to let the ideas he has presented sink into your mind. His eyes are either on the audience or on the words of the Bible he is holding in his hand. You feel as though he is talking right to you, and you cannot help but listen to him.

You would walk away from "Preacher B" with a vastly different impression of the message than you would from "Preacher A," even though the verbal content was exactly the same. "Preacher A" would get low marks from you and most everyone in the audience. "Preacher B" would get raves.

This imaginary example illustrates a simple but essential truth: No matter how strong your content is, no preacher is very effective

---

practitioner of preaching in this tradition is Robert Smith Jr. His *Doctrine that Dances* (Nashville: B&H, 2008) is a homiletical gem. When it comes to delivery, we commend his chapter on "The Preacher as a Doxological Dancer" (103–26). It may not be exactly what you expect, but we promise you will be blessed. We also suggest that you take a look at E. K. Bailey and Warren Wiersbe, *Preaching in Black and White* (Grand Rapids: Zondervan, 2003).

without good delivery. A few minutes of lousy delivery can instantly negate hours and hours of solid preparation.

It is true that some preachers are guilty of having all style with little substance. They are adept at saying almost nothing and making it sound good. Certainly, we should guard against that error. But there is also the error—which may be more common and more harmful—of having excellent sermon substance that never receives a full hearing because of an ineffective delivery style. For preaching to be truly engaging exposition, substance and style must be wedded so that the preacher skillfully delivers a strong message.

OVERVIEW OF THE DELIVERY DIMENSION

The delivery dimension of preaching begins by understanding how the human voice works and the way to use it with skill and success. We will give that subject careful attention. We will consider the nonverbal, physical elements of delivery such as eye contact, gestures, facial expression, posture, and movement. We will discuss the options of delivering your message with full notes, short notes, or no notes at all. Your style of communication helps determine the way your audience receives your message, and so we will examine elements of an effective preaching style, and ways to analyze and understand your audience. Because we are preaching to an increasingly visual culture, we will talk about using video, computer graphics, drama, and props in preaching. Finally, we will examine the connection between a preacher's personal life, his walk with God, and his public behavior.

As you begin this section of *Engaging Exposition*, it is imperative that we caution you of something: from time to time you may feel as though you are reading information that is somewhat unrelated to preaching. Discussion of subjects such as the way your voice works, how gestures can help a speaker, and audience analysis and adaptation may seem more appropriate to a public speaking or communication textbook. However, the principles presented in this section are crucial for delivering God's Word effectively to your congregation. Throughout this section, we will make the connections between the general communication materials we are presenting here and the specific application of expository preaching.

PREACHING AND THE
COMMUNICATION PROCESS

The goal of preaching is to communicate a message from God's Word, in cooperation with the Holy Spirit's desire to change the hearts and lives of our listeners. If preaching were merely a human endeavor, this goal would be impossible to attain. After all, how can our words and our efforts ever change another person's heart?

We would be foolish even to attempt to preach were it not for the fact that God has commanded the preaching of His Word with the intention that preaching transform the listeners. Paul instructed Timothy: "Preach the word! Be ready in season and out of season. Convince, rebuke, exhort, with all longsuffering and teaching" (2 Tim 4:2 NKJV). Notice that the command "preach the word" is accompanied by four transformational intentions of preaching: (1) convincing, which is the Greek elenchon, a word meaning to show to be wrong and to bring to conviction; (2) rebuking, or epitimao, which means to warn; (3) exhorting, or parakaleo, which means to comfort or to encourage; and (4) teaching, or didache, which is transformation through patient instruction. Teaching, the last transformational intention, is actually the means to the other three, as indicated by the phrase "*with* all longsuffering and teaching."

When preachers faithfully communicate the message of God's Word, Scripture indicates that our efforts will meet with success. God makes this promise: "For as the rain comes down, and the snow from heaven, / And do not return there, / But water the earth, / And make it bring forth and bud, / That it may give seed to the sower / And bread to the eater, / So shall My word be that goes forth from My mouth; / It shall not return to Me void, / But it shall accomplish what I please, and it shall prosper in the thing for which I sent it" (Isa 55:10–11 NKJV). While we may tend to judge our success on our skill in preaching and the results thereof, God has said that success comes when His Word simply goes forth. He will use us in spite of our weaknesses to communicate His message to people so that their lives will be changed for His purposes and His glory.

The teacher's task is to communicate God's Word. When we deliver His message, we are engaged in public communication. For that reason, preachers will profit from a working knowledge of how communication operates, just as they benefit from understanding the principles of hermeneutics and sermon construction.

Human communication is an inevitable and ongoing process. A long-standing axiom is that one cannot *not* communicate. When one person is with another person, they are unavoidably communicating with one another, even if neither person says a word. Think about it, even if you and a loved one are angry and refuse to speak to one another, you are *still* communicating! And, even when we are alone, we are communicating with ourselves through the inner dialogue that goes on in our minds constantly.

Not only is the process of communication inevitable, though; it is also a describable process. Communication theorists call our inner dialogue *intrapersonal communication*, our communication with others in groups of two or three *interpersonal communication*, and our communication in a setting such as delivering a sermon *public communication*. Other levels of communication are *group communication*, which is the type of communication that occurs in groups larger than two or three, such as a committee or a board meeting, and *organizational communication,* which is the type of communication that

The Communication Process

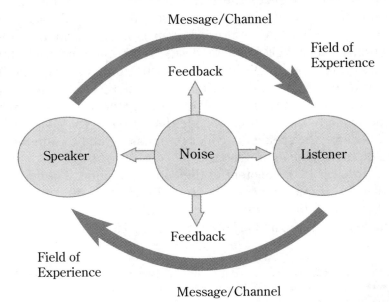

Message/Channel

Field of Experience

Feedback

Speaker ← Noise → Listener

Field of Experience

Feedback

Message/Channel

Diagram 21.1

occurs between departments in a business or school or between ministry areas in a church.

Though communication is often subtle and complicated, the core elements of communication can be identified and described. Below is a basic diagram of the communication process.[2]

Notice the major components of this model. They are the speaker, the message, the channel, the listener, noise, feedback, and fields of experience. If we were to describe the communication process in a narrative manner, we might say: *In communication, a speaker sends a message through a channel to a listener, who in turn provides feedback to the speaker. Both the speaker and the listener communicate based on their unique fields of experience. Noise can interfere with the process of communication.*

Consider the role each of the elements of this model plays in communication.

The *speaker* affects communication through his skills as a communicator, through his knowledge of the subject matter, and through his relationship with his listeners. In Christian preaching, the speaker's relationship with God and his spiritual and emotional maturity also affect tremendously his ability to communicate.

The *listener* influences the communication process by many of the same factors that affect the speaker. We can understand our listeners by noting their age range; their gender distribution; their educational levels; their occupations and socioeconomic levels; their attitudes, values, and beliefs; and their differing goals and motivations for listening. All of these elements make up the listener's *field of experience*. The listener uses all of the elements of his or her field of experience to interpret or decode the message the speaker has sent. Likewise, the speaker encodes his message and communicates based on his field of experience.

The *message* is the content of the communication. The message includes the formal speech we are delivering. In the expository preacher's case, the sermon that comes directly from a passage of Scripture is a significant part of the message. However, the message

---

2.   This type of diagram is very similar to the one proposed by David Berlo in *The Process of Communication: An Introduction to Theory and Practice* (New York: Holt, Rinehart, and Winston, 1960). Often, this model will be referenced as the Berlo model of communication.

also consists of the nonverbal signals the speaker sends with the tone of his voice and the use of his body to deliver the message.

The communication *channel* includes everything that helps get the message from the speaker to the listener. The words we use are part of the communication channel, as are gestures, movement, facial expressions, vocal tone, props or object lessons, images projected on a screen with presentation software, interactive note-taking pages, and anything else that is used to communicate the message. Notice that in a public speaking event such as preaching, communication is taking place through multiple channels. The speaker's attitude and demeanor also form the channel. When a speaker has a relationship with his listeners, when he communicates with energy and vigor, and when he works to engage the audience, he creates a more effective channel for communicating with his audience.

Noise is anything that distracts from or disrupts the communication process. In the preaching event, noisemakers can include literal noise, such as loud heating and air units, crying babies in the auditorium, or a malfunctioning sound system. Other distractions can also cause noise, such as poor lighting, room temperature that is either too hot or too cold, a speaker who is unprepared, video equipment that does not work properly, or starting or ending late. The pastor of a church is largely responsible for working to reduce noise in the worship experience.

Feedback is the mechanism in communication by which the speaker determines how the listener is receiving and responding to his message. Preachers are wise to include a wide range of opportunities to receive feedback. These means of getting feedback can include: (1) paying attention to the immediate feedback of body language, receptivity, and even verbal response of the listeners as you are preaching the message; (2) giving an occasion for questions and answers by e-mail, in discussion groups, or by some other means; (3) providing comment and question cards to determine audience needs and responses; (4) asking trusted friends and family members to give their viewpoint about your effectiveness as a speaker; and (5) listening to yourself or watching yourself on video on a regular basis. We cannot overemphasize the importance of the last item. Throughout these chapters, we will assume that you are monitoring yourself regularly by listening or watching your own preaching. This is an advantage that preachers of past ages did not have, and we do well to avail ourselves of the opportunity, even though it is often painful to hear or see our own preaching as we noted in the previous chapter.

PREACHING AS A CALLING AND A SKILL

Because preaching is a form of the communication process, we can develop skills to improve our preaching ability. Occasionally, we will hear from well-meaning people who say, "You can't teach a man to preach. He's either got it or he hasn't." There is a germ of truth to that type of thinking. Certainly no preaching professor and no preaching textbook can turn a man into a preacher. Preaching is first a calling and a gifting that comes from God. But it's untrue to think that unless a person is born with fully developed, natural preaching skills, he will never become a better preacher. True, some people do have natural gifts such as a strong voice, a quick mind, a winning personality, or a naturally compelling physical delivery style, while others are lacking in some or all of those areas. However, if God has truly called a man to preach, God will also develop that man into a stronger communicator of His Word. And, God can use the example of other preachers, college and seminary preaching courses, and books like this one to improve a God-called preacher's skill level.

So, resist the notion that good preachers are born, not made. God can make you a better preacher. But, also resist the misconception that good sermon delivery will be easy for you right away. Professional trainers in nearly every field agree that there are four stages in gaining any skill. The first stage is *unconscious incompetence.* This is when a person is terrible at doing something but has no idea how bad he is. Watch the early audition shows on *American Idol* just one night, and you'll see ample proof of people at this stage. We have also seen this phenomenon more than a few times with beginning preachers. They take a preaching class not to improve themselves (for in their minds, they have no room for improvement) but only to be affirmed in how wonderful they already are! Usually, a person who is honest with himself will move beyond this stage pretty quickly. The next stage is *conscious incompetence.* This stage happens when a person begins to understand his faults and weaknesses at a certain skill. He may even be learning the principles for improvement, but he has not yet learned how to integrate those principles into his performance. Most beginning preachers find themselves in this stage. They know some things that they should and should not do, but they have trouble applying what they know. This stage can be frustrating and may take some time and pain to get past. Eventually, however, one moves into the next stage: *conscious competence.* Conscious competence is when a person can execute a skill successfully but requires great concentration and effort in order to do it. By the end of a preaching course, most students find themselves in some form of this stage. They are able to preach with greater skill, but it requires great concentration to do so. The final stage is *unconscious competence.*[3] This is when one can perform a skill competently in a way that seems natural and even effortless. At this level, public speaking actually becomes very enjoyable, and the preacher is able not only to deliver his message, but to pay closer attention to audience response and to make unplanned adjustments to enhance his delivery.

We're not certain that any preacher ever completely reaches the stage of unconscious competence. Most preachers, including your authors, still have to remind themselves regularly of the basic skills that make preaching effective. Two elements, however, will take you on the journey to this final level of competence. One element is learning the right principles for sermon delivery. That is the purpose of this section. The other element is spending time in the pulpit. The more time you spend speaking in front of people, preaching God's Word to the best of your ability and in reliance upon Him, the more you will become comfortable and self-forgetful in your sermon delivery.

Paul told the Thessalonian believers: "He who calls you is faithful, who also will do it" (1 Thess 5:24 NKJV). We know from the context that he was referring to God's commitment to sanctify Christians in

---

3.   Placing this stage in its spiritual context, D. Martin Lloyd-Jones said, "be natural; forget yourself; be so absorbed in what you are doing and in the realization of the presence of God, and in the glory and the greatness of the Truth that you are preaching . . . that you forget yourself completely . . . Self is the greatest enemy of the preacher, more so than in the case of any other man in society. And the only way to deal with self is to be so taken up with, and so enraptured by the glory of what you are doing, that you forget yourself altogether." *Preaching and Preachers* (Grand Rapids: Zondervan, 1971), 264.

every part of their lives. The same spiritual principle, though, can be applied to those who have been called to preach God's Word. God, who has called us to preach, will also be faithful to accomplish in us what needs to be done for us to become effective communicators of His Word. So, preach at every opportunity. Profit from your mistakes. Follow good examples. Learn the basic principles of delivery. Commit yourself to be a lifelong student of effective communication, because God has entrusted to you the most wonderful message anyone could ever deliver![4]

---

4. The great Baptist preacher of London, Charles Spurgeon, said it quite well, "When I have thought of the preaching of certain good men, I have wondered, not that the congregation was so small, but that it was so large. The people who listen to them ought to excel in the virtue of patience, for they have grand opportunities of exercising it. Some sermons and prayers lend a color of support to the theory of Dr. William Hammond, that the brain is not absolutely essential to life. Brethren, you will, none of you, covet earnestly the least gifts, and the dullest mannerisms, for you can obtain them with the exertion of the will . . . Labour to discharge your ministry, not with the lifeless method of automation, but with the freshness and power which will render your ministry largely effectual for its sacred purposes." *An All-Around Ministry* (Edinburgh: Banner of Truth, 1960), 316–17.

CHAPTER 22

HOW WE PRODUCE SPEECH

Y our voice is one of the most individual and identifiable things about you. In fact, your voice print is as distinctive and unique as your fingerprint. When you call a friend on the phone, he or she can often recognize you—even without caller ID—simply by the sound of your voice. Your manner of speaking reveals a lot about your background, education, upbringing, and personality. For these reasons and many more, your voice is an essential element for effective preaching. Your voice can cause people to respond either negatively or positively to the content of your message.

In this chapter we will discuss the mechanics of how speech is produced. People who speak for a living, such as preachers do, need to know how the voice works as surely as a professional cyclist should know the way the gears, brake system, and other equipment of a bicycle operates. Based on the foundation we build in this chapter, we will focus on ways to improve your speech in the pulpit in the next chapter.[1]

In order to understand the way the voice works, one must examine the four physical processes that are involved in creating speech. Each process performs an important function. (1) *Respiration* provides

---

1. A short but fine discussion on the voice can be found in Bert Decker and Hershael York, *Speaking with Bold Assurance* (Nashville: B&H, 2001), 82–85. A more extensive, but equally helpful treatment is found in Vines and Shaddix, *Power in the Pulpit* (Chicago: Moody, 1999), 263–90. Few preachers have given more careful study to the voice than Jerry Vines.

power for speech. (2) *Phonation* provides *sound*. (3) *Resonation* provides *volume* and *quality*. (4) *Articulation* provides *meaning* and *clarity*. Every one of these processes can be called an *overlaid function*. By that, we mean that each process has a biological purpose that is more essential than producing speech. Respiration, for instance, sustains life. The parts of your body used in phonation and resonation also help with breathing. The parts of your mouth used for articulation are primarily intended to help you chew and ingest food. Nevertheless, while speech production is an overlaid and secondary function biologically, it still plays an integral and primary part in the process of human communication.

POWER FOR SPEECH: RESPIRATION

Respiration is the means by which oxygen is delivered to your body. This process is achieved by the physical act of breathing air in and out. While the biological function of respiration involves extremely complicated chemical activity at the cellular level, the aspects of respiration involved in producing speech are relatively simple.

Breathing is a muscular activity controlled primarily by the *diaphragm*, a muscle shaped like an inverted bowl, dividing the upper part of the body from the abdomen. When the diaphragm is relaxed, the "bowl" rests in an upward position toward the lungs. When contracted, the diaphragm pushes downward and forward. In this position, the diaphragm exerts pressure on the front of the abdomen and, in so doing, enlarges the space in the thorax, which includes the lungs.

Inhalation occurs as air fills the vacuum created by the diaphragm, entering into the lungs through both the mouth and nose. *Exhalation* occurs as the diaphragm is relaxed to the upward position, expelling air from the lungs through the mouth and nose.

A simple way to understand respiration is to lie on the floor on your back. Make sure your head is straight and your shoulders are firmly against the floor. This position will ensure that your head and chest are aligned for proper breathing. Place one hand on your chest and the other hand on your stomach. Inhale slowly, trying to push the hand on your stomach as far upward as possible. As the diaphragm flexes, you will feel your stomach go up rather dramatically, and even the sides of your abdomen will push out slightly.

Once your lungs are fully inflated, exhale slowly. Now, as the diaphragm moves upward, you will feel your stomach and your sides go down. Notice that, while your stomach moves upward during inhalation and downward during exhalation, your chest stays in the same position. It should barely move, if it moves at all. Repeating this process slowly eight to ten times will actually provide a sort of workout for your diaphragm. After you have finished, you may feel a slight sense of tiredness in your abdomen.

Take a moment right now to try the exercise we have described. Now, consider how this type of breathing transfers into your preaching. When you are delivering a sermon, you should aim for this same type of diaphragmatic breathing. The stomach should go out when you breathe in, and go in when you breathe out. The shoulders and chest should remain stationary during inhalation and exhalation.

SOUND FOR SPEECH: PHONATION

Phonation means "to make sound." In speech, phonation is a function of the *larynx*, commonly known as the "voice box." The larynx is in fact a very complicated box-shaped structure made of cartilage, which sits right at the top of the trachea. When a person speaks, exhaled air passes through the *vocal bands*, a pair of fibrous sheets of muscle on either side of the larynx. During vocalization, the vocal bands move close together so that they resist the movement of air, and vibrate. This vibration produces a sound, similar to how the twin reeds of an oboe vibrate to produce sound when air is passed through them, or how your lips vibrate to make a sound when you hold them together and blow. Three significant aspects of vocal production are influenced by phonation: *pitch*, *range*, and *inflection*.

Vocal pitch refers to the place on the musical scale that your voice most normally operates. To a great extent, the pitch of a person's voice is caused by anatomical factors. The length and thickness of the vocal bands work to create the pitch at which a person speaks. Just as an electric bass guitar with long, thick strings plays lower notes than a violin with short, thin strings, people with longer, thicker vocal bands will have deeper voices than people with shorter, thinner vocal bands. While vocal pitch is affected by physical factors, it is also strongly influenced by habit and personal choice.

Range refers to the variety and breadth of pitches that your voice uses. Range is most noticeable in singing, where the various vocal ranges are given specific names. Women's voices are typically divided into three groups: soprano, mezzo-soprano, and contralto. Men's voices are classified as tenor, baritone, and bass. In every pitch classification—from the highest soprano to the lowest bass—human voices normally have a range of about two octaves. Most people have the same vocal range, with the only difference being where that range begins and ends. Speakers do not usually employ as wide a range as singers; however, a good speaking voice displays a variety in range.

While similar to general variety in pitch, *inflection* refers more specifically to changes in pitch within a sentence or even a word. Using inflection, a preacher may emphasize a word within a sentence by raising or lowering his pitch, or a preacher may indicate a question by raising his pitch at the end of a sentence. Inflection can be crucial in shaping the meaning of what the speaker says. In Western culture, downward inflection communicates strong affirmation, while upward indicates a question. A circumflex inflection can express doubt or sarcasm. Flat inflection connotes disappointment or disgust.[2]

Consider, for example, a straightforward sentence such this one: "I am not angry." The meaning of this sentence can be shaped dramatically by a simple use of inflection. If the preacher emphasizes the first word with a higher inflection, he suggests that while he is not angry, someone else is: "*I* am not angry." If he uses inflection to emphasize the word "not," the preacher may imply that he really is angry, even though he is protesting that fact: "I am *not* angry!" Finally, by raising the pitch on the last word in order to emphasize it, the preacher indicates that he is asking a question: "I am not *angry*?"

---

2. Duane Litfin notes, "a variety of intonation and inflection gives color, texture, and meaning to your words." *Public Speaking*, 2nd ed. (Grand Rapids: Baker, 1992), 325.

VOLUME AND QUALITY FOR SPEECH: RESONATION

Resonation can be defined as the reverberation of any sound. The initial sound of the human voice which originates in the larynx is extremely weak and lacks a pleasing quality. While the structure of the vocal bands has some bearing on the way a person's voice sounds, by far the most important factor is resonation. Resonators in the speaker's body work to amplify the volume and modify the tone of the voice. The way resonators in your body operate might be compared to the sound board of a piano. A piano string, if suspended in space, stretched tightly, and struck, would barely make a noise and would sound tinny and metallic. However, when stretched across the sound board—usually a thin panel of spruce that underlies the strings—the piano string resonates so that it makes a full and pleasing sound when struck. Spinets, studio uprights, baby grands, and grand pianos have slightly different sound qualities partially because of the differences in their sound boards and other resonators. In the same way, your voice is modulated and amplified by a number of resonators in your body, so that you speak with your own unique voice.

There are seven areas of your body that play a part in resonation. Moving from the top of your body downward, the resonators are the *sinuses,* the *nasal cavity,* the *oral cavity,* the *pharynx,* the *larynx,* the *trachea,* and the *chest.* The sinuses, trachea, chest, and larynx make only minimal contributions to the way one's voice sounds, mainly because the size and shape of these resonators are somewhat fixed, and therefore are not within the control of the speaker. The most important resonator is the pharynx, or upper throat, because of its size, position, and degree of adjustability. The oral cavity, which is also adjustable, is the second most effective resonator, followed by the nasal cavity, which, though fixed in size, can dramatically affect both the volume and quality of the voice.

The *volume,* or loudness, of the voice refers to the amount of force the speaker uses to deliver the message to the listener. The human voice is capable of achieving a surprising level of volume. For most of the history of the church, preachers did not have sound systems to support their voices, and yet they were able to preach before large congregations and still be heard. For instance, when George Whitefield preached outdoors in the mid-1700s in Philadelphia,

Benjamin Franklin was impressed by the preacher's loud and clear voice. Franklin became curious about how far Whitefield's voice could be heard and began backing up farther and farther away from the preacher until he was at the farthest point from which he could still hear Whitefield clearly. Franklin wrote his conclusion: "Imagining then a semi-circle, of which my distance should be the radius, and that it were filled with auditors, to each of whom I allowed two square feet, I computed that he might well be heard by more than thirty thousand."[3] Consider how powerful the human voice is— it can be loud enough to be heard by thousands, even in the open air! Preachers today should have no trouble being heard if they learn to use their voices well. When the voice is being used properly, a preacher can preach with sufficient volume to be heard by his audience several times a day with no strain or harm to his voice.

MEANING FOR SPEECH: ARTICULATION[4]

The sound generated by the larynx and then amplified and modified by the resonators is shaped into meaningful expression by the articulators. Articulators include the tongue, teeth, gums, gum ridges, hard palate, lips, soft palate, and the glottis. Through the manipulation of these parts of your body, you are able to form *phonemes*, which are the smallest parts of vocal expression. Phonemes blend together to make the words that you speak. While vowels as well as consonants are phonemes, the articulators mainly have to do with forming consonant sounds.

There are six categories of consonant sounds that the articulators produce. *Stops* or *plosives* are sounds that briefly stop the flow of the voice. Pressure builds between the articulators and then "explodes" to produce the sound with a sudden release of breath. *Nasals* are produced as the soft palate is lowered so that there is resonance in the nasal passages. *Fricatives* are sounds caused by friction between the articulators. *Affricatives* are combinations of a stop and a fricative.

---

3. Benjamin Franklin, *Autobiography*, chapter 10, earlyamerica.com/lives/franklin/chapt10 (accessed November 5, 2009).
4. Vines and Shaddix, *Power in the Pulpit,* 275–79, provide a helpful treatment of articulation that complements our discussion.

Glides are produced by moving the articulators as sound is made. Finally, the "l" sound is a *lateral* consonant, formed by placing the tip of the tongue at the ridge of the gums as air is released around the sides of the tongue. Other than the "l" sound, every consonant sound can be either *voiced* or *unvoiced*. A voiced consonant requires some vocalization. An unvoiced consonant is essentially articulated breath without any vocalization. For instance, the "p" sound and the "b" sound are both made exactly the same way—by stopping the flow of air briefly with the two lips and then releasing the air. The "p" sound is unvoiced. If you make a "puh-puh-puh" sound, you will notice that you are not vocalizing but merely releasing air through your lips. The "b" sound is voiced. If you make a "buh-buh-buh" sound, you will notice that you are using your voice as well as your lips to produce the consonant. Below is a chart listing all of the consonant sounds used in speaking English, along with a description of how they should be articulated.[5]

Type of Consonants			
Category	**Sound**	**Sample Word**	**Articulators**
Voiced Stops	"b"	"Bethlehem"	both lips
	"d"	"Damascus"	tongue tip, gum ridge
	"g"	"Gabriel"	tongue back, soft palate
Unvoiced Stops	"p"	"Peace"	both lips
	"t"	"Tower"	tongue tip, gum ridge
	"k"	"Caleb"	tongue back, soft palate
Voiced Fricatives	"v"	"Vine"	top teeth, bottom lip

---

5. A discussion of consonants is also found in G. Robert Jacks, *Getting the Word Across: Speech Communication for Pastors and Lay Leaders* (Grand Rapids: Eerdmans, 1995), 181–86. Jacks also provides a consonant chart (185). A companion volume to *Getting the Word Across* is entitled *Just Say the Word: Writing for the Ear* (Grand Rapids: Eerdmans, 1996).

	"TH"	"This"	tongue tip, top teeth
	"z"	"Zoar"	tongue tip, gum ridge
	"zh"	"Vision"	tongue blade, gum ridge
	"h"	"Heaven"	Glottis
Unvoiced Fricatives	"f"	"Fullness"	top teeth, bottom lip
	"th"	"Thanksgiving"	tongue tip, top teeth
	"s"	"See"	tongue tip, gum ridge
	"sh"	"Shield"	tongue blade, gum ridge
Voiced Affricatives	"dj"	"Joy"	tongue tip, gum ridge
	"dz"	"Beds"	tongue tip, gum ridge
Unvoiced Affricatives	"ch"	"Chains"	tongue tip, gum ridge
	"ts"	"Pizza"	tongue tip, gum ridge
Nasals (all voiced)	"m"	"Man"	both lips
	"n"	"New"	tongue tip, gum ridge
	"ng"	"Sing"	tongue back, soft palate
Lateral	"l"	"Last"	tongue tip, gum ridge
Voiced Glides	"hw"	"Why"	rounded lips
	"y"	"Yes"	tongue blade, soft palate
	"r"	"Redeem"	rounded lips, tongue tip, gum ridge
Unvoiced Glide	"w"	"Wine"	rounded lips

While articulation has to do primarily with consonant sounds, it is important at this point also to note that the articulators work to alter the shape of the mouth in order to form distinguishable vowel sounds. The tongue has a prominent role in this process. The jaw position and lips also play a major part. Think, for instance, about how your mouth works to form the "ah" sound in "father." The tongue placed behind the bottom row of the teeth and the back of the tongue is lowered so that the mouth and throat are opened to the maximum extent. When you make the "ee" sound in "feet," the back of the tongue raises, narrowing the vocal cavity in shape. To make the "oo" sound in "food," the tongue is again slightly down in the back, and the lips are rounded.

Another aspect of speech that is closely connected to articulation is *rate*. Your rate of speech is how quickly or slowly you speak. An average rate of speech between 150 and 200 words per minute sounds most natural and is most intelligible in public speaking situations.[6] A simple way to determine your rate is to record yourself preaching, select a one-minute section of your message, and then count the number of words you have said. At fast rates, articulation tends to become sloppy and hard to understand. Often, preachers will have gusts of verbiage that rise much higher than 200 words per minute. While speaking quickly can communicate urgency and passion for your subject matter, it is extremely difficult for listeners to pay attention to speech that is consistently rapid-fire, even when the articulation is clear.

PUTTING IT ALL TOGETHER

Based on what we have discussed in this chapter, you can put together the way speech production works by thinking for a moment about the journey of one molecule of air in the process of saying one word. First, the molecule of air is inhaled into the body by *respiration*. That molecule is then released in a careful and controlled manner, regulated by the diaphragm, and directed toward the vocal mechanism for *phonation*. The air vibrates the vocal bands, producing a

---

6. Appropriate rates of speech vary from author to author. For example, Litfin, *Public Speaking*, 326, says it is closer to 120 to 160 words per minute.

sound. That sound is modified and amplified as the molecule of air reverberates through the nasal cavity, oral cavity, and other *resonators*. Finally, the molecule of air is *articulated* into meaning by the tongue, teeth, lips, and other parts of the mouth, and then released to form meaningful speech. This procedure repeats hundreds and even thousands of times over as a preacher delivers a message.

It is important, then, not only to understand how the process of vocal production works, but also to learn how best to use the voice and how to avoid common vocal mistakes. In the next chapter, we will consider how to speak with your best voice.[7]

---

7. For some helpful insights from a female perspective on the issues discussed in this chapter, see Carol Kent, *Speak Up with Confidence* (Colorado Springs: NavPress, 1997), 115–19.

CHAPTER 23

SPEAKING WITH YOUR BEST VOICE

T hink for a moment about some of your favorite preachers. Recall the times you have heard them preach and the statements you have heard them say. You probably can almost hear their voices in your mind as you think about them. You can remember how they emphasized words, whether they spoke loudly or softly, what their tone and inflection sounded like, and whether their voice was airy and light or deep and resonant. The human voice is a remarkably expressive and distinctive instrument, and it creates an impression on the mind of the listener that lingers long after the sermon is over.[1]

In this chapter, we will talk about speaking with your best voice. Notice that we are advocating that you speak with *your* voice. Do not make the mistake that some preachers make of mimicking the sound of another preacher's vocal style or mannerisms. When you do that, you deprive yourself and your listeners of the joy of hearing

---

1. Aristotle in *Rhetoric* 3.15–35 put it this way: "For it is not enough to know what we ought to say; we must also say it as we ought; much help is thus afforded toward producing the right impression of a speech . . . It is essentially the right management of the voice to express the various emotions—of speaking loudly, softly, or between the two; of high, low, or intermediate pitch; of the various rhythms that suit various subjects. These are the three things—volume of sound, modulation of pitch, and rhythm—that a speaker has in mind." We located this quote in David W. Fetzer, "Now, Deliver the Goods!," in *The Moody Handbook of Preaching*, ed. John Koessler (Chicago: Moody, 2008), 367.

what you really sound like. God made you. He gave you your voice. Since He called each to preach with the voice He has given him, each preacher should preach with his own voice rather than sounding like the echo of other preachers. At the same time, you should preach with your *best* voice. Within the context of your own personality and giftedness, you can take some steps to improve your speaking voice. Consider the following 10 principles for strengthening your voice, and work on applying them as you preach.

SUPPORT YOUR BREATHING

The stress and tension that often accompany public speaking may cause preachers to breathe the wrong way. Instead of focusing on supporting their breathing with the diaphragm, they will attempt to take deep breaths by elevating the shoulders, collarbones, and chest. This type of breathing is called *clavicular* breathing. The concentration of energy is placed on the clavicles, which are the bones at the front of the shoulders. Clavicular breathing is typically shallow and strained and, thus, is unsatisfactory in providing the necessary power for speech.

Often, the phrasing of preachers who have not learned to breathe properly sounds disjointed. Instead of saying,

"For God so loved the world that He gave His only begotten Son, that whoever believes in Him should not perish but have everlasting life" (John 3:16 NKJV),

they might say,

"For God so loved the world (breath) *that He gave His only begotten* (breath) *Son, that whoever believes* (breath) *in Him should not* (breath) *perish but have everlasting* (breath) *life."*

Try reading John 3:16 out loud the way we have formatted it above, with all of the extraneous breaths left in. You will probably notice that catching your breath so often in such a short period of time will actually leave you feeling breathless and winded. This breathlessness results because the breaths you are taking are not enough to sustain your speech. You will also notice that the meaning of the verse becomes harder to understand, and that your delivery lacks authority and confidence.

Now, try saying all of John 3:16 in one breath. Begin by standing up with a good posture. Take a deep breath using the diaphragm. Then concentrate on sustaining your volume and energy throughout the entire verse. If at first you need to pause for a breath, take one at the comma between "Son" and "that," but continue practicing until you can say the whole verse. Make sure that you do not run out of breath as you get to the end of the verse. Be careful not to rush through the words. Keep repeating the verse until you can say it at a normal rate of speech from start to finish, with full volume and projection and with confidence and authority. This simple exercise illustrates how important breathing can be in relaying meaning.

AIM FOR A PLEASING VOCAL QUALITY

The particular tone and resonance of every person's voice are unique and form part of our individuality and personality. There is no standard "preacher voice" that every pastor should make it his aim to use. In fact, speaking with what has been called a "stained glass" tone of voice can sound affected and artificial. It is best to use the natural vocal tones that God has given us, rather than attempting to be something that we are not when we are on the platform. Even so, some qualities of voice are ones to which most people respond positively, while other qualities are almost universally perceived negatively. When our vocal quality is displeasing, people will have a tendency to pay attention to how we speak rather than what we are saying. Most people enjoy listening to a tone of voice that is authoritative and easy to hear, yet varied and pleasant.[2] This type of voice can be produced by supporting your voice with proper breathing; by relaxing your upper body, including your shoulders, neck, and abdominal muscles; and by keeping the vocal mechanism open.

Preachers should try to avoid a number of vocal problems. A *harsh* voice, that is, a gravelly and rough tone of voice that manifests itself as hoarseness at low volume levels and can sound

---

2. Fetzer notes, "Today's audiences prefer a natural, spontaneous, conversational delivery . . . This open style of speaking communicates honesty, sincerity, trust, and a transparency . . . Make your speaking come alive with a personal touch. Talk to and with people, not just at them" ("Now, Deliver," 367).

strident when more intense, makes speakers seem unsympathetic, overly stressed, abrasive, and even angry. Harshness is caused by the constriction of the throat or by tension or damage to the vocal mechanism. A *breathy* voice sounds thin and weak. Such a voice is often childish or effeminate sounding and lacks authority and power. Breathiness is caused both by inadequate breath support and by allowing a large amount of unvocalized air to escape from the vocal bands. *Nasal* or *denasal* vocal tones result from an incorrect flow of air through the nasal passages. In *nasal* voices, too much air passes through the nose, producing a whiny sound. *Denasal* voices occur when not enough air is being directed through the nasal passages, producing a stuffed-up and thick-headed tone of voice. Some of these vocal faults are caused by anatomical factors and may require surgery or therapy to correct. For the most part, however, preachers can improve their vocal tone simply by monitoring themselves, listening to audio recordings of their messages, and working to improve their voice quality.

ELIMINATE UNNECESSARY WORDS AND SOUNDS

One hallmark of novice and nervous speakers is an overabundance of vocalized pauses. By this, we mean "filler" words, phrases, and sounds such as "um," "uh," "er," "OK?," "y'know," "see," "like," "and so on and so forth," "in other words," "whatever," "anyway," and "right?" Preachers have their own set of vocalized pauses, including "Amen?," "beloved," "my dear friends," and others. When our speech is filled with these types of non-fluencies, a straightforward sentence such as, "When we were lost, Jesus died on the cross in our place to pay for our sins" becomes, "OK, when we were, like, lost, y'know, Jesus, see, um, died, like, on the cross, y'know, like, in our place, uh, to pay the, er, price for our, like, sins. Amen?" You might read the sentence and think that no one would actually speak like that, but we have heard examples that egregious and even worse. Speeches filled with vocalized pauses not only become unclear but also cause the speaker to sound unprepared and lacking in authority and confidence. These pauses can also rob the sermon of its prophetic power.

Other extraneous sounds that speakers make can include lip smacking, tongue clicking, throat clearing, sniffling, and even giggling after every sentence. Amazingly, when speakers are made aware of vocalized pauses in their presentations, they are often caught by complete surprise. In one public speaking class, a student had said, "OK?" more than 75 times in a 10-minute speech. After the speech was finished, his professor asked, "Frank, did you know that you said, 'OK?,' over and over in your presentation?" Frank answered embarrassedly, "I didn't know I said it even once!"

Listening to recordings of your messages on a regular basis and having trusted friends provide feedback can help you identify vocal pauses that creep into your speaking. When you become conscious of a habitual word or sound you are making, you will begin to notice it more while you are speaking and learn to leave it out. Perhaps the best cure for vocalized pauses is to learn to be comfortable with actual pauses when you are speaking. An effective speaker learns that he does not have to fill every silence with the sound of his voice.[3]

AVOID PITCH AND VOLUME PATTERNS

When we are speaking naturally, our pitch and volume usually match the content we are communicating. We emphasize important words and phrases by getting louder or softer or by going to a higher or lower pitch. In public speaking, however, it is very easy to develop a singsong pattern in our pitch and volume. That pattern can especially develop when we are reading or reciting something or if we are not giving careful attention to the meaning of the words we are saying. Even worse, preachers sometimes adopt a pattern of pitch and volume that they think "sounds like preaching." Often, this pattern involves starting a sentence with high volume and then getting lower in pitch and volume at the end of the sentence. To illustrate this pattern, read the following three sentences out loud, starting higher and louder at the beginning, and then getting lower and softer at the end of each sentence:

---

3. In *Speaking with Bold Assurance,* Decker and York have a good discussion of the issue. They especially emphasize "the power of the pause" (Nashville: B&H, 2001), 86–91.

Many of you have come to this place with great questions. You are wondering whether Jesus will save you. I promise you, He will save everyone who calls on His name.

If you have read the sentences above as we have suggested, then your voice will have sounded much like the stereotypical "preacher's voice." Now, try reading the same sentences as you would in normal speech, emphasizing the important words by using your pitch and volume. While our voices should be somewhat amplified in intensity and drama when we are preaching, our speech should still sound normal. Using habitual pitch and volume patterns makes preaching seem artificial and can lead to drooping eyelids in the congregation.[4]

ENUNCIATE CLEARLY

If you ask your friend, "Jeetyet?," he probably understands that you mean, "Did you eat yet?" However, slurred words and mushy articulation in the pulpit can lead to miscommunication and can undermine the speaker's credibility. D. L. Moody, the famed evangelist of the nineteenth century, reportedly had such poor enunciation that he pronounced "Jerusalem" as a two-syllable word. While that story is probably true, Moody's effectiveness as a preacher certainly did not come from his sloppy articulation. It is important for preachers to have crisp and precise enunciation. Clear enunciation means that the preacher does not mumble, slur words together, or leave out syllables or sounds. For instance, do not say "thinkin'" for "thinking," or fail to leave on the "g" in any "-ing" word. Do not say "hunnerd" for "hundred" or "goverment" for "government." Be careful to use your tongue, teeth, and lips to pronounce each part of the words you are saying.

Also, remember that clear enunciation does not mean affected, pretentious, or exaggerated articulation. Never using contractions, overly emphasizing consonants, pronouncing words like "marked" as two-syllable words, or other such things that speakers sometimes do to make themselves seem more proper or erudite, actually make

---

4. James Merritt, a pastor in Atlanta, Georgia, and a former president of the Southern Baptist Convention, says a preacher should begin just a little lower in pitch and a little slower in rate. If you start too high, you will strain to go higher. If you start too fast and try to go faster, you will run out of gas!

speakers sound amateurish, patronizing, and a little silly. So, avoid pronouncing "the" as thee when you should say "thuh" or pronouncing "often" as "off ten" rather than "offen." Aim for speech that is both articulate and natural.

SPEAK AT A RATE YOUR LISTENERS CAN FOLLOW

Preaching at a consistently high rate of speech can make it hard for your listeners to stay focused on your message. When you are talking about things with which the audience is familiar or when you are using speed to communicate excitement or passion for your message, a faster rate may be appropriate. New ideas such as explanations of textual concepts or important ideas such as your sermon points or steps of application will usually call for a slightly slower rate of speech.

Closely related to your speaking rate is your use of pauses. Sometimes, preachers are so interested in getting to the next idea that they fail to let a concept they have just presented make its full impact with the audience. Especially before and after you make a significant statement, pause long enough for the weight of your words to sink into your listeners' thinking. As a simple rule of thumb, it is good to remember that a brief pause in speaking is for absorption of an idea, a longer pause is for getting attention, and a medium-length pause is for making transitions.

In our years of teaching preaching, we have never even once told a student to pause less and speed up. We have, however, told students to slow down and pause more on many occasions. Do not underestimate the power of pacing and timing in delivering your message.[5]

USE AN APPROPRIATE VOLUME

Speaking with an overly loud voice is a common stereotype of preaching. Perhaps our tendency to think that preaching should be loud is

---

5. See also Hershael York and Bert Decker, *Preaching with Bold Assurance* (Nashville: B&H, 2003), 248–49. They note that "the pause can be one of your dynamic communication tools" and then add, "The problem with pausing is that most of us have never tried it" (248).

a holdover from days when preachers did have to "speak up" just to be audible in a big room with no amplification. In today's context, most preachers do not need to speak as loudly as in past times. We have microphones and speakers to help us. Instead, your voice needs to be loud enough to be heard clearly in the room in which you are speaking.

Preachers need to project when they are speaking. Vocal projection is using the voice loudly and clearly in order to be heard. Even with microphones and sophisticated audio systems, a preacher who does not project his voice clearly either will not be heard, or his voice will lack the ability to arrest and maintain the listeners' attention throughout the sermon.

We have found that a good rule of thumb is to speak loudly enough so that you can hear your voice slightly reverberating off the walls of the room. Think in terms of filling the room with your voice. Some sermon material will call for you to become softer, though still clear and audible. Other parts of your message will require a slightly louder voice. Your volume will vary depending on the size of the room in which you are speaking and the size of your audience. In a small room, optimal volume should not be too loud, though it does need to be loud enough to be heard. In a larger room, optimal volume will probably be significantly louder than your normal volume, although you certainly want to avoid shouting or speaking with a voice that no longer sounds conversational.[6]

BE EXPRESSIVE

Preachers who never vary their pitch, rate, and volume tend to be boring, unexpressive, and—almost literally—monotonous. Such preaching easily loses the interest of listeners and can keep them from hearing the vital message the preacher is proclaiming. When you preach, match your voice to the content you are communicating. Celebrative sermon material will call for speaking in the higher

---

6. For a good treatment of the voice, see Steven and Susan Beebe, *Public Speaking: An Audience-Centered Approach*, 3rd ed. (Needham Heights, MA: Allyn and Bacon, 1997), 290–94. They have a brief discussion of "using the microphone" (294).

range of your voice with greater speed and volume. Words of sorrow or rebuke can be communicated with the deeper parts of your vocal register and are often spoken more slowly or quietly. Most importantly, use enough variety in your voice to keep the listeners' interest and to enliven your sermon content.

DISCOVER AND USE YOUR OPTIMAL PITCH

Your optimal pitch is the pitch at which your voice functions best. Many preachers use a habitual pitch that is far different from their optimal pitch. We have known some preachers who grew up speaking with a voice that is slightly higher than their optimal voice. Their vocal pitch sounds strangely high or thin. Other preachers make a conscious decision to lower the pitch of their voice artificially in order to make themselves sound more profound or important or to emulate other preachers they admire. It is also very common for preachers to get stuck on a habitual pitch that is too high because they become passionate and highly energized as they preach. They hit a certain pitch and then stay there for the rest of the sermon.

There are numerous problems with using a habitual pitch that is significantly different from one's optimal pitch. From a vocal health point of view, the practice can put unnecessary stress on the vocal bands and can cause long-term damage to the vocal mechanism. From a vocal performance standpoint, speaking far below or above your optimal pitch limits your ability to express yourself with your voice. From a personal perspective, preachers who insist on using an artificial pitch may reveal a lack of confidence about who they are and how God made them.

We use pitch to emphasize words and to convey emotions. Excitement and passion, for instance, are typically communicated by a higher vocal pitch, whereas disappointment or sorrow can be indicated by dropping one's pitch. If, however, a preacher consistently speaks at the top of his vocal range, he has nowhere to go when he wants to raise his pitch to emphasize something. Likewise, a preacher who uses an unnaturally deep voice in order to sound more authoritative will find his vocal flexibility severely restricted. One of the best things a preacher can do early in his ministry is to learn what his optimal pitch is, and then train his voice to stay near that pitch when he is preaching.

Finding your optimal pitch is a simple process. There are a number of methods for doing so. Some vocal coaches recommend discovering one's optimal pitch by quietly humming a familiar song, such as "Happy Birthday." The pitch to which your voice naturally gravitates will probably be your optimal pitch. Another way is to lie down, relax, and vocalize the "ah" sound, almost as a sigh. This sound will be near your optimal pitch. The method that we have found to be most helpful is to go to a piano and begin singing down the scale until you reach the lowest note you can sing comfortably. Then, go up five keys from there. That note, five tones above your lowest comfortable note, will be your optimal pitch.

Once you have found your optimal pitch, test yourself from time to time to see if you are speaking around that pitch when you preach. Listen to a recording of yourself and see whether you are consistently above or below your optimal pitch. Using your optimal pitch does not mean that you will always stay on the same note, as though you were chanting your message. It does mean, however, that you will speak in the general neighborhood of that pitch most of the time. Preaching at your optimal pitch will protect your voice from strain and hoarseness. It will also give you greater expression in using your vocal range.

PRONOUNCE WORDS CORRECTLY

Pronunciation differs from enunciation in that while enunciation refers to saying words clearly, pronunciation has to do with saying words properly. Our pronunciation may be influenced by a regional accent. For instance, a person from New England may talk about "pahking the cah," or a person from the southern United States may tell someone to "look ovuh thayuh." Generally, listeners will forgive a regional accent unless they have a strong bias against some part of the country. In fact, a slight regional accent can be appealing and charming to your listeners. However, if your regional dialect includes saying things like "warsh" for "wash," or "ax" instead of "ask," then your accent can keep people from understanding you. Even within the confines of their distinctive regional accents, speakers can work to pronounce words properly.

Poor pronunciation harms both your intelligibility and credibility. When we say a word improperly, our listeners either will not understand us or take our mispronunciation as a sign that we are ill-informed or uneducated. We usually mispronounce words by omitting sounds, by adding sounds, by changing the order of sounds, by substituting one sound for another, or by placing the accent on the wrong syllable of the word. To pronounce words properly, use a dictionary to look up words that are unfamiliar to you or that you are unsure about. The pronunciation guide in most dictionaries will help you to say words properly. For Bible names and terminology, a Bible dictionary will often be helpful in determining the right pronunciation. Below are some common pronunciation errors. Look over the list and think about whether you make these or other mistakes.

Common Pronunciation Errors		
Word	Correct Pronunciation	Incorrect Pronunciation
ACROSS	a CROSS	a CROST
ADULT	a DULT	AD ult
CAVALRY	CAV al ry	CAL va ry
COMPARABLE	COM per able	com PARE able
COMPULSORY	com PUL sory	com PUL so rary
CREEK	CREEK	CRICK
DROWNED	DROWN'D	DROWN ded
ERR	UR	AIR
ESCAPE	es CAPE	ex CAPE
FEBRUARY	FEB ru ary	FEB u rary
GET	GET	Git
JUST	JUST	JIST
LARYNX	LAR inks	LAR niks

Common Pronunciation Errors		
LIBRARY	LI brary	LI berry
MISCHIEVOUS	MIS che vous	MIS CHEE vee us
NUCLEAR	NU clee ar	NU cyou lar
PERSPIRATION	PER spir a tion	PRESS pir a tion
PICTURE	PIC ture	PIT chur
REALTOR	REAL tor	REAL a tor
RECOGNIZE	REG og nize	REK a nize
RELEVANT	REL e vant	REV e lant
STRICT	STRICT	STRICK
SURPRISE	sur PRISE	sup PRISE
THEATER	THEE a ter	thee A ter

These 10 principles have prescribed helpful steps to strengthen your voice and, as a result, your preaching. John Connell says it well, "It all comes out in the voice. Joy, nervousness, anticipation, authority, boredom. The voice gives the audience its first real clue about you. Yet the voice is often neglected."[7] Do not neglect the instrument that God has given you to communicate His Word. Instead, apply these 10 principles and use your best voice forward to edify the church and glorify God.

---

7. Quoted in Ron Huff, *I Can See You Naked,* rev. ed. (Kansas City: Andrews and McMeel, 1992), 122.

CHAPTER 24

PREACHING WITH YOUR ENTIRE BODY

Designed by Sir Christopher Wren, St. Paul's Cathedral in London is an architectural landmark of that city. The cathedral has long been praised as one of the most famous church buildings in the world. For most of its history, crowds came to admire the architecture of St. Paul's Cathedral but rarely came to hear preaching. Everything changed in the mid-1800s, however, when Henry Parry Liddon began preaching there. Possessing a brilliant mind, a passionate heart, and a rich, flexible voice, Henry Liddon brought multitudes to gather at St. Paul's Cathedral. His fervor caused him to use his entire body to communicate his message. A listener in 1868 described Liddon this way: "His eyes glow and flash, every line of his face quivers with emotion, his gestures are so free, so expressive, so illustrative, that you might almost say his body thought. He leans far out from the pulpit, spreading himself, as if it were, over the congregation, in an act of benediction."[1]

The way we use our eyes, hands, feet, and faces on the platform can make a huge impact on our listeners. In the next two chapters, we will discuss the physical aspects of sermon delivery. This chapter will address eye contact and gestures, both of which are essential in using the entire body to preach. In the next chapter, we

---

1. Clyde E. Fant and William Pinson, *A Treasury of Great Preaching: An Encyclopedia of Preaching, Volume 5* (Dallas: Word, 2000), 101.

will talk about the overall impression we make by our appearance, movement, and demeanor on the platform.

EYE CONTACT[2]

You have probably heard people say things such as: "Look me in the eye when I'm talking to you," "Her eyes are always smiling," "I don't trust something about his eyes," or even the old proverb, "The eyes are the windows to the soul." It may be difficult to ascertain psychologically why the eyes have such significance, but the fact remains that our eyes are extremely important non-verbal indicators.

The ancient rhetorician Cicero (106–43 BC) noted that the use of the eyes is second only to the voice in making a speaker effective. He wrote: "The expressive power of the human eye is so great that it determines, in a manner, the expression of the whole countenance."[3] You cannot control everything that your eyes express. You can't make them sparkle with delight or burn with fiery passion or melt in sadness. However, you can control whether you are looking at your listeners.

What Eye Contact Accomplishes

Eye contact communicates a wide variety of things to your audience.[4] It shows that you are prepared, that you are confident, that you are honest, and that you are interested in your subject matter and your listeners. Avoiding eye contact with your listeners tells them that you are unfriendly, nervous, unprepared, and insincere.

Consider just a few of the things that eye contact accomplishes when you are preaching:

---

2. Decker and York, *Speaking with Bold Assurance*, have a fine chapter on this subject (Nashville: B&H, 2001), 65–69.
3. Cicero, quoted in Charles Koller, *How to Preach without Notes* (Grand Rapids: Baker, 2007), 35.
4. Huff says, "If you're not going to use eye contact in your presentation, you might as well Federal Express your message . . ." *I Can See You Naked* (Kansas City: Andrews and McMeel, 1992), 117.

1. It establishes rapport between you and the audience.
2. It shows the audience that they are the focus of your attention.
3. It enhances your believability.
4. It helps you monitor audience response.
5. It creates accountability with your audience.
6. It will give you greater confidence.

You will discover that when you keep your eyes on your listeners, they will also keep their eyes on you and pay closer attention to your message. You can make adjustments in your message as you gauge your listeners' reaction and attention. Not only does eye contact communicate poise and assurance to the audience, it also gives them increased confidence in you as a speaker. Their positive nonverbal feedback, in turn, will create a higher level of comfort and boldness in you.

Improving Eye Contact

Essential as it is, making eye contact can be one of the hardest things for speakers to do. Novice speakers, as well as some who have been speaking for a long time, may have trouble keeping their eyes on the audience. The simple act of looking at the audience can make a speaker feel intimidated and frightened. So, nervous speakers may avoid eye contact altogether. They keep their eyes focused on their notes throughout the message. Or they continuously look at a spot four feet in front of them on the floor, or at the ceiling or at the walls. As a result, they seem impersonal and disinterested.

Perhaps even worse, some speakers employ techniques they falsely believe will create the appearance of eye contact. They look over the heads of the listeners. They speak to the empty seats rather than the ones that are filled. (Generally, this technique will guarantee a larger number of empty seats!) Or, they dart their eyes from person to person without ever fixing their gaze on anyone, which can make the speaker look dishonest or apprehensive. These "tricks" never work. Your listeners can always tell whether or not you are really looking at them. The only way to give the impression that you are making eye contact is actually to make eye contact.

Here are some guidelines for effective eye contact:

Establish eye contact at the beginning of your message. Even if you are using notes, make sure that you are looking up for the first several minutes of the sermon. Plan your opening words carefully and commit these concepts to memory so that you can begin the message by giving your listeners your full attention. Doing this will communicate your preparedness and energy to the audience.

Maintain strong eye contact with your audience throughout the message. Aim for spending 75 to 90 percent of your time with your eyes on your audience. If you are using notes, practice with them enough so that you do not have to look down very often. Make it your goal only to look away from your congregation for an extended period when you are reading your Bible.

Look directly into listeners' eyes. While you should avoid staring, which can make listeners feel singled out and uncomfortable, you do want to connect with the eyes of individuals in your audience. When you look into the eyes of an audience member, hold your gaze for two or three seconds. (That's longer than it sounds!) In audiences of 100 to 150, it is feasible for a preacher to look meaningfully into the eyes of every person in the room several times in the course of a sermon. For larger audiences, looking at individuals in each section will cause each person in that section to feel connected with you. If you are preaching in a very large place that uses camera and image magnification screens, recognize that many in the audience will perceive that you are looking at them only when you make sustained eye contact with the camera.

Guard against looking at or avoiding the same people or places repeatedly. Some parts of the congregation are simply easier to look at than others. A face that smiles at you when you are preaching is pleasant; a scowling face makes you want to look away. Nevertheless, try to be equitable in looking at every section in the audience. Be extremely cautious that you do not look at one person over and over again. We have noticed that some preachers have a tendency to make continuous eye contact with those in the audience they perceive to be important, as though seeking their approval. This is very noticeable and detracts from the preacher's effectiveness. Reviewing your preaching on video from time to time can help you determine how long you sustain eye contact and whether you favor one section of the auditorium over others as you are looking out. York and Decker believe, "You convey the power of your message through your eyes more than through any other single avenue of communication, so it is worth all the effort and practice."[5] Bottom-line: do not neglect this crucial area of public speaking. Outside of your voice, few things communicate more effective than your eyes.[6]

GESTURES

The effective use of gesture is also very important in connecting with your audience and keeping their attention. Think about it: if we were asked to choose between listening to someone who stands still with his arms glued firmly to his sides or one who gestures freely while he speaks, most of us would vote for the more active preacher.

Gesture can be defined as any movement of the hands, arms, or even the head that emphasizes or reinforces what you are saying. In normal conversation, we use gestures instinctively and spontaneously. Rarely would we become overly concerned about the timing, the variety, or the effectiveness of our gestures when talking to a friend at a coffee shop or telling a story to our family around the dinner table.

However, as with so many other aspects of speaking in public, being on the platform can make us uncomfortably aware of things to which we normally pay no attention. Standing before our listeners, we suddenly notice our hands and arms and wonder, "What am I supposed to do with these appendages?" As contradictory as it may sound, it takes practice, experience, and thought to learn how to gesture naturally and effortlessly.

Purposes of Gestures

Gestures in your speech work in much the same way as type size, underlining, and bold print in books or magazines. They help your

---

5.   Hershael York and Bert Decker, *Preaching with Bold Assurance* (Nashville: B&H, 2001), 229.
6.   Beebe and Beebe state plainly, "Of all the delivery features discussed in this chapter, the most important one in a public speaking situation is eye contact." Steven and Susan Beebe, *Public Speaking: An Audience-Centered Approach*, 3rd ed. (Needham Heights, MA: Allyn and Bacon, 1997), 289.

listeners to see what is important in your message. Consider a few of the purposes gestures can achieve in your speech:

They can repeat. Repeating gestures have a literal meaning that directly corresponds with your words. When you hold up three fingers to talk about three points, your gestures are visually reiterating your verbal content.

They can contradict. Nodding your head in the affirmative while saying, "No," creates a disagreement between your gestures and your words. Saying, "I think he's exactly right," while rolling your eyes, shows that you don't believe he's right at all. This type of contradiction can be used for a humorous effect in your message. Be aware that any time there is a conflict between what you are saying verbally and what you are signaling nonverbally, the listener will tend to perceive the nonverbal message as your intended meaning.

They can substitute. If you say, "He caught a fish about this long," as you hold your hands 12 inches apart, you are using gesture to take the place of words. While we often use gestures to substitute for words in conversation, problems arise when someone is listening to a sermon in an audio-only format, such as radio or Internet broadcast.

They can complement. A preferable alternative to using gestures to substitute for words, complementary gestures visually reinforce the verbal message. Using this technique, for instance, the preacher might say, "He caught a fish about a foot long," while holding his hands 12 inches apart.

They can emphasize. A gesture can highlight the importance or the emotion of what you are saying. A preacher might hold up a clenched fist to indicate anger or passion. Or he might lift his hands in the air to indicate praise or joy. Emphatic gestures are perhaps the most common gestures used in conversation and public speaking. While they don't have literal meaning, their emotional content is usually understood by the audience.

They can regulate. You can use gestures to manage and guide your communication to your listener. Palms extended toward the audience indicate that you are asking them to stop or withhold judgment about a statement that you have made. Hands turned upward can express frankness and good humor. A slight wave of the hand as you move from one section of your message to the next can indicate a transition of thought.[7]

Guidelines for Effective Gestures

Eliminate unnecessary gestures. We offer this guideline first because it is by far the most important and helpful. Regularly watching yourself or asking a trusted listener about any monotonous or repetitious gesture you are using will help tremendously in improving your gestures. A passionate preacher may unknowingly begin to gesture emphatically with nearly every word or every syllable, stabbing the air repeatedly with his index finger, chopping his hand furiously, or shaking his fist over and over again. While any of these gestures can be appropriate if used sparingly, overdoing a gesture has a similar effect as putting every word in a printed piece in italics or shouting all the time when you're speaking. Gestures become ineffective when they are overused.

Identify your nervous gestures. Some gestures are distracting because they are just plain weird. One preacher developed the odd custom of lifting up on his toes and clicking his heels after making an important point, as though he were Dorothy trying to get back to Kansas. A word of correction from his wife cured him of this habit quickly. Every preacher has the tendency to develop nervous gestures from time to time. These can include gripping the pulpit with white knuckles, folding your arms like a judgmental Pharisee, tugging at your sleeves, buttoning and unbuttoning your coat, fiddling with your eyeglasses, putting your hands in your pockets, playing with your keys (something best left in your study!), scratching your nose continually, or some other nervous mannerism. Even experienced speakers will find themselves slipping into bad habits without regular monitoring and feedback.

Do not choreograph your gestures. We are amazed that a number of preaching books advocate planning gestures ahead of time and

---

7. Adapted from Wayne V. McDill, *The Moment of Truth: A Guide to Effective Sermon Delivery* (Nashville: B&H, 1999), 97–98. Also see Beebe and Beebe, *Public Speaking,* 284–87; Decker and York, *Speaking with Bold Assurance,* 70–73; Huff, *I Can See You Naked,* 83–86.

rehearsing them when preparing to preach.[8] We have seen a number of preachers and other speakers (usually beginners) who have used planned and choreographed gestures. These gestures tend to look wooden and awkward, and often have an unintended comedic effect. John Broadus gave sound advice that still holds today: *"Never make any gesture from calculation. It must be the spontaneous product of present feeling, or it is unnatural."*[9] The best gestures arise almost unconsciously as you react to the content of your message.

Gesture from the shoulders, not the elbows. When speakers are self-conscious or uncomfortable, many of us have a tendency to stiffen and to hold our upper arms against our torso. With this posture, our gestures will tend to come from the elbows rather than the shoulders. This makes our gestures look too subdued and creates greater physical tension and anxiety. Simply remembering to move your upper arms and shoulders when you gesture can work wonders in making your gestures more free and expressive.

Match your gestures to the speaking situation and the message content. Just as you would speak more loudly in a large auditorium, you need broader and bigger gestures when you are speaking in a larger venue. When the setting is more intimate, smaller gestures are more appropriate. Likewise, the content of your sermon will help direct your gestures. If you are telling a humorous story, large, imitative gestures may be in order. When you are getting more personal in making application, simply emphasizing your words with slight hand and arm motion is effective. It's also important to be aware that your gestures almost always seem bigger to you than they do to your audience, especially when you are new to public speaking. York and Decker write: "If you are basically introverted and unaccustomed to using gestures, the slightest hand movement may feel like you are making windmills with your arms. If you watch yourself on video, however, you will see that your movement is not exaggerated at all."[10]

Time your gestures appropriately. Gestures work best when they come slightly before or in concert with the words they emphasize.

---

8.   Roy Debrand, "The Visual in Preaching" in *Handbook of Contemporary Preaching,* ed. M. Duduit (Nashville: Broadman, 1992), 401–3.

9.   John A. Broadus, *A Treatise on the Preparation and Delivery of Sermons,* 23rd ed., ed. E. C. Dargan (New York: A. C. Armstrong and Son, 1898), 506.

10.   York and Decker, *Preaching with Bold Assurance,* 231.

Some preachers gesture too late. For example, one prominent preacher from the not-too-distant past almost always gestured after he spoke. He would say, "It was a wide, wide desert," and then, half-second later, spread his arms wide. This became a noticeable part of his preaching style that many others imitated.[11] His overall skill at preaching was probably not enhanced by gesturing late. Instead, he overcame this faulty mannerism with his other considerable strengths. For the rest of us, the best method is to time our gestures with our words. Beebe and Beebe provide a helpful conclusion to this topic: "Use gestures that work best for you. Don't try to be someone that you are not . . . your gestures should fit your personality. We believe it is better to use no gestures than to counterfeit someone else's gestures. Your nonverbal delivery should flow from *your* message."[12]

---

11. Steve Brown, Hadden Robinson, and William Willimon, *A Voice in the Wilderness: Clear Preaching in a Complicated World* (Sisters, OR: Multnomah Books, 1993), 31.
12. Beebe and Beebe, *Public Speaking,* 287.

CHAPTER 25

MAKING A LASTING IMPRESSION

Master preacher and respected homiletician Haddon Robinson has observed that there are three kinds of preachers: those to whom you cannot listen, those to whom you can listen, and those to whom you must listen. The listener decides which type of preacher you are during the first few moments of the sermon.[1] The old saying often attributed to Will Rogers is proven true again and again: *You never get a second chance to make a first impression.* A great deal of a speaker's initial appeal has to do with nonverbal elements of his delivery. Psychologist Albert Mehrabian's studies in human communication indicate that only 7 percent of a speaker's message comes through his words, while 78 percent comes from the voice, and 55 percent from facial expressions.[2]

Skillful nonverbal communication helps you to make a positive first impression when you are preaching. However, your demeanor and behavior also create a long-term impression on your audience. This lasting impression affects the way the listener perceives you and, by extension, your message. In this chapter, we will consider how facial expressions, posture, and movement can influence the success of your sermon delivery.

---

1. Haddon Robinson, *Biblical Preaching: The Development and Delivery of Expository Messages,* 2nd ed. (Grand Rapids: Baker, 2001), 75.
2. Ibid., 203.

YOUR FACIAL EXPRESSIONS

Facial expressions result through the complicated motions of the numerous muscles in the face. These movements are extremely important in communicating your emotions to your listeners. Many emotions are fairly easy to detect based on the expressions on a person's face, and the interpretation of facial expression has a great degree of cross-cultural acceptance. For instance, a genuine smile communicates happiness to just about anyone in the world, no matter what their culture, while a furrowed brow and a down-turned mouth usually indicate anger. Raised eyebrows and an open mouth show surprise, a pleasant look expresses contentment, and so on. Other expressions, such as disgust and fear, can be harder to distinguish from one another.

Because they are closely tied to our emotions, facial expressions often occur involuntarily. Our inner feelings automatically show up on our face. Most people have a hard time suppressing emotion from their countenance. When you feel nervous, happy, irritated, sad, excited, uncomfortable, disgusted, relaxed, stressed—or whatever other human emotion you are experiencing—your face will almost always communicate it. Even when you try to conceal your emotions, those who know you best can still read the look on your face.

A great deal of the content preachers communicate has an emotional component. Our listeners read our faces for the emotions were are expressing, and they assign a high degree of credibility to what our faces communicate. To relay the full meaning of our material, preachers can voluntarily adopt facial expressions to communicate emotional content to the audience. The follow ing guidelines can help you make a stronger impression with yo' facial expressions.

Avoid a deadpan look. After years of teaching preaching class' have discovered that most preaching students are not nearly as sive as they believe they are. This is true with vocal expre' even truer regarding facial expression. The natural express' people's faces tends to be emotionless. To confirm this, ju faces of people sitting in the congregation at church or v the sidewalks of a city. Most of them are unsmiling and When a preacher stands on the platform to speak, a com' own nervousness, his concentration on his message, and his natural tendency to be poker-faced will result in an expression that conveys nothing. As you preach, be aware that your face communicates, and work to make your expressions animated and lively.

Match your facial expression to your sermon content. Remember, if there is a perceived discrepancy between your nonverbal message and your verbal message, the listener will almost always take your nonverbal communication to be your intended meaning. Imagine someone saying, "God loves you," with a scowl on his face or warning, "Sin will take you to hell," with a broad, toothy smile. In both cases, the words do not match the expression. The result either becomes comical or appears insincere. Make sure that the words you say and the look on your face correspond to one another.

Practice your facial expressions. A number of preaching textbooks make the excellent suggestion of testing out the way your face looks. A good way to do this is to get a handheld mirror and to practice. With the mirror facing away from you, make a happy face. Now, turn the mirror toward you. Do you look as happy as you thought you did? Most people are surprised that their expressions are not as animated as they had supposed. Try the same exercise with facial expressions for confusion, anger, surprise, disgust, and sorrow. Now, with the mirror in front of your face, adjust your expressions until your face is communicating what you intend it to say.

Exaggerate your facial expressions slightly. Because of our tendency to think that we are being more expressive than we are, but also because preaching is a public communication forum that requires a degree of amplification, exaggerating your facial expressions often helps to connect with the audience. We have discovered that it's almost impossible to overdo it or go "over the top" when trying to be expressive from the pulpit. In one preaching seminar, students were offered a prize if they could be so expressive in their vocal and facial expression when reading Scripture as to appear ridiculous or outrageous. Though the students all tried their hardest to overdo their expressions, their classmates voted and discovered that *no one* succeeded in going over the top. Instead, the seminar participants agreed that the Scripture readings were consistently improved when facial expressions were exaggerated.

Smile, brother, smile! Most preachers would make a more favorable impression in the pulpit if they simply smiled more. Men who are called to ministry have a responsibility to God, our families, and those in our ministry to be continually cheerful. Though many people find it difficult at first to smile while talking, it is an ability that you can learn and improve. Bert Decker and Hershael York observe that one of the reasons that little children wanted to be around Jesus may have been because He smiled. Decker and York contend that children are naturally attracted to a smiling face: "Very early they learn that smiling people comfort them, care for them, coddle them. People who don't smile tend to neglect them, scold them, even hurt them. For the rest of our lives we feel drawn to smiling people."[3] You have cause to smile most of the time if for no other reason than the fact that you are going to spend eternity in heaven!

Work on actually feeling the emotional content of your message. Make no mistake: we are not advocating that you preach with a fake, plastered-on smile, a contrived look of sorrow, or some other false face. Our listeners can tell when our facial expressions are not genuine. For that very reason, preachers must learn to feel the content of the message they are preaching. As you experience the emotions of your sermon, you will be more likely to convey those emotions on your face while you preach. Your response to the truths you are proclaiming will show on your face, and the audience will connect with your message more deeply.

YOUR MOVEMENT AND POSTURE

Two aspects of speaking that have a positive long-term influence or listeners are a confident posture and lively and appropriate mo ment on the platform. By posture, we are talking about the way hold yourself. By movement, we are referring to going from p' place on the platform.

Before you even begin speaking, your posture and move your audience a clue as to your energy level and your at' preaching. If you stand with slumped shoulders or lumbe'

---

3. Bert Decker and Hershael York, *Speaking with Bold Assurance*
    a Persuasive Communicator (Nashville: B&H, 2001), 73

pulpit, it's the equivalent of announcing: "I don't want to be here, I'm not interested in what I have to say, and I don't care much about you." Conversely, good posture and a sprightly step indicate enthusiasm and vigor. As your message continues, movement helps to keep the listener's attention, and the right posture ensures proper breathing and vocal power. In the last chapter, we talked about gesture, which is a specialized form of movement primarily involving the hands and head. Here, we offer some guidelines for good posture and platform movement.

Stand with a confident and energetic posture. Communication expert Dale Leathers asserts that communicators with a relaxed, open, and flexible posture are perceived as more powerful and credible. Also, he writes that speakers who lean forward when speaking establish high rapport with their audiences. On the other hand, rigidity, crossed arms, and overall tension indicates a lack of energy and assertiveness.[4] An energetic posture helps to communicate that you are confident, that you know your subject matter, and that you are glad to be speaking to your audience. This type of posture will communicate energy and vitality to your audience. It will help you to achieve full vocal production and provide a healthy air supply as you speak. It will also prepare you for free and flexible movement on the platform. A simple way to correct posture problems is to stand against a wall with your heels, buttocks, shoulders, and the back of your head touching the wall. Step out from the wall, maintaining the same posture and alignment. Though this posture may feel strange at first, it is the best posture to maintain. Over a period of time and practice, you can train yourself to hold this posture without feeling stiff or rigid.

Dale Leathers, *Successful Nonverbal Communication* (New York: Macmillan, 1986), 162.

Checklist for a Good Posture

- The crown of the head is the highest part of the body
- The chin is parallel to the floor, neither raised up nor tucked into the chest.
- The shoulders are held back and down, not up and tight.
- The chest is slightly out, not caved in or puffed up.
- The spine is in a natural curvature, rather than rigidly straight or unnaturally curved.
- The arms are resting naturally at the sides.
- The hips are aligned with the shoulders.
- The legs are bent slightly, so that the knees are flexed and weight is placed on the balls of the feet.
- The feet are positioned six to eight inches apart.
- One foot is placed a few inches in front of the other, so that any shift of weight from foot to foot results in front to back movement instead of side to side movement.

Keep your arms at your sides when not gesturing. As we have observed before, our arms and hands—which we carry with us all the time—can become strange appliances that we don't know how to operate when we are in a public speaking situation. All of a sudden, they seem awkward and we wonder what we should do with them. As a general rule, it is best to keep your arms resting at your sides unless you are gesturing. This may feel uncomfortable and unnatural at first. However, if you observe seasoned speakers who have learned to hold their arms this way, you will see that it looks very normal and relaxed. When you gesture, move your arms freely, then bring them back against your sides. If you are speaking from a pulpit, an alternative is to have your hands resting lightly on the top of the podium. However, be careful to avoid bracing your arms, grasping the pulpit desk tightly, or leaning on the pulpit.

Some Postures to Avoid

➤ *Pocket jangle.* Hands are placed in the pockets (or in one pocket) throughout the message. The preacher then proceeds to jangle any keys or loose change or to fiddle with whatever else might be in his pockets. Learn to keep your hands out of your pockets altogether. Pinning your pockets shut for a few Sundays will usually cure you of this habit.

➤ *Parade rest.* Hands are clasped behind the back, much as a sailor or soldier under command would do. Hands stay in this position for a long period of time. This stance makes the hands disappear and causes the preacher to look officious and harsh.

➤ *Fig leaf.* The exact opposite of the parade rest, the fig leaf involves clutching the hands together and holding them just below the waistline. Not good at all, for a number of reasons.

➤ *"I'm freezing."* Crossing your arms may seem natural and relaxed, but it usually communicates closeness, discomfort, and even judgmentalism to your audience. In addition, folded arms tend to collapse the chest, making it harder to achieve full vocal production.

➤ *Wounded warrior.* A variation of crossing your arms, this involves crossing one arm across your front and grabbing your other arm at the elbow. The other arm drops down at your side. The overall effect is that of one arm serving as a tourniquet for the other lifeless, dangling limb. Again, your breathing is restricted, and you look incredibly unnatural.

➤ *"Superman."* Both arms are bent at the elbows, with the hands resting on the belt, creating the classic "Man of Steel" pose. Its close cousin, *the broken wing*, uses only one arm bent at the elbow. Both postures communicate that the speaker is ill-at-ease.

Some Postures to Avoid

➤ *Hand steeple.* This position involves placing the palms together or folding them as in prayer, and then holding them at the chest. Other variations include *the spider on a mirror* where the fingertips are pressed together, *the big potato* with the hands locked to form a large fist, and *the hand washer* which adds movement to the basic hand steeple, as though the speaker were scrubbing up for surgery. All of these postures tend to make the preacher look nervous, pedantic, or self-consciously pious.

Use the center of the platform as your base. The most powerful place on the stage is front and center.[5] During the first few minutes of your speech, stay at that central position to establish it as the home base for your message. As the content of the message calls for movement, you can leave your base, returning at the appropriate time. Even while standing at front and center, you can take two or three steps in different directions to keep the listener's attention.

Move purposefully for emphasis in your message. When you are telling an illustration, you might move to act out parts of the story. Or when you are making personal application, you will move to the side or a few steps closer to the audience in order to be more personal. Your movement on the platform can also help your listener to visualize ideas you are discussing. For instance, you might move to the right side of the platform to talk about the past, go to the middle to talk about the present, and then move to the left of the platform to talk about the future. For the rest of the message, movement (or even gesturing) to the right will represent the past to your audience, while referencing the left of the stage will cue them to think about the future, and going to the middle will remind them of the present. Movement on the platform should never be random. It should always have a purpose in helping to communicate your message. Also, be careful to take two steps or more when you move. Taking one step makes a speaker look halting or hesitant.

---

5. Wayne McDill, *The Moment of Truth: A Guide to Effective Sermon Delivery* (Nashville: B&H, 1999), 96.

Eliminate impediments to free movement. Anything that keeps you from moving freely on the platform should be eliminated, if possible. The platform should allow for free movement from right and left as well as from front to back. For preachers, the biggest impediment to movement is the pulpit itself. The pulpit communicates the centrality of the Word of God in the worship service. However, if the pulpit is a large and bulky piece of furniture that obscures the preacher and that keeps him from moving as he speaks, it can be an encumbrance to effective communication. For this reason, we advocate using the smallest and least visually obstructive pulpit available. If you use a pulpit, make sure it matches your height. A pulpit that is too short will cause the preacher to look as though he is hunched over it. A tall pulpit can hide everything but the preacher's neck and face from the audience's view.

Consider your audience's sightlines. Make sure that you do not move in such as way as to keep your listeners from seeing you. Descending from the platform to the floor can be an effective way to create closeness and intimacy with your audience. However, if large numbers of people cannot see you well on the floor, it is better to stay on the platform. Likewise, moving too far to one side of the platform may keep people from being able to see you as well. Generally, auditoriums are designed so that the front and center point and the area within a five-foot radius of that point offer the best sightlines. You might consider sitting in various seats throughout your auditorium and determining if there are any places on the platform where a listener would have a hard time seeing you, then marking those boundaries on the platform.

Keep moving, but avoid pacing. While movement on the platform is almost always perceived positively by listeners, pacing creates the impression that the speaker is nervous, underprepared, or new to speaking in public. The difference between effective movement and pacing is very easy to discern. When a speaker is moving effectively, he walks a few steps, stops, and stands for while, and then moves to another place on the platform, stops, and stands still again. Movement occurs as the speaker transitions from one idea or section of his message to the next, and there is a pause in motion. A preacher who paces never stops walking. He walks and talks constantly, and his movement never has any significance. Instead, he is merely releasing nervous energy through his feet.

CHAPTER 26

YOUR DELIVERY SYSTEM

R alph Lewis, who taught preaching for many years at Asbury Theological Seminary, told about a time that he was invited to speak at a community-wide worship service in a Michigan resort town. About 600 people gathered in a beautiful outdoor setting near a lake. As soon as he began preaching, a breeze from the lake snatched up his note cards and scattered them into the crowd. Then, as he scurried, red-faced, to retrieve his notes, the host pastor good-naturedly called out, "That's okay. The cows won't eat 'em!"[1]

Which is best—preaching with lots of notes, with a few notes, or with no notes at all? It is a question that preachers have been asking for a long, long time. Over a century ago, John Broadus, regarded by many as the father of American homiletics, wrote his reflections: "Though so often discussed, this question constantly recurs, not merely for the young preachers whom every year brings forward, but for many of maturer age, who are not satisfied that they have been pursuing the wisest course. It is a question affecting not only one's manner of delivery, but his whole method of preparation, and in fact all his habits of thought and expression."[2]

---

1. Ralph Lewis, "Preaching With and Without Notes," in *Handbook of Contemporary Preaching,* ed. Michael Duduit (Nashville, TN: Broadman, 1992), 409.
2. John A. Broadus, *A Treatise on the Preparation and Delivery of Sermons,* 23rd ed., ed. Edwin Charles Dargan (New York: A. C. Armstrong and Son, 1898), 431.

In this chapter we will consider your delivery system, or the means by which you communicate your message to your listeners. We will introduce the methods used most often for delivering a sermon, briefly review the use of those methods in the history of preaching, and then offer some practical suggestions for strengthening your own delivery system.

METHODS OF SERMON DELIVERY

Four major methods are available for delivering a sermon, only two of which are viable options for most preachers. For the sake of discussion and completeness, however, we will present each method.

Impromptu Delivery. This method involves standing to preach with no notes and without formal preparation ahead of time at all. As a pastor and a preacher, you will have to speak this way from time to time. Since people tend to assume that preachers always have something to say (or that preachers always want to say something), sometimes they will ask you to come to the platform and share a few words.

What do you do when asked to speak off the cuff? Do not make excuses. Everyone in the room knows that you have been put on the spot, so you do not need to acknowledge that. Keep the message relatively brief, remembering that it is hard to preach a bad short message. Consider using a pattern such as greater to lesser, contrasting the good versus the bad, talking about a cause and its effect, or moving from past to present to future. These paradigms will provide you with a quick outline.

As for the content of an impromptu message, preach about your quiet time from that day or share your testimony. Expound a single verse or a popular biblical story. After you have become more experienced, you will probably have a few favorite messages that you can preach in a shortened form without preparation.

Although you inevitably will have to preach some impromptu messages, it is by no means the best way to preach. Jeffrey Arthurs noted that impromptu messages are sometimes necessary to answer questions or to address crises, writing: "An IV is necessary during triage, but it shouldn't replace a balanced diet."[3]

Memorized Delivery. Phillips Brooks called the recited sermon "a method some men practice, but I hope nobody commends."[4] Using this method, the preacher commits a word-for-word manuscript to memory and then recites the sermon in the pulpit. Memorization and recitation has been used by a number of very successful preachers in the past; however, this method is not advisable for most preachers. The obvious danger with memorization is that you are likely to forget what you have memorized. Most trained actors would have trouble memorizing and reciting a 30-minute, uninterrupted soliloquy.

Even if you can successfully commit your entire sermon to memory, a recited sermon usually sounds like just that—a *recited* sermon. The message seems canned, as though the preacher were reading it off of the back of his mind. We have noticed that even the most skillful preachers who memorize have a tendency to sound artificial and seem more intent on performing the message just as they had written it rather than communicating with their audience. For these reasons and others, we have warned hundreds of preaching students across the years: Memorization is death. Don't do it.

Delivery from a Manuscript or Full Notes. This method involves writing a manuscript or extensive notes, and then reading the manuscript or notes expressively from the pulpit. Some preachers who use this method create a complete manuscript that includes everything they will say in the sermon. Others do not have a fully worded script for the sermon but instead have pages of notes that include nearly everything they are going to say, minus transitions and some other elements.

Using full notes or a manuscript provides you close control and planning of the words you will say during the message. This method can be helpful when pastors preach on a controversial subject and want to be certain of the wording and need a record of what they

---

3. Jeffrey Arthurs, "No Notes, Lots of Notes, Brief Notes," *The Art and Craft of Biblical Preaching: A Comprehensive Resource for Today's Communicators,* ed. Haddon Robinson and Craig Brian Larson (Grand Rapids: Zondervan, 2005), 600–601.

4. Phillips Brooks, *The Joy of Preaching,* reprint, originally published as *Lectures on Preaching* (London: H. R. Allenson, 1895; Grand Rapids: Kregel Publications, 1989), 129.

have said. On the downside, extensive reading from the pulpit is usually not as expressive or passionate as natural speech. Eye contact becomes dramatically lower when a preacher is reading from his notes or manuscript, and the preacher's movement is severely limited by his need to be at the podium to see his notes. For every preacher who *can* read a sermon well, there are thousands who *think* they can.

Using a Manuscript or Full Notes
Advantages
➤ The completed manuscript or notes provide the preacher confidence.
➤ The preacher has greater control over the timing of the message.
➤ Details of explanation and illustration have higher accuracy.
➤ Word choice is more literary, varied, and precise.
➤ The preacher is less likely to ramble and add unnecessary material.
Disadvantages
➤ Eye contact is greatly diminished.
➤ Reading is often much less expressive and energetic than natural speech.
➤ Language may be designed to be read more than to be heard.
➤ Delivery may sound stilted or artificial.
➤ Preachers will find it difficult to adjust the message to the demands of the particular preaching event.

Extemporaneous Delivery. This kind of delivery is sometimes called preaching *ex tempore,* a Latin term that means "out of the moment." While *extemporaneous* can be a synonym for *impromptu,* in the jargon of preaching and public speaking, extemporaneous speech refers to delivery in which the basic flow, structure, and content of the message are carefully planned, while the precise wording of the message is composed during the delivery of the speech itself. Extemporaneous delivery can be done with brief notes or using no notes at all. Broadus offered an excellent description of this type of speech:

The phrase extemporaneous speaking is applied to cases in which there has been preparation of the thought, however thorough, but the language is left to be suggested at the moment. Still further, when notes are made, as a help to preparation, when the plan of the discourse is drawn out on paper, and all the principal points are stated or suggested, we call it extemporaneous speaking, because all this is regarded only as a means of arranging and recalling the thoughts, and the language is extemporized.[5]

Extemporaneous delivery offers the best advantages of every other delivery system, with fewer disadvantages. A preacher who delivers his message in this manner will make extensive preparation of his sermon, developing full notes without having to take the intensive time required to write a word-for-word manuscript. He will reduce those notes to one or a few short pages that provide a "roadmap" for the general direction of his message. He will then preach either with his reduced notes in the pulpit or without notes, choosing his words as he preaches. Using this method, the preacher maximizes eye contact, has freedom to move about the platform, and engages his personality more fully in the preaching event, while also delivering a message that is prepared and purposeful.

As a side note, extemporaneous preaching is often confused by listeners—and by some preachers—with both impromptu and recited preaching. This confusion may result from the perception that the extemporaneous preacher is either just making up his message as he goes along or that he has memorized all that he is saying, since there are few notes in front of him. In fact, preaching extemporaneously is like neither of these methods. Instead, it is a much more conversational approach to preaching, in which the preacher is speaking from his heart about ideas from the Scripture into which he has immersed himself in the study.

---

5.   Broadus, *A Treatise,* 457.

Preaching Extemporaneously
Advantages
➤ Makes efficient use of the preacher's study and preparation time.
➤ Enhances eye contact and audience rapport.
➤ Allows the preacher to communicate with his natural personality.
➤ Produces a more conversational platform style.
➤ Enables natural and unrestricted platform movement.
➤ Allows easy alteration of the material when necessary.
➤ Encourages a simple and memorable sermon structure.
➤ Creates a nearly universally positive audience response when done well.
Disadvantages
➤ Can become an excuse for lack of preparation.
➤ May cause the preacher to leave out important sermon material.
➤ Preacher may rely on often-repeated phrases rather than developing precise wording.
➤ Message may become loose and unfocused.
➤ May be too stressful for some preachers.

DIFFERENT DELIVERY METHODS IN PREACHING HISTORY

Has one of these four methods of delivering a sermon been uniquely blessed of God in the history of the church? The answer to that question is an emphatic "no." In fact, the argument can be made that every method has been used effectively in the history of preaching, including the impromptu and recitation methods.

The Bible certainly does not require one method of delivery. The methods that seem to be most used in Scripture could best be described either as impromptu or extemporaneous without notes. We do not imagine Jesus using a manuscript when preaching the Sermon on the Mount, Peter flipping pages as he preached at Pentecost, or Paul holding note cards as he preached at Mars Hill.

We must recognize that preachers in the Bible were preaching *revelationally*, bringing a new word from God to His people, whereas today's preachers speak *explanatorily*, taking the revealed text of Scripture and bringing it to bear upon our listeners. Accordingly, preaching in the Bible is in a class by itself and possesses unique qualities that extend even to the methods of delivery used. However, it is instructive that sermons in the Bible were preached freely and not read, even by men like Paul who were also great writers. The early Christian centuries following the closing of the canon were characterized by preaching that was much like the preaching of the apostles, both in content and in form.

By the fourth century, Christian preaching had become more influenced by the rhetoric of the Greeks and Romans. Preachers such as John of Antioch and Augustine were trained in rhetorical studies, and their messages mark a shift from the simple structure of the apostolic age to a more formal model. Even so, since one of the canons of classical rhetoric was memory, it can be assumed that even these more complicated messages were delivered from memory without extensive notes.[6] Indeed, some of Augustine's ancient homilies, which were transcribed, display a reliance on the text of Scripture for their structure, and appear to have been preached extemporaneously.

During the sixteenth and seventeenth centuries, it became more common for preachers to use full manuscripts in the pulpit. Indeed, in the Church of England, extemporaneous preaching became so identified with the scandalous Independents and Puritans that one London preacher was removed from his pulpit because he dared to lift his eyes from his manuscript and look at his congregation while he preached. But manuscripts gained favor in wider circles as well. Jonathan Edwards delivered his famous sermon, "Sinners in the Hands of an Angry God," from a manuscript that he held closely to his face, barely looking at his audience as they writhed in agony under his graphic descriptions of judgment. Later in his ministry, however, Edwards became an advocate of extemporaneous preaching. G. Campbell Morgan and Alexander Maclaren, great expositors of the late nineteenth and early twentieth centuries, felt that notes or

---

6. Adapted from Ralph Lewis, "Preaching With and Without Notes," in *Handbook of Contemporary Preaching*, 409–16.

a manuscript would interfere with eye contact, and took little or no notes into the pulpit.[7]

The great Baptist orator R. G. Lee memorized his messages word for word and recited them. When you listen to his famous message "Payday, Someday," recorded in the 1940s, and compare it to a version of the message recorded in the 1970s, you will discover that most parts of the message are absolutely identical though he uses no notes. Adrian Rogers, Lee's eventual successor at Bellevue Baptist Church in Memphis, Tennessee, used extensive notes very skillfully and preached with incredible power. W. A. Criswell, famed pastor of the First Baptist Church of Dallas, Texas, preached extemporaneously, almost always without notes.[8] If you were to survey prominent contemporary preachers, you would find some who use extensive notes, some who use a few notes, and some who use none at all.

CHOOSING YOUR SYSTEM

Now, we come back to the question we asked at the beginning of this chapter: Which is best—preaching with lots of notes, with a few notes, or with no notes at all? Since we can rule out impromptu preaching or memorization, we are left with two live options: using full notes and preaching extemporaneously. Based on the advantages we have discussed earlier, we advocate extemporaneous delivery as the best method to use for most. Even so, the amount of notes a preacher uses in the pulpit depends on several factors:

Your own comfort level. Some preachers will never be at ease if they are "flying without a net" and preaching with no notes at all. You may discover that you feel greater freedom in the pulpit with the assistance of a few notes to prompt your thinking and to quell your nerves.

Your personal loquaciousness. A loquacious person is someone who is talkative and chatty. Some preachers are naturally talkative. They never lack words and always are ready to chime in with their

---

7.   Ibid.
8.   For more information about the delivery styles of these preachers, as well as others from the Southern Baptist preaching tradition, see Al Fasol, *With a Bible in Their Hands* (Nashville, B&H, 1994).

opinions and feelings. Oddly enough, this kind of preacher may be more in need of notes than someone who is naturally quiet and reserved. Those with the "gift of gab" may find that they use their ease of speech as an excuse not to prepare, or that they have a hard time staying on point without some notes to guide them.

The needs of the particular preaching event. Among the three authors of this text, we sometimes use no notes, brief notes, or even extensive notes, depending on the circumstances under which we are preaching. For the Sunday morning message, which receives the most time and attention in preparation and which is more likely to be televised or broadcast on the internet, we try to reduce our notes to as few as possible, if we use any notes at all. For Sunday evening or midweek services, we often use more notes because we have not had time to internalize the message as much as we would like or because we need the security of having our outline in front of us. For formal events such as weddings, funerals, or academic ceremonies and addresses, we may use even more extensive notes to make sure we get the wording right.

To learn to preach extemporaneously, we would advise that you begin by preaching with no notes at all in a safe environment. Whether speaking for a Wednesday night prayer meeting, a classroom preaching laboratory, or some other low-risk situation, take the bold step of preaching without notes. After the initial nervousness passes, you will begin to experience the freedom and joy of interacting with your listeners, relying on the Holy Spirit to guide you in the preaching event, using the Bible itself to prompt your thinking, and expressing the passion of your message unencumbered by pages of notes in front of you. Over time, you can add some notes as needed. However, you will probably discover that you do not need as many notes as you may have once thought you did.

SOME PRACTICAL SUGGESTIONS

Whether you are preaching extemporaneously with or without notes, the following suggestions will help you to deliver your message effectively:

Simplify your structure. Keep the design of your sermon uncluttered and uncomplicated. Eliminate sub-points whenever you can. The biggest problem with sub-points and infinitesimal division in the sermon is that a complicated structure looks a lot better on a page of notes than it sounds when you are delivering it. The listener has trouble distinguishing between main points, sub-points, and sub-sub-points. Moreover, both the preacher and listener will have an easier time remembering the message's main ideas if the structure is simple.

Follow the text of Scripture. The best way to keep your structure simple is to follow the order of ideas presented in the passage of Scripture from which you are preaching. If you have no notes at all in front of you, you still have your Bible. When the content of the message reflects the content of the text, your text actually serves to prompt you about what to say next in the sermon. Underline and circle important words and phrases that you want to talk about. When you refer to your Bible for your points rather than looking at notes, it actually enhances the authority of your message in the perception of your listener.

Condense your notes. Although you may write extensive notes or even a full manuscript in preparation for your sermon, it is best to condense your notes into one or two pages. You may take these brief notes into the pulpit with you, or you may keep them on hand to review right before you preach. We have found that taking the time to condense sermon notes on a single sheet of paper is very helpful in internalizing the message.

Prepare for special materials. If you have a quote that you want to read or statistics you plan to cite in a sermon, prepare note cards with that information on them, or put the materials on a sticky note attached to the pages of your Bible. More extensive special materials can be placed in a small notebook on half-sheets of paper. You will appear more professional and prepared if you have special materials arranged neatly in a form that is easy to access while you are preaching.

Memorize your main idea and major points. These sentences are essential for communicating the core content of your message. The main idea of the text (MIT) and your message (MIM) is the one thing you want people to remember when the message is over. For that reason, you should know it by heart. It is also important to be able to state your major points from the pulpit without having to look down at notes. You may want to write these sentences in the margins of your Bible or attach them on sticky notes; but even so, you need to have these important concepts committed to memory.

Internalize the message. While memorizing the entire message is always inadvisable, you will find it very helpful to spend some time, especially in the hours right before you preach, internalizing your message. Do not try to repeat your message word for word. Instead, talk through the major movements of your sermon. Get the order of the ideas locked into your mind. Review what you will explain for each point, how you will illustrate each point, and what application you will make. Think through how you will begin the message and how you will end it. As you internalize the message, you will discover the sermon becomes smaller in your consciousness. Instead of being a long assortment of ideas, it will become one unit that you are ready to communicate to your audience.

Pay attention to your transitions. Extemporaneous preachers are most likely to lose their train of thought during transitions from one section of the message to the next. For that reason, it is important to think about how you will get from the introduction of the sermon to the body, from point to point, from the body to the conclusion, and then to the invitation. Also, focus on the smaller transitions from explanation to illustration to application within each division of the sermon.

Think intent rather than content. Your task in preaching is not to get through your message. Your task is to get through to your audience. Thinking in terms of what you are trying to accomplish with the message is more profitable than focusing on remembering what you intend to say. An outline that displays a sequence of motivations offers an intentional model: (1) Get attention. (2) Awaken interest. (3) Show the need. (4) Satisfy the need. (5) Call for action. Thinking about your intention will give your message passion and purpose. It will enhance and strengthen your delivery as you convey to your people the unsearchable riches of Christ.

CHAPTER 27

STYLE CAN MAKE A DIFFERENCE

The ancient Romans wrote on wax tablets, using a writing instrument called a *stylus*. The Latin word *stylus* was eventually employed to describe a person's handwriting and, by extension, to denote the manner by which a writer expressed his thoughts. Later, the same term came to be used in reference to a person's way of speaking. Today, we use the word "style" to refer to the fine arts, dress and fashion, and other distinctive manners. In preaching, a person's style is "his characteristic manner of expressing his thoughts."[1]

Just as you have a distinctive handwriting style, you also have a personal communication style that is all your own. Our purpose in this chapter is two-fold. First, we will discuss the elements that produce an effective preaching style. Then, we will offer suggestions for strengthening and improving your preaching style.[2]

---

1. John A. Broadus, *A Treatise on the Preparation and Delivery of Sermons*, 23rd ed., ed. Edwin Charles Dargan (New York: A. C. Armstrong and Son, 1898), 339–40.
2. For an excellent study that looks at this issue through the categories of classic rhetoric, see Paige Patterson, "Ancient Rhetoric: A Model for Text-Driven Preachers," in *Text-Driven Preaching*, ed. Daniel Akin, David Allen, and Ned Matthews (Nashville: B&H, 2010), 11–35. Patterson examines carefully the canons of *ethos, logos*, and *pathos*. Also see R. Kent Hughes, "The Anatomy of Exposition: Logos, Ethos, and Pathos," *SBJT* 3.2 (1999): 44–58.

ELEMENTS OF EFFECTIVE STYLE

In *Communication in Pulpit and Parish,* Merrill Abbey describes the six qualities that work together to form a desirable communication style. They are (1) purity, (2) precision, (3) clarity, (4) energy, (5) beauty, and (6) naturalness.[3] By examining each of these qualities, we can gain a fuller understanding of what an effective preaching style includes.

Purity

Preachers should aim for language that conforms to the basics of proper grammar. When we fail to speak properly, many in our audience will question our education and our knowledgeableness. Listeners may wonder whether the preacher truly understands the truths of Scripture and the nuances of theology if he consistently fouls up verb tenses or if the verbs rarely agree with the subjects in his sentences. In whatever language you are preaching, make sure you understand the rules of good grammar and proper usage.

If you ask just about any non-native speaker of English, you will learn that our language is notoriously difficult. Nearly all English grammar rules have exceptions. The forms that verbs take as they move from past to present to future or that nouns take as they shift from singular to plural can be irregular and illogical. Accordingly listing all of the potential grammatical missteps a speaker might make would be impossible. The following list represents some of the most common grammatical errors.

1. *Subject-verb disagreement.* The subject and verb of a sentence should agree in number. If the subject is singular, then the verb should be also. If one is plural, the other should be as well. A speaker should say *a boy runs* or *boys run,* not *a boy run* or *boys runs.* Agreement becomes especially difficult in public speaking when we add several clauses or phrases in between the subject and verb. A speaker might say, "The epistles of Paul, though written over a relatively short amount of time, *reflects* a wide variety of subject matter."

---

3. Merrill R. Abbey, *Communication in Pulpit and Parish* (Philadelphia: Westminster Press, 1973), 194–95.

It is far easier to see the problem when it is printed on a page. We recognize that "reflects" should be "reflect." When we are speaking, however, it can be more difficult to detect the error. Keeping your sentences simple and making sure that subjects and verbs stay close to one another can help guard against this type of error.

2. *Pronoun-noun disagreement.* Pronouns and the nouns to which they refer should agree in number. We often make this error when we are referring to a person in a generic sense. We might say, "A sinner can be forgiven of *their* sins." Here the noun "sinner" is singular, and the pronoun "their" is plural. This problem can be fixed in two ways. The speaker could say, "A sinner can be forgiven of his or her sins." A more natural expression, however, might be "Sinners can be forgiven of their sins."

3. *Wrong verb form.* If we are not cautious, we may make an error such as saying, "He *come* into the house late last night," when we mean, "He *came* into the house late last night." Or we might say, "I *set* down at the table," instead of "I *sat* down at the table." Other common verb form errors are saying "I *seen*" rather than "I *saw*," or "He *give* it to me yesterday," in place of "He *gave* it to me yesterday."

4. *Confusing adjectives and adverbs.* English speakers regularly use the word "good" when they should use the word "well." The simple corrective is to remember that "good" is an adjective, while "well" is an adverb. It is wrong to say, "He preaches *good*," but it is equally wrong to say, "She was not having a *well* day." Confusion of adjectives and adverbs can be very tricky. Saying, "We've got to dig down *deeper*," may sound right, but the correct form is actually, "We've got to dig down *more deeply*." The rule here is very simple to remember: Adjectives modify nouns. Adverbs modify verbs, adjectives, and other adverbs.

5. *Pronouns in the wrong case.* Pronouns can be in two cases: the nominative and the accusative. When a pronoun is the subject of a sentence or a predicate nominative, it is in the nominative case. When a pronoun is a direct object, an indirect object, or the object of a preposition, it is in the accusative case. The nominative pronouns are "I," "we" "he," "she," and "they." The accusative pronouns are "me," "us," "him," "her," and "them." "You" takes the same form in both the nominative and accusative cases. Thus, while, "Jesus died on the cross for you and *I*" may sound right, the correct form is actually, "Jesus died on the cross for you and *me*." "I am going to the

store with you and she" should be "I am going to the store with you and her." Putting pronouns in the wrong case may be the most common error speakers make because the incorrect form often sounds more proper to our ears than the correct form.

Precision

Our preaching style should demonstrate detail and accuracy so that the words we are using are communicating exactly what we intend our listeners to hear and understand. To speak precisely, we should use concrete language rather than abstract language, and we should make certain we include accurate details in our descriptions.

Abstract language is broad and general, while concrete language is specific and exact. When we fail to use concrete language, our audience will have a hard time grasping and visualizing what we are talking about. This lack of comprehension can be especially true when we are telling illustrations. Consider the drastic difference, for example, between saying, "The farmer had very little," and saying, "The only thing Farmer McGillis had to his name was a broken down and dried up Jersey cow named Bessie, who stood out in a barren pasture every day, searching for just one blade of grass to chew." Now, one might argue that the second description is too elaborate or extravagant. This much is undeniable, though: it paints a precise and vivid picture in the mind of the listener, which the first description fails to do. Precise language engages the imagination.

Precision also requires getting our facts straight. If you want to use the illustration of the football player who mistakenly ran the ball the wrong way all the way up the field, gather the details. A quick Internet search will reveal that the player was Roy "Wrong Way" Riegels, that he played for the University of California, Berkeley, football team, that his team was playing Georgia Tech in the 1929 Rose Bowl, that he was just 30 yards away from scoring when he somehow got turned around and ran 65 yards in the wrong direction, that he was tackled at the three-yard line by his own teammate, Benny Lom, that Georgia Tech scored a safety for a 2-0 lead, and that Riegels had to be talked into returning to the game for the second half. Those types of details grab the attention of your audience and keep their interest in your message. With search engines, Bible software programs, and other research tools at our disposal, there is no reason for preachers not to find the precise details and to get them right.

Clarity

Clarity in style is the act of making our meaning plain and simple. Speaking with clarity involves "speaking in such a way that no reader or hearer can misunderstand."[4]

Clarity depends on presenting cogent ideas in a logical manner.[5] Clear messages have an unmistakable main idea and several points that are easy to identify and follow. When a message is clear, everyone listening should have a good idea of where the preacher is in his message, where he is headed, and what his over-arching theme is. Outlining your message clearly is important in achieving the goal of clarity, but it is equally important to communicate the outline plainly when you are preaching.

Good transitions help make the message clear to your listeners. Tell them when you are moving from point to point. Enumerate your points so that your listeners know how many there are. At each transition from one point to another, also remind your audience of your main idea. These simple procedures can make a tremendous difference in helping your listeners follow the logic and flow of your message.

Clear messages also use plain language. As much as possible, rid your messages of unexplained theological terminology, spiritual jargon, and elevated vocabulary. If you have a choice between a simple word and an obscure word, and if both terms communicate essentially the same idea, choose the simple word every time. According to Jo Sprague, Douglas Stuart, and David Bodary, "the clear speaker is more like the sharp-shooter who takes careful aim and makes every word count."[6] The most helpful and beloved preachers are the ones who make concepts in God's Word clear to the listener.

---

4.   John A. Broadus, *On the Preparation and Delivery of Sermons*, 4th ed., ed. Vernon L. Stanfield (New York: Harper and Rowe, 1979), 210.
5.   William H. Kooienga, *Elements of Style for Preaching*, The Craft of Preaching Series (Grand Rapids: Zondervan, 1989), 63.
6.   Jo Sprague, Douglas Stuart, and David Bodary, *The Speaker's Handbook* (Boston: Wadworth, 2010), 260.

If you are unable to explain a biblical concept simply, you may not understand it completely yourself.

Energy

Effective preachers learn to speak with force. Forcefulness does not simply mean speaking loudly or being dictatorial in the pulpit. Instead, it means using personal, direct, and sensate language to communicate with your listeners.

Personal language creates energy. A preacher who speaks in the third person most of the time will wind up sounding remote and distant to his audience. For example, saying, "A Christian should demonstrate love to his fellow man," is not nearly as powerful as saying, "If you are a Christian, you'll show love for the people around you." Using the words "you" and "we" makes messages more immediate and applicable. William Kooienga notes that using "you" shortens the distance between the speaker and the listener.[7] As a word of caution, be careful to refrain from using "you" in an accusatory way. A good rule of thumb is to say "you" when your comments are encouraging and uplifting, and to say "we" when your message includes correction or rebuke.

Direct and active language is more forceful than passive language. In a sentence written in the active voice, the subject does the action of the verb. In a sentence written in the passive voice, the subject receives the action. "He was run over by the bus," has a verbal phrase in the passive voice. "The bus ran him over," has a verb in the active voice. Generally, sentences with the passive voice are less energetic than ones with the active voice. As much as possible, seek to use the active voice when you are preaching.

Sensate language arouses the emotions and invites your listeners to imagine details. Use language that appeals to your audience's sense of sight, touch, taste, hearing, and smell. By using sensate terms, you will maintain the interest of your listeners, and you will make your message more memorable.

---

7. Kooienga, *Elements of Style for Preaching*, 102.

Beauty

Beauty is the element of style that makes the message pleasing to the ear. Figurative language can be a powerful tool to enhance the beauty and artfulness of your sermon. Following are some figures of speech and stylistic devices that can enliven your language.[8]

1. *Simile* makes a comparison between two things that are otherwise dissimilar, usually using the words "like" or "as." Isaiah used simile when he wrote these lines : "Though your sins are like scarlet, / They shall be as white as snow; / Though they are red like crimson, / They shall be as wool (Isa 1:18 NKJV).

2. *Metaphor* creates an equation that implies two unlike things are the same. The words of Jesus, "Most assuredly, I say to you, I am the door of the sheep" (John 10:7 NKJV), are a metaphor.

3. *Personification* imbues ideas or objects with the qualities of human beings. The book of Proverbs personifies wisdom as a woman, stating, "Wisdom calls aloud outside; / She raises her voice in the open squares" (Prov 1:20 NKJV).

4. *Hyperbole* overstates something in order to make a point. When Jesus said, "It is easier for a camel to go through the eye of a needle than for a rich man to enter the kingdom of God" (Mark 10:25), He was using hyperbole.

5. *Repetitive language* makes listeners feel that the ideas you are presenting are snowballing to a logical conclusion. Psalm 118 repeats the phrase, "His mercy endures forever," several times in order to drive home the main idea that the psalmist is communicating.

6. *Antithesis* contrasts two ideas in order to dramatize the difference. This pattern is the one that Jesus used in the Sermon on the Mount when He said, "You have heard that it was said to those of old, 'You shall not commit adultery.' But I say to you that whoever looks at a woman to lust for her has already committed adultery with her in his heart" (Matt 5:27–29 NKJV). The contrast between "you have heard . . ." and "but I say . . ." creates antithesis.

Look for way to beautify your message so that the sermon has some degree of artistry and aesthetic appeal. Through practice and attention over a period of time, preachers can learn to use

---

8.   This summary of figures of speech and stylistic devices is only a brief synopsis of what we covered earlier in section 1 on hermeneutics.

figures of speech naturally in their speech, even when preaching extemporaneously.

Naturalness

A natural preaching style is one that sounds like normal speech rather than sounding stiff, contrived, or artificial. Although there is a performance aspect to preaching, delivering a sermon is not a mere performance, and the preacher is not playing a part. Instead, what we say from the pulpit and the way we say it should flow naturally from our personality.

A conversational preaching style emphasizes naturalness. Wayne McDill notes that a conversational style does not mean using a style that is chatty, light, or of little importance. Instead, the emphasis is on natural, or normal, communication with the listeners. He makes these observations: "The conversational style is simply the preacher's natural manner. This means that the preacher uses his normal way of talking in the pulpit, enlarging his expression as necessary to reach his audience."[9]

Conversational preaching aims to use the natural cadences of normal speech rather than high oratory and flowery eloquence. Conversational preaching allows for a wide variety of expression, similar to how we express numerous emotions in one-on-one conversations, and often do so with great passion. Because this style of preaching also is dialogical, it feeds on the interplay between the preacher and the audience during the preaching event.[10]

Broadus and Stanfield, who advocate using a conversational style in preaching, also caution against preaching with a "casual, not to say careless conversational style."[11] While a preacher should deliver his sermons as one person talking to another person, "there are

---

9.   Wayne McDill, *The Moment of Truth: A Guide to Effective Sermon Delivery* (Nashville: B&H, 1999), 119.
10. We note this preaching style is currently a popular one in the United States of America. We would also note that the popularity of a particular preaching style ebbs and flows over time.
11. Broadus, *On the Preparation and Delivery of Sermons*, 207.

levels of conversation, and the pulpit is not a park bench, nor is the subject the weather."[12]

STRENGTHENING YOUR PREACHING STYLE

Several guidelines can help you improve your style and incorporate the elements of effective style we have discussed in your preaching.

1. *Prepare your message to be heard rather than to be read.* Often, the sermon manuscript or notes are prepared as written documents rather than oral documents. Oral style uses repetition to remind the listener of important concepts, has the rhythm and sound of conversational speech, and favors short, simple sentences over longer and more complex sentences. Writing your message in an oral style will help you communicate with greater naturalness in the pulpit.[13]

2. *Use personal pronouns often in your preaching.* Especially when you are making application, keep your message in the first person plural (we, us) or the second person (you). Doing so gives your message a greater sense of immediacy and force.

3. *Read and listen widely to develop good models for style.* If you spend the bulk of your time reading commentaries, works on theology, or even preaching textbooks like this one, your language may wind up being dry and stale. Read other contemporary preachers to see how they express God's truth in their messages. Listen to gifted communicators. Reading popular magazines and even novels also can help you learn to use figures of speech and add variety and spice to your language.[14]

---

12. Ibid.
13. Wilbur Ellsworth, *The Power of Speaking God's Word* (Ross-shire, Great Britain: Christian Focus Publications, 2000). Ellsworth takes a technical look at orality and preaching. While not agreeing at every point, you will certainly benefit from reading his work. G. Robert Jacks, *Just Say the Word: Writing for the Ear* (Grand Rapids: Eerdmans, 1996) is also helpful on this subject.
14. A work that addresses this very issue is T. David Gordon, *Why Johnny Can't Preach* (Phillipsburg: P&R, 2009). The reason men cannot preach today, Gordon observes, is two-fold: they cannot read or write. In many ways, societal changes in communication are largely a contributor to this problem, but the ultimate responsibility falls on the preacher of God's Word. Gordon proposes a three-fold solution: (1) Arrange for an annual review of your preaching by the church. (2) Cultivate the sensibility of reading a text closely. (3) Cultivate the sensibility of composed communication [i.e., writing well] (95–12).

4. *Be ready to adapt your style to your audience and setting.* Skill as a communicator means being able to bring a timely message in the right way, no matter what kind of audience you are addressing. As a preacher of the gospel, you should not be content in just "being yourself" without respect to your audience or speaking situation. A situation such as a funeral, a graduation, or a worship service in a more formal church calls for a formal approach in the pulpit. Speaking to the college group on Wednesday night calls for a more relaxed presentation. Addressing the children at summer camp will require a still different choice of words and structure. In every circumstance, you can connect with your audience by adapting your style. As Paul well reminds us, "Be ready in season and out of season" (2 Tim 4:2 NKJV).

CHAPTER 28

PREACHING TO THE PEOPLE IN FRONT OF YOU

One mark of an effective preacher is that he connects his message to the people who sit in front of him. He does not preach to people who are not there or to people as he wishes they were. Instead, he delivers the message so that those who are actually listening can understand, appreciate, and respond. Preaching to the people in front of you requires asking questions like these: *Who are my listeners? What are they looking for in my message? How are they receiving what I say?* These questions look simple and straightforward, but they are actually very tricky to answer. We have learned that how you think the listener is responding to your preaching may not be the case at all.

One preacher was speaking for the first time in a small church that featured an unusual layout in its auditorium. The normal configuration of pews had been put in front of the platform, and then two pews had been placed on either side of the stage, so that people sitting in those seats had a side view of the preacher. Everyone in the congregation was sitting in front of the platform, except for one solitary, rather large, muscular man. He sat by himself in one of the pews along the side, with his arms folded, his brow furrowed, and his lips twisted into a sort of half snarl. He looked as though he may have been the meanest, angriest man in the world at the beginning of the sermon, and he only looked meaner as the message wore on.

If you have preached even once or twice, you know that an inner conversation goes on in the head of the preacher the entire time he is speaking. That unspoken, intrapersonal communication inside the mind includes the preacher telling himself what is next in the sermon, debating over whether the word he is about to use is the best one, and interpreting audience response. During that message, the preacher's mental dialogue was dominated by one subject: that man sitting just a few feet from him. Here is a rough transcript of that internal discussion:

Who is this guy? Why does he look so angry? He must not like what I'm talking about. Maybe he doesn't like me personally. How could that be, when we've never even met? Maybe I remind him of someone he despises from his childhood. What can I do? Maybe if I tell a funny story . . . no, that didn't work either. I'm dying out here. If I don't look at him, maybe I'll forget he's there. Rats! I can't keep from looking at him! Could it be that Satan has incarnated himself and come to hear me preach tonight? Lord, please deliver me!

The inner conversation went on like that through the entire message, as the preacher did his best to focus on the rest of the audience, to concentrate on the content of the Scripture he was expounding, to remember his points, to rely on the working of the Holy Spirit, and somehow to keep from being distracted by the angry-looking man in his peripheral vision. After the services were over, the preacher stood at the back door of the little church, shaking hands with the members of the congregation as they filed out. There, near the back of the line, was the man who had sat on that side pew. When he took the preacher's hand, the big man could barely speak. Instead, he blubbered through tears that were streaming down his face.

"Pastor," he said, "that message was just what I needed. You'll never know how God used you in my life tonight. Thank you, brother, thank you." With that, the tears overcame the man to the point that he could no longer speak. He hugged the preacher tightly and then walked away from the church, wiping his eyes with the blue bandana he had pulled from his back pocket.

ANALYZING YOUR AUDIENCE

What is going on in your audience will always be something of a mystery. It is nearly impossible to know all the ins and outs about who the people in your audience are, how their backgrounds have affected their thinking and attitudes, where they are spiritually in their relationship with Jesus Christ, whether they understand the biblical truths you are proclaiming to them, and what they are thinking, feeling, and believing as the message unfolds.

Delivering a sermon effectively, however, requires understanding as much as you can about your audience. If they are not getting the message, then the sermon is a washout, no matter how well-intentioned and well-prepared it may be. Preachers must learn to analyze the audience—the collection of individuals gathered in front of him. Audience analysis includes the following criteria: size, demographics, interest, attitude, and spiritual condition.

The Audience's Size

Variations of size in your audience will require you to change the approach of your communication. You will discover that sermon delivery and material that communicates extremely well in a large audience can have the opposite effect when presented to a smaller audience.

For example, we have noticed that some funny stories almost always work better in larger groups and more crowded rooms. Because laughter tends to be contagious, a larger crowd seems to build its own momentum for humorous stories. So, if we are preaching to a smaller group or in a half-empty auditorium, we know that the humor we use is unlikely to produce the same effect that it does in larger places. Those contexts do not mean that the preacher should ditch all of the humorous stories from his sermon. It simply means that he should be prepared for a different kind of response, and then adjust accordingly.

Conversely, as audience size decreases, the preacher gains the advantage of being able to get specific feedback about the message. With a smaller group, you can ask and answer questions, check the listeners' attention more accurately, and then adapt your preaching to the feedback you receive. In a larger group, where you cannot see into the faces of all of your listeners, you may be left to guess whether they are comprehending your message or not.

The Audience's Demographics

Demographics involve characterizing your audience in terms of certain variables. While assuming all people in a particular demographic group think, behave, and listen in the same way is naïve, the preacher should be aware that demographic characteristics can affect the audience's response. Following are four important questions to ask regarding demographics:

1. *What is the age range and age distribution of my audience?* Younger people tend to be more idealistic. They are strongly influenced by the values of their peers; usually like faster-paced, fluidly organized messages; and appreciate the use of a diversity of communication tools. Older listeners may prefer hearing sermons organized in a more linear structure and delivered in a slower, more deliberate manner. Because they have a greater stake in the status quo, they tend to be more resistant to calls for change.

2. *What is the gender breakdown of my audience?* While men and women have increasingly grown closer together in the way they receive messages, on some subjects, men and women may desire a slightly different approach in the sermon. Men tend to prefer a persuasive intent in the messages they receive. Women often desire an attitude of negotiation and sharing as they listen to a preacher.[1]

3. *What is the educational and socioeconomic level of my audience?* In general, listeners with broader educations and more varied social experiences will be more open to new ideas. However, they will also tend to argue mentally with the preacher, raising silent objections to the points you make in your message. Those in the audience who are not as educated will be less likely to object to your message, but they will be more likely to cling to previously held ideas. From a persuasive standpoint, dealing with a predominantly blue-collar audience as compared to a more professional group presents a separate

---

1. For a book that looks at this issue, see Alice Matthews, *Preaching that Speaks to Women* (Grand Rapids: Baker, 2003).

challenge. Knowing the educational and social levels of your audience also will help you decide how to explain concepts from the biblical text, what level of vocabulary is best suited for the sermon, what types of illustrations to use, and what the direction of the message's application should be.

4. *What ethnic and cultural groups are represented in my audience, and what is the proportion?* One of the most encouraging things about the twenty-first-century church is that local congregations are becoming more ethnically and racially varied. Ethnic and cultural distinctions among your audience members most likely will cause them to differ in their understandings about what preaching should accomplish and differ in their preferences in communication. Different congregational cultures may show distinct preferences regarding how long the sermon should be, whether the message should be more instructive or more emotional, and how the sermon should be delivered.

The Audience's Interest

Your audience's interest level affects the way you should approach the preaching of your message. The audience's interest can be classified in the following categories:

The *casual audience* has almost no unified attention in the subject matter. Teenagers at a youth event or a passerby on the sidewalk in a street preaching context are examples of casual audiences. The major task in addressing such an audience is gaining attention.

The *passive audience* consists of listeners who are listening because circumstances dictate that they must. A congregation at a funeral or a wedding is an example, as well as an audience for such times as Easter, Christmas, or Mother's Day, when societal and family expectations may require church attendance from those who are normally disinterested. The preacher must gain the passive audience's interest in his subject matter.

The *selected audience* is gathered for a reason that is important to them. They have a greater interest to receive the message the preacher is communicating than the causal and passive audiences do. The normal Sunday morning crowd would be most like a selected audience. The preacher should make an impression on these listeners and motivate them.

In a *concerted audience*, a great majority of the listeners are interested in accomplishing a task and have enthusiasm for the speaker and his subject matter. A deacon body and a church council would be examples of concerted audiences. The preacher's job here is to persuade the listeners and lay out a plan.

Finally, the *organized audience* is a group over which the speaker has considerable influence or even a degree of control. In the secular world, military units and athletic teams are organized audiences. The pastor's staff and most motivated lay leaders would be typical organized audiences in the church setting. When addressing an organized audience, the preacher's task is primarily to direct the listeners' actions.

Understanding your audience's interest level will help you determine what kind of material to include in the message, the style of communication to use, and the way to organize the message. For the most part, we find it best to assume that the typical congregation falls somewhere on the spectrum between passive and concerted. That means that the majority of our listeners have a motivation to be in church, worshipping God and hearing the Bible proclaimed, but they may be rather passive in terms of their interest in the specific subject we are addressing. Therefore, we should design our sermons to get listeners' attention, address real needs in their lives, proclaim the message of the biblical text, and then call listeners to faith and obedience based on the central truth of the message.

The Audience's Attitude

Listeners in your audience will fall into one of three stances in relationship to you and your message. Many will be *favorable,* that is, they will already agree with most of what you are saying and will feel good about you. Your goal, then, will be to reinforce their positive attitude, to deepen their commitment to and understanding of the truth they already believe, and to encourage them to act on that commitment.

Others in the audience will be *indifferent.* They will not have made up their minds about the subject of your message. This attitude usually means that listeners simply need more information and instruction.

Some listeners will be *opposed* to your message. They will disagree with the basics of what you are saying. Often, they disagree because they have a lifestyle that conflicts with your message's content. Sometimes members of the audience will be opposed simply because they are not favorable to you as a speaker. When addressing an opposed audience, the speaker aims to find common ground if possible, to address objections, and to present himself as a person of good will.

Often, the listeners' attitudes in today's audience will be profoundly influenced by a post-modern way of thinking about truth. Graham Johnston offers the following distinctives as some of the hallmarks of post-modern people: rejection of objective truth, skepticism and suspicion toward authority, a search for self-identity, blurred morality and expediency, a desire for the transcendent, media saturation, a quest for community, and a constant exposure to materialism.[2]

The preacher must recognize that his audience interacts nearly every waking hour with a worldview that is often diametrically opposed to the message of the Bible. In order to gain a hearing and to meet our listeners' need for understanding, we must give consideration for what their attitudes are and how the biblical message communicates to them.

The Audience's Spiritual Condition

In addition to assessing the audience by the other measurements mentioned, Christian preachers must also consider very carefully the spiritual condition of the people to whom they deliver their messages. The way listeners receive the message we preach depends greatly on whether they have a relationship with Jesus Christ and whether they are growing in that relationship.

At the most elementary level, only two kinds of people live in the world—those who are lost and those who are saved. Jerry Vines and Jim Shaddix make this observation: "Although many passages of Scripture address issues that are equally applicable to believers and

---

2.   Graham Johnston, *Preaching to a Postmodern World* (Grand Rapids: Baker, 2001), 26.

unbelievers, most texts address either the people of God or unregenerate mankind. The preacher must be very clear in his mind regarding the primary audience of his particular text."[3]

As you think about the people in front of you, consider which preaching opportunities should be more oriented toward unbelievers and which should be geared toward the gospel needs of Christians. Remember that the ratio between Christians and non-Christians changes with the season of the year and the different services of the week, even when you are preaching in the same location.

Within the regenerate portion of your audience, there are believers who are obeying God while others are living far from Him. Some are stagnating in their spiritual lives, while others are growing. The application you make in the message and the way you present the truths of Scripture should be, to some extent, determined by the spiritual status and maturity of those who listen to your sermon. But, again, remember that the gospel speaks to and meets the deepest and most genuine needs of believers and unbelievers alike. As Dennis Johnson says, following the insights of Tim Keller, "what both the unbeliever and the believer need to hear in preaching is the gospel, with its implications for life lived in confident gratitude in response to amazing grace."[4]

WHAT OUR LISTENERS NEED

Frank Harrington, who served for 27 years as the senior pastor of Peachtree Presbyterian Church in Atlanta, Georgia, offered an insightful observation about preachers and their audiences. He said audiences significantly influence preachers: "Great people encourage great preaching. Many people say that the preacher makes the church, but the very opposite is true. The church makes the preacher. I have been encouraged immensely by members of this church to go into the pulpit and preach what God has laid on my heart."[5] Identifying

3.   Jerry Vines and Jim Shaddix, *Power in the Pulpit* (Chicago: Moody, 1999), 128.
4.   Dennis Johnson, *Him We Proclaim: Preaching Christ from All the Scriptures* (Phillipsburg: P&R, 2007), 55. Keller's preaching may be accessed at "The Redeemer Sermon Store" at sermons.redeemer.com/store.
5.   Quoted in Michael Duduit, *Conversations on Preaching* (Franklin, TN: Preaching Press, 2004), 11.

the needs of your congregation and designing your communication to connect with those needs can make your preaching stronger, more lifelike, and more relevant. Consider three major needs that our listeners have and how we can respond to those needs.

Listening. People in the audience want to be heard. They need a preacher who is thinking about their questions, identifying their struggles, considering their opinions, and paying attention to their feelings. When you are off the platform and out of the pulpit, look for ways to get to know who your people are and what they are thinking and experiencing. While a preacher may be tempted to think of the sermon as one-way communication, the listener craves interactive openness. The message must be designed to draw out a response, either inward or overt. Include elements in your delivery of the message that engage the listener and require them to interact—even if only nonverbally—with the truth you are proclaiming.

Contribution. Many listeners have a heartfelt longing not just to take up space in the auditorium but to make a difference in God's kingdom. They should be made to understand that the church–both in its local and global expressions—needs them and offers them a place to use their abilities. Consider what "takeaways" you can include in the sermon's application. Also, occasionally include action responses for your audience while you are preaching the message. For instance, one preacher talked about feeding the hungry, and dismissed the congregation early so that they could go buy grocery items to supply local food pantries for the poor. Another preacher asked his congregation to take off their shoes and leave them at church as part of a drive to provide shoes for the homeless. These simple acts of contribution make a lasting impression on the listener.

Hope. Often listeners are experiencing a discouraging and unpromising life situation. Listeners desire someone who cares that they are listening and who values their presence. They deserve a message worth hearing, a sermon that is carefully prepared as well as skillfully and passionately delivered. Moreover, they want to see possibilities beyond their present as the preacher proclaims how faith in God has transformed both his own life and the lives of others. They need a word from God. As God's man, you must be faithful to give it to them.

CHAPTER 29

PREACHING WITH VISUAL APPEAL

P owerPoint presentations that are out of sync with the sermon outline, video clips that malfunction and misfire, corny or histrionic dramas in which the actors have not learned their parts, and object lessons that require more explanation than the meaning of the scriptural passage are several real-life, all-too-common examples of why we were tempted to leave this chapter out altogether and advise you to just preach your sermon. Do not use video. Do not use drama. Do not use computer presentations. Do not use an object lesson. Just stand with a Bible in your hands and preach your message.

However, we have resisted that temptation and have written this chapter for two compelling reasons:

1. Preachers today (including your authors) are almost unquestionably going to use visual support in their messages and need some guiding principles for using it well.
2. Although there are major pitfalls to avoid, visuals in the message can enhance and enrich the verbal content of the sermon when employed skillfully.

It is inescapably true that preachers must communicate visually. Our listeners, especially in the United States of America, are used to seeing visual support for the verbal content they are hearing. When we watch the news on television, visuals always accompany verbal messages. When we surf the Internet, we have words and pictures to help us understand the information we are receiving.

People have different learning styles and preferences that we need to consider in our delivery. Rick Blackwood cites a research study of 1,500 adults who had dropped out of school in the eighth grade. Nearly 100 percent of the study subjects were "sensing-dominant" learners, who needed visuals and interaction to help them learn and understand. On the other end of the educational scale, researchers discovered that 83 percent of a group of finalists for National Merit Scholarships were intuitive type learners who relied on visuals.[1] So, every segment of our audience has a tremendous need for visual images to help listeners comprehend, understand, and remember our message.

Biblical preachers have often used visual images to enhance their message. For instance, Matt 18:2–4 says that Jesus placed a child in the midst of the people to whom He was speaking, and then said, "unless you are converted and become as little children, you will by no means enter the kingdom of heaven" (NKJV). The Lord instructed Jeremiah to make bonds and yokes and to put them on his neck in order to illustrate that He would bring the nations deliverance through submission to Babylon. Jeremiah used this visual illustration—a prop, really—as he proclaimed a message to several different kings (see Jer 27:1–7).

Before we begin examining the various tools and methods preachers can use to enhance the visual appeal of their message, it is important to note that communicating visually does not mean only using external visual aids in the message. In many ways, the preacher himself is a one-person, multimedia event. Consider all of the different media that you use when you simply stand in front of a group of people to preach. You are using sound as you speak. You are using visuals as you gesture and move. You are using the written word as you have them read along with you in their own Bibles. You may even use drama as you act out portions of the biblical narrative or tell your stories. While putting pictures on a screen or showing video clips can be effective, preachers would do well to remember that describing something clearly and imaginatively or telling a story with vivid imagery and sensate language can create a visual image in the listener's mind. In fact, when your listeners imagine a

---

1. Rick Blackwood, *The Power of Multi-sensory Preaching and Teaching* (Grand Rapids: Zondervan, 2008), 71. This source covers all the information from this paragraph.

scene as you are describing it to them, your description may make a deeper and more lasting impact on them because they have taken the effort to construct the images in their own minds.

USING PRESENTATION SOFTWARE

Certain equipment used to be standard in a church auditorium. A church building would almost always have platform furniture, pews, a choir loft, and a pulpit. These days, a church auditorium may or may not have any of the aforementioned items. Nearly every new church, however, will be outfitted with video screens and some sort of projection system. Video projection has become very widely used in our worship services, and graphics generated by programs such as PowerPoint, Keynote, Impress, or some other presentation software have become more common than hymnals and pew Bibles.

Presentation software has made many positive contributions to modern worship. In our estimation, having images and words projected on screens accomplishes the following: (1) It aids in congregational singing and praise by getting peoples' noses out of their hymnbooks so that their eyes are up and their voices project more loudly and joyfully. (2) It makes transitions between musical elements more smooth, since the music leader no longer has to instruct people to turn from page to page in their hymnals or shuffle through the pages of a printed set of lyrics. (3) It unifies the congregation during the reading of Scripture, since everyone is able to read from the same words, in the same version of the Bible, and at the same time. (4) It helps the preacher communicate the main idea and the points of his sermon clearly, with visual as well as oral support of the sermon content. (5) It facilitates the preacher's use of cross-references without his having to laboriously instruct the congregation to turn from one passage to another.

Along with these helpful aspects of presentation programs, there are a number of negative features and potential dangers: (1) Having the Scripture verses on the screen could discourage listeners from bringing their Bibles or following the message in their own copies of God's Word. (2) The images on the screens can distract the audience from listening to the preacher. (3) In venues where the preacher's magnified image is projected on large screens, even listeners seated

Using Presentation Programs Well

1. *Design and develop the sermon first.* An unclear main idea and outline will not be made better by the addition of flashy graphics, animations, and creative typefaces. The preacher should skillfully design and develop his sermon *before* he works on a computer presentation.
2. *Use images to communicate.* Because of computer presentation programs the preacher can easily integrate photos, illustrations, and other images into the delivery of his sermon. These images create visual metaphors that tend to embed themselves into the memories and hearts of our listeners.
3. *Aim for simplicity rather than impressiveness.* Dramatic transitions and striking animations become overused in a very short time. Simple but clear presentations are almost always better. Choose color schemes and typefaces that are easy to read and pleasing to the eyes.
4. *Limit words per slide and slides per presentation.* Twenty-five words are about the maximum that you should place on a single slide. More words cause the type to become too small for listeners to read easily and make the screen look cluttered. Presenting 12 to 15 slides per program is also a good rule of thumb. If it is longer than that, the presentation can become the "star of the show," overshadowing the rest of the preaching event.
5. *Do it well, or do not do it at all.* For a video presentation to be effective, it needs to be artfully designed and skillfully presented. A pastor's congregation or his staff usually includes people who are gifted in putting together appealing and effective presentations. A wise preacher will ask for the assistance of these individuals. In the preaching event itself, the computer operator must be trained to follow the message carefully, so that the graphics appear on the screen at the right time. A poorly executed presentation is much worse than no presentation at all.
6. *Do not use it as a crutch.* Preachers need to know how to communicate the structure and flow of their messages orally, so

that the audience can follow the logic of the message simply by hearing. Even when you use a computer presentation, be careful to communicate the main idea and major points of your message clearly.

7. *Think about what to leave out.* We know some preachers who deliberately omit a couple of Scripture passages from the presentation, knowing they will read these verses in the sermon. They reason that doing so will keep their listeners in the habit of following along in their own Bibles.[2]

near the platform will tend to watch the screens rather than interacting with the preacher himself. (4) Video projection of the preacher creates a mediated version of the pastor, which can separate him from the congregation to some degree and make him seem larger than life. (5) Poorly designed presentations can make the message more confusing rather than helping the pastor communicate it. (6) When presentations are not presented seamlessly and accurately, they can greatly distract the listener. (7) Because presentation programs are so widely used now in classrooms and business settings, listeners may grow tired of seeing them, and may be less likely to pay attention to them.

While today's preachers will almost inevitably use presentation software to some extent, preachers must understand how to use PowerPoint or other similar software programs in a way that maximizes the communication power of their messages. Below are some guidelines for using presentation programs.

---

2. Some material adapted from Kenton Anderson, "In the Eye of the Hearer," in *Art and Craft of Biblical Preaching: A Comprehensive Resource for Today's Communicators*, ed. Haddon W. Robinson and Craig B. Larson (Grand Rapids: Zondervan, 2005), 607–9.

Before moving away from our discussion of using presentation programs, we must note that many preachers today are combining low-tech presentation formats with computer-generated graphics with great effectiveness. Writing your points on a blackboard or whiteboard, giving people handouts to follow, or even using an overhead projector and transparencies may create a retro, handmade feel in your delivery that is refreshingly different from the slicker presentations to which our listeners have grown accustomed.

PLAYING VIDEO CLIPS

Screens and projection systems used for presentation software also allow the preacher to use videos to support his message. Videos are forms of illustrative material and should be chosen by using the same guidelines a preacher would use for selecting other illustrations in the sermon. The best video illustrations fit the idea the preacher is communicating. Referring to an illustration that does not quite match the concept being presented in the sermon, John Koessler, a preacher and a professor, makes this observation: "It fits the sermon like those baggy jeans on a teenage boy. Increasingly, we're hearing video clips as illustrations. Some work very well, but they tend to be general; sometimes I wonder what a pastor was doing watching that film."[3]

Some video clips may come from films or television programs. Others may be produced by companies that create video illustrations exclusively for use in sermons. These videos are readily available for download via the Internet. Preachers also may make their own videos to use in their sermons. Filming parts of the sermon at home, on the mission field, or in some other location can keep the message fresh and add excitement to it.

One preacher made a powerful use of video by having two sets of rolling numbers appear on video screens throughout his message. One number represented the people dying worldwide without a relationship with Christ, with three dying per second. The other

---

3.   John Koessler, quoted in Lee Eclov, "Lessons from *Preaching Today* Screeners," in *Art and Craft of Biblical Preaching*, 706.

number tallied the people dying in the United States without Jesus, with one person dying every 15 seconds. By the end of the message, the video screens displayed hundreds who had died without Christ in the United States, and thousands who had died around the globe. The video served as a constant illustration of lostness as the pastor preached his message.

Following are some guidelines for using video clips in the message.

Using Videos Well

1. *Obey the law.* Do not use a video clip from a copyrighted work without getting the consent of the owner. To do so is dishonest and unethical. If you plan to use copyrighted video material, get permission to use it, and pay any fees required. If you are not willing to obtain consent and pay for the use of the video, you do not need to use the video.

2. *Short videos are best.* Just as with an illustration you would relay verbally, a video that requires extensive explanation or that goes on too long is not the best material to use in the message. About two or three minutes is long enough.

3. *Integrate the video smoothly into the message.* Few things are more awkward or distracting in a sermon than a preacher trying to show a video, only to have it miscued or to have the video equipment malfunction. As with computer presentations, if you cannot do it well, it is better not to show a video at all. A good rule of thumb is that you should be able to segue into a video element of your message as seamlessly as you would transition into telling a story in your sermon.

4. *Do not show a clip from a film you could not totally endorse.* When you show a video clip from a movie, you are implying, to a great extent, that you, as a man of God entrusted to shepherd His people, approve of all of the film's content. It may seem like a hackneyed sentiment, but if you would not want Jesus to go with you to see the movie you are showing, do not show it in His church. We believe it is best not to

use clips from movies that use profanity, deal with sexual themes, or feature excessive or graphic violence. If you have any doubt at all about a clip, you are better off just not showing it. Remember this advice: when in doubt, don't!

5. *Beware of overusing video.* Any time you direct your listeners to watch a video in a sermon, you are losing precious time to interact with them personally. We have noticed that when audiences are viewing videos, they tend to go into "TV mode" and actually may become less engaged in the message. Watching multiple videos in a message, or even watching a video every week, can become tiresome for your audience after a while.[4]

PREACHING WITH PROPS AND OBJECT LESSONS

Object lessons and props are simple and yet offer an extremely effective means of communicating visually with your audience. While we often associate object lessons with children's sermons, they are actually more suited to messages for grown-ups. Children often have a hard time connecting the object with the lesson, whereas adults enjoy making those mental connections. Props may not actually teach an analogical lesson, but they do help the listeners visualize something the preacher is describing verbally. Additionally, artwork such as paintings and photographs can be extremely powerful in getting the attention of the audience and communicating a message. Here are some guidelines for using props and object lessons.

---

4. Some material has been adapted from Kenton Anderson, "In the Eye of the Hearer," in *Art and Craft of Biblical Preaching*, 607–9.

Guidelines for Props and Object Lessons

1. *Use props and objects sparingly.* When preachers use object lessons every week, the effectiveness is greatly diminished. One can almost hear the audience asking, "I wonder what he is going to pull out of the box this time?" It's better to use objects only once in a while.
2. *Consider when the audience will see the prop.* Sometimes a preacher creates curiosity and a sense of intrigue by having an unexplained object on the platform throughout the message, and then finally telling the audience why the prop is there. Other times, it might be better to hide the object until you are ready to talk about it in the sermon.
3. *Make sure your audience can see the object.* Especially in large places, it is important to consider how large the object needs to be or how you should display it so that everyone can see it.
4. *Always connect the dots.* Object lessons are analogies. The preacher must never assume that the listener sees the relationship between the object and the truth he is presenting. Make the connection clear. The words "in the same way" are always helpful in doing this.

DRAMA IN WORSHIP

Live drama on the platform can communicate powerfully to the audience and can help set the stage for the truths that the preacher will present in the message. We find that the best time for drama is usually either right before the sermon begins or at an earlier point in time in the worship service. Pastor Rick Blackwood offers the following characteristics of effective drama in worship.

Characteristics of Effective Drama

1. *Relevance.* The theme of the drama must connect to the message.
2. *Excellence.* Well-written scripts, extensive rehearsals, and skillful actors make drama effective. As with other visual elements, if drama is not done well, it should not be done at all.
3. *Engagement.* If a drama is not done well, it can become boring and disengaging. An amateurish or poorly prepared drama is embarrassing to everyone involved, including the audience.
4. *Creativity.* Drama should be characterized by variety and freshness. Avoid using the same type of drama over and over again.
5. *Seamlessness.* The preacher, actors, and other worship leaders should be prepared to transition smoothly from other worship elements to the drama.[5]

---

5.   Blackwood, *The Power of Multi-sensory Preaching,* 136–41.

CHAPTER 30

THE PREACHER'S PERSONAL LIFE AND PUBLIC BEHAVIOR

Nearly this entire book has focused on getting a message ready to preach. In this final chapter, we are addressing something even more important: preparing the preacher to preach. Warren Wiersbe and David Wiersbe observe that "In every part of his being—physical, mental, emotional, spiritual—the preacher must be a prepared vessel to contain, and then to share, the message of life."[1] As we consider the preacher's personal life and public behavior, we will discuss the importance of pursuing a strong walk with Christ and keeping the right attitude and demeanor toward ourselves, others, and the work of preaching. We will also discuss the importance of maintaining a professional and effective physical appearance and participating in public worship.

STRENGTHENING YOUR WALK WITH CHRIST[2]

In order to preach effectively and to live faithfully, a preacher must pursue a constant and growing fellowship with Jesus Christ. One

---

1. Warren Wiersbe and David Wiersbe. *The Elements of Preaching: The Art of Biblical Preaching Clearly and Simply Presented* (Wheaton, IL: Tyndale House, 1986), 19–20.
2. In this context, we enthusiastically commend the classic by J. Oswald Sanders, *Spiritual Leadership* (Chicago: Moody, 1967). See also Bill Bennett, "The

essential element in strengthening your walk with Christ is prayerful and personal study of the Bible. Paul instructed believers: "Let the word of Christ dwell in you richly in all wisdom" (Col 3:16 NKJV).

In this book, we have presented a Bible study methodology that will help you get at the core meaning of a passage of Scripture so that you can preach it to your people. We have found that the study we do for preaching is powerful not only in helping us prepare messages, but also in helping us grow spiritually.

Having said that, we also recommend that you read the Bible devotionally, that is, separately from your study for sermon preparation. Whether you are reading through the Bible in a year, journeying through a devotional guide with daily Scripture readings, or using some other plan for systematic feeding on God's Word, you need to spend time reading the Bible for your own spiritual growth.

Prayer is vital in your walk with Christ as well. A preacher was sitting in his study one afternoon, after having spent an hour in prayer and personal Bible study. As he was coming to the close of his devotional time, he was struck by a question. "What would happen," he wondered, "if I prayed more and did other things less?"

He began to think about the different activities of his day. What if he prayed more and read the newspaper or magazines or even the latest books on leadership or theology less? What if he prayed more and slept less? Or what might happen if he prayed more and watched television less?

That series of questions led him to another big question. He asked himself, "Is there any area of my life that would suffer if I prayed more?"

He began to examine his life. Would he be less effective as a pastor and teacher if he prayed more? Would he be less loving as a husband or less wise as a father if he prayed more? Would he be a lesser man or a less effective leader if he prayed more? Of course, the answer to every one of those questions was, "No."

Secret of Preaching with Power," in *Text-Driven Preaching,* ed. Daniel Akin, David Allen, and Ned Matthews (Nashville: B&H, 2010), and Ned Matthews, "The Disciplines of a Text-Driven Preacher," in *Text-Driven Preaching,* idem; Greg Heisler, *Spirit-Led Preaching* (Nashville: B&H, 2007); C. J. Mahaney, *Living the Cross-Centered Life* (Sisters, OR: Multnomah, 2006); David Platt, *Radical: Taking Back Your Faith from the American Dream* (Sisters, OR: Multnomah, 2010).

He recognized, as we are sure you just have, that no area of anyone's life would suffer as a result of more prayer. That day was a life-changing one for that preacher because it began him on a road of seeking God in prayer.

Prayer is indispensable for preaching because it is so essential for the Christian life itself. The Bible summarizes the prayer life of Jesus by saying that "He Himself often withdrew into the wilderness and prayed" (Luke 5:16 NKJV). Jesus was not haphazard in His approach to prayer. He deliberately and sacrificially set aside time to spend with the Father.

Mark records a specific prayer time in Jesus' life and ministry: "Now in the morning . . . a long while before daylight . . . He prayed" (Mark 1:35 NKJV). Jesus chose to pray before the rush of His day began. Jesus lived His life by prayer, ordered His ministry through prayer, and found great power in prayer. His preachers should do no less.

Haddon Robinson spoke of some of the occupational hazards of ministry: "The administrative load preoccupies pastors with scores of details that won't go away. Emotional weariness from dealing with people problems drains creative energies. And speaking several times weekly outstrips your capacity to assimilate truth fully into your life."[3] The way to combat fatigue and to bring perennial freshness to ministry in the service of God is through continual prayer and feeding on the Word of God.

A close walk with God brings His anointing and power into our lives and invites His blessing to our preaching ministry. As preachers and men of God, we should regularly ask ourselves some questions:

- Are we deliberately making time for prayer and Bible study, or are we giving God the time left over after all of our other daily business is done?
- Do we give God the best part of our day—when we have energy and a fresh mind with which to concentrate on Him—or are we praying and studying during the times when we are worn out?
- With all of the demands on our schedules in mind, how can we intentionally make time for God in our day?

---

3. Haddon Robinson, "Busting Out of Sermon Block," in *Art and Craft of Biblical Preaching: A Comprehensive Resource for Today's Communicators* (Grand Rapids: Zondervan, 2005), 535.

E. M. Bounds puts all of these questions in context:

> The Bible preacher prays. He is filled with the Holy Spirit, filled
> with God's Word, and filled with faith. He has faith in God; he
> has faith in God's only begotten Son, his personal Savior, and he
> has implicit faith in God's Word. He cannot do otherwise than
> pray. He cannot be other than a person of prayer. The breadth
> of his life and the pulsations of his heart are prayer. The Bible
> preacher lives by prayer, loves by prayer, and preaches by prayer.
> His bended knees in the place of secret prayer advertise what
> kind of preacher he is.[4]

KEEPING THE RIGHT ATTITUDE

Your attitude is the place where your personal life intersects with
your public behavior. Although we may try to hide it, our inner attitude eventually expresses itself in the words we say, the things we do,
and the ways we relate to people. For those who are called to preach,
a Christlike attitude will demonstrate itself in three directions.

First, we must have the right attitude about ourselves. The Bible
says, "Be clothed with humility, for 'God resists the proud, but gives
grace to the humble'" (1 Pet 5:5 NKJV).[5] Preachers should view themselves with genuine humility. Humility requires understanding how
holy God is and how sinful we are. It also requires placing the interests of others above our own.

There is a difference between insecurity and biblical humility.
When we lack confidence or focus on our personal inadequacies, we
are not demonstrating humility. Actually, we are displaying a subtle
form of pride and thinking unduly about ourselves. Another sign
of the absence of humility in our lives is arrogance. Preachers who
always look out for their own concerns, who do not regard others as
important, and who strut in the pulpit or insist on having their own
way demonstrate through their attitudes that they are not walking

---

4.   E. M. Bounds, "The Prayerlessness in the Pulpit," in *The Complete Works of
      E. M. Bounds on Prayer* (Grand Rapids: Baker, 1990), 414. When it comes to
      the discipline of prayer, few equal this man's passion and insights.
5.   Note this text follows immediately upon Peter's instructions to his fellow
      elders in 1 Pet 5:1–4.

with Christ. Godly humility will result in our placing supreme confidence in God to do through us what we cannot do on our own.

George Morrison, a Scottish pastor, reminds students preparing to preach, "Be good and true, be patient; be undaunted. Leave your usefulness for God to estimate. He will see to it that you do not live in vain."[6] The apostle Paul did this very thing, "Not that we dare to classify or compare ourselves with some of those who are commending themselves. But when they measure themselves by one another and compare themselves with one another, they are without understanding" (2 Cor 10:12 ESV). Our basis for comparison, as preachers, is not in relation to our fellow brothers in the ministry. We must seek to be pleasing to one person—the Lord Jesus Christ. When we compare ourselves to another and do not match up, we burn with envy, but when we compare ourselves to another and feel we are better, we glow with pride. Envy and pride fill the hearts of more homiletic students than they probably want to admit. Instead of boasting in our skills or moping because of our lack of skills, let us follow Paul, who gets to the heart of it all by saying, "'Let the one who boasts, boast in the Lord. For it is not the one who commends himself who is approved, but the one whom the Lord commends'" (2 Cor 10:17–18 ESV).[7]

Second, we must have the right attitude about our listeners. Paul's admonition, "Let this mind [or attitude] be in you which was also in Christ Jesus" (Phil 2:5 NKJV), was given in the context of instructing believers to put the interests of others above themselves. Wayne McDill offers a helpful contrast between having an exhortative stance toward the audience and having an adversarial one. A preacher with an adversarial stance accuses and scolds his listeners, setting himself up as their opponent. On the other hand, a preacher with an exhortative stance seeks to encourage the listeners, even when he brings words of challenge or rebuke. McDill makes this observation: "This stance brings you alongside your hearer rather than against him, exhorting him rather than accusing him."[8]

---

6. Quoted by Warren Wiersbe, "The Patented Preacher," in *The Art and Craft of Biblical Preaching*, 77.
7. For a wonderful treatment of this difficult virtue to cultivate, see C. J. Mahaney, *Humility: True Greatness* (Sisters, OR: Multnomah, 2005).
8. Wayne V. McDill, *The Moment of Truth: A Guide to Effective Sermon Delivery* (Nashville: B&H, 1999), 173.

Third, we must have the right attitude about preaching. The key to the right attitude is to understand the focus of preaching. Authentic preaching is centered on God, Jesus Christ, the Bible, and the listeners. The preacher should aim for an attitude that conveys this perspective: I am bringing a word from God, pointing the listener to faith in Him. I am preaching Jesus, the only power to save and change lives. I am preaching the biblical text, not my own ideas, and I am preaching with a heart of compassion for my audience and their needs.

In all of this, the preacher must remember that preaching is never about the preacher. A number of tell-tale signs indicate preacher-centered preaching. One sign is uncontrollable nervousness. A tinge of nervousness is both natural and helpful in preaching. Because we are speaking about the most important subject in the whole universe, we should enter the pulpit with a degree of fear and trembling. A certain amount of nervousness will animate and energize our sermon delivery. Uncontrollable nervousness, however, occurs when we are afraid of whether we will forget our message, how people will perceive us, and whether we will appear foolish before others. All of these fears are self-centered. If you struggle with uncontrollable stage fright, it may very well be an issue of whether you are placing your trust in yourself or in the Holy Spirit.

Another sign of self-centered preaching is frustration in the pulpit. In this case, the preaching event becomes an opportunity for the preacher to rant or to vent his emotions, rather than to bring a word from the Lord. Other signs can include preoccupation with performance and image, fear of offending the listener for the Gospel's sake, and a lack of self-forgetfulness on the platform. A preacher must have an attitude of servanthood and self-sacrifice as he relates to his audience. This type of attitude will move the preacher to adapt to his audience and to make any adjustment he can in order to preach God's Word to the listeners.

PROJECTING A GOOD PERSONAL APPEARANCE

Even before a preacher steps onto the platform to speak, the audience is already evaluating him to some degree on his physical condition, clothing, and grooming. While some might argue that judging a person on his personal appearance is grossly superficial, the way we look does, in fact, communicate who we are, how we think and feel about ourselves, and the way we regard our audience.

We will wisely refrain from dictating the exact type of clothes a preacher should wear in the pulpit. Those standards vary from congregation to congregation and from culture to culture, and they are changing constantly. Someone, though we cannot remember who, has factitiously defined "fashion" as that which is so unattractive that it must be changed each year. What was standard attire in one generation may become outdated and old-fashioned very quickly.

While we will not attempt to prescribe your wardrobe choices, some basic and timeless questions regarding your appearance as a preacher can guide you:

1. *Are you staying physically fit and watching your weight?* We recognize that this subject is touchy. Most adults struggle with their weight. For pastors, however, watching our weight and maintaining an exercise program are essential for several reasons. First, our weight dramatically affects our health. To ensure a long and energetic ministry, pastors should guard their weight. Second, the ministry is a great place to overeat. Most pastors feel that they are constantly being offered food or being asked out to dinner as part of their interaction with their congregation. Without carefully monitoring their intake and rigorously pursuing physical exercise, pastors will put on unwanted pounds. Third, obesity communicates negatively in the pulpit. It is also sinful in many cases. We will have a hard time convincing our audience to be disciplined in other areas if our lack of physical discipline is obvious. As an act of stewardship of our bodies, we should exercise regularly and eat sensibly.[9]

2. *Is your hair arranged in a pleasing way?* Whether you wear your hair in a buzz cut, spiked on top, parted on the side, or in some other style, keep it trimmed and combed neatly. As we get older, most men's hairlines recede at least slightly. Some men go bald on top or in the back. These changes may call for a new hairstyle. Combing over your hair across a bald spot almost always makes you look older, and perhaps a little out of touch with your appearance. A better choice is to cut the hair short and show the bald spot. Every

---

9. Jerry Vines and Jim Shaddix, *Power in the Pulpit* (Chicago: Moody, 1999), 78–81.

preacher needs to evaluate his hairstyle as he gets older to make sure it does not look dated or inappropriate to his age. Honoring what God has naturally given you is always the better choice. Do your best with what you have.

3. *Are you dressed appropriately for the occasion?* Every church has its own slightly nuanced congregational culture regarding appropriate dress for Sunday. Some churches are very intentionally casual. Others continue the tradition of wearing their "Sunday best." To a large extent, whom we are trying to reach and connect with will guide our clothing choices. The pastor should be sensitive so that he wears clothing appropriate for the place where he is preaching. If his church is largely a group whose men wear a suit and a tie, then the pastor probably will also wear a suit and tie, unless he is interested in changing that aspect of the church culture. If the church members wear casual clothes, the preacher will likely look out of place wearing a suit. Public speaking teachers advise that a speaker dress a little more formally than the average person in his audience. If, for instance, you are preaching to crowd who wears T-shirts and blue jeans, it is fine to wear a nice T-shirt and blue jeans as well, although wearing a golf shirt and slacks would also be appropriate. Wearing a suit would be too formal in that situation. However, wearing a muscle shirt, cutoff shorts, and flip-flops would be underdressed. Use this guiding rule in choosing clothing: Be sensitive and appropriate.

4. *Are you neat and orderly?* Whatever your style of clothing and hair, be well-groomed. If you have facial hair, keep it trimmed, being careful to cut back any facial hair that would obscure your mouth or keep people from seeing your expressions clearly. Comb your hair and use a product on your hair to keep it from looking messy. If you are wearing pants that will hold a crease and shoes that will hold a shine, make sure you press and polish accordingly. Also, remember that neatness is important in casual contexts as well as more formal ones. A potential problem with casual attire is that it can degenerate into sloppy attire. Wrinkled clothing, soiled clothing, or clothing with holes in it does not communicate well, no matter what your venue may be.

5. *Does your appearance distract or detract from your message?* This last question precipitates every question preceding it and actually is the basis for bringing up clothing and appearance in a book about preaching. Because appearance communicates, we need to

make sure that the way we look does nothing to distract or detract from the message we are delivering. No preacher should desire that the dominant impression made on the listener after hearing a sermon would be the color of his suit, the print of his tie, the holes in his jeans, or the pattern on his shirt. Generally, the best physical appearance is that which draws the least attention to itself, allowing for the greatest attention to be placed on the message we are preaching from God's Word.

PARTICIPATING IN WORSHIP

Part of the pastor's leadership role is to help the congregation worship. A preacher should guard against conveying the attitude that the time of singing and praise at the beginning of the worship service provides only a preliminary to the main event—his sermon. On the contrary, the pastor should passionately worship for the sake of honoring his Lord, strengthening his own soul, and serving as an example to his people. Following are some principles for participating in worship.

Be present and engaged in the service. We are disturbed by the number of pastors who come into worship services late, missing the majority of the congregational praise and worship time. Equally alarming are preachers who sit down throughout the musical portion of the service, review their sermon notes as though they were in a study carrel in a library, and refuse to join the church in singing. People are watching us during the worship service. They are looking to see if we are interested in what is going on as the praise team sings and the music minister leads in worship. If we desire for our people to worship, we must worship as well. More than that, participating in worship and praise prepares us to preach God's Word as much as it prepares our congregation to hear.

Lead well in public prayer. While preachers often focus on the words of their sermon as the central message they communicate during a worship service, many people who attend worship long for the blessing of their pastor praying meaningfully and fervently for them. Though reading prayers is usually not advisable, we do recommend mentally preparing your pastoral prayer ahead of time, praying through it in the study as you get ready on Sunday morning, and then seeking the guidance of the Holy Spirit as you stand before your people to pray.

PUBLIC PRAYERS IN WORSHIP	
Type of Prayer	**Description and Purpose**
Invocation	The first prayer in worship. Usually a shorter prayer. Its purpose is to acknowledge the presence of God among the worshippers.
Pastoral Prayer	A longer prayer with four parts: acknowledgment and worship of God; confession of sin; supplications for needs of the world, nation, and community; and requests on behalf of the worshippers. Its purpose is for the pastor to voice the corporate prayers of the congregation.
Offertory Prayer	A shorter prayer. Its purpose is to give thanks for God's provision and to ask God's blessings on the tithes and offerings given for the work of His kingdom.
Prayer for Illumination	Occurs immediately before the sermon. Its purpose is to ask for the Holy Spirit to search the hearts of the worshippers and to apply the truth of God's Word to their lives.
Prayer of Decision	Occurs at the end of the sermon. Its purpose is to voice the possible responses of the listeners to the message that they have heard.
Benediction	A very brief concluding prayer. Its purpose is to ask God's blessing on worshippers as they depart.

Read Scripture with enthusiasm and meaning. In some churches, the reading of Scripture is separated from the preaching of the Word. Others incorporate the reading of Scripture into the preaching event itself. Regardless of its placement, the reading of Scripture is the most significant element of verbal communication in the worship service and deserves careful attention and care on the part of the preacher. As a regular course of action, we recommend that the pastor read the Scripture in worship, rather than having someone else read it. Reading the Scripture is part of his calling as a preacher of the Word.

Keep the following principles in mind as you read Scripture aloud in worship:

1. *Prepare your reading.* Failure to prepare will cause you to stumble over words or keep you from emphasizing the words you should. As you prepare your message, read the Scripture aloud in the study, using the version of the Bible from which you will be preaching.
2. *Consider the genre of biblical material you are reading.* Language works differently in the various types of biblical material. In narrative, the words move the action. In poetry, words express emotion. In didactic material, words convey ideas and logic.
3. *Read to communicate.* Effective oral interpretation of Scripture is not merely calling out words. Read so as to convey the intellectual, emotional, and aesthetic content of the Scripture passage.
4. *Read with confident humility.* Someone has wisely said that a preacher should read the Scripture aloud as though he were *reading* it, not as though he had *written* it. A heart of humility and submission to God's Word will show up in your voice and attitude as you read.[10]

Use time wisely. Warren Wiersbe has well said that a sermon "does not have to be eternal to be immortal."[11] When you are a guest speaker for another church or a meeting, always ask your host what time you need to be finished. If your host says, "Don't worry about that," ask him again until he tells you the time he has in mind. Then, no matter what else happens in the service, abide by your time limits. When you are preaching in your own church, you bear responsibility for protecting your own preaching time. Work with other worship leaders to make sure ample time is given for all of the worship elements. Some churches are insistent that the service begin and end within one hour, while others allow for a longer time span. Even so,

---

10. Chapter 13 of this book also addresses at some length the public reading of Scripture.
11. Warren Wiersbe and David Wiersbe, *The Elements of Preaching,* 42.

since all worship services operate within time limitations, learn to keep your message within your time frame. Almost every preacher would love more time to preach, but pastoral sensitivity and integrity demands we use good judgment and exercise wisdom in this area. However, remember this: if you have something to say and you say it well, your people will not fuss or complain. They will honor and bless you by returning week after week to hear God's man preach God's Word. What more could we ask? What could we hope for? So, preach the Word, for God has promised that his Word "will not return to me void" (Isa 55:11 NKJV).

CONCLUSION

The chapters through which you have come have shown you how to exegete a selected text in its context, based on sound hermeneutical principles, how to develop expositional sermons based on the text and read within the grand redemptive story line of Scripture, and how to stand each week and deliver God's word to His people. The only task left to do is to "Preach the word!" (2 Tim 4:2 NKJV).

To be sure, the task before you will not be easy. George Barna reports that "only 4% of adults [in America] have a biblical worldview as the basis of their decision making."[1] That observation, though sobering, is not shocking. However, his next discovery should really get our attention as preachers of God's Word: "Only 9% of born again Christians have [a basic, biblical worldview]."[2] What did he mean by a biblical worldview?

> For the purposes of the research, a biblical worldview was defined as believing that absolute moral truths exist; that such truth is defined by the Bible; and firm belief in six specific religious views. Those views were that Jesus Christ lived a sinless life; God is the all-powerful and all-knowing Creator of the universe and He still rules it today; salvation is a gift from God and cannot be earned; Satan is real; a Christian has a responsibility to share their faith in Christ with other people; and the Bible is accurate in all of its teachings.[3]

---

1. "A Biblical Worldview Has a Radical Effect on a Person's Life," Barna Research Group, Ltd. (December 1, 2003), http://www.barna.org.
2. Ibid.
3. Ibid.

How did this happen? How did one of the most religious countries in the world become a nation of biblical and theological illiterates?

The fault surely falls on the shoulders of those who stand to preach but have forsaken "rightly handling the word of truth" (2 Tim 2:15 ESV). Walt Kaiser is exactly correct when he says, "One of the most depressing spectacles in the church today is her lack of power . . . . At the heart of this problem is an impotent pulpit."[4]

This lack of power is the result of neglecting to preach the whole counsel of God's Word and the theology of God's Word. Too many of our people know neither the content nor the doctrines of the Scriptures. Preaching the cross of Christ and the bloody atonement accomplished by His death and resurrection is the exception rather than the norm.

Ours is a day when people are more familiar with the characters of the most recent box office hit than they are the men and women of the Scriptures. The three authors who have penned this book hope that this unfamiliarity will radically change in the days ahead. Indeed, we must change if we are to build vibrant Great Commission churches whose members will take the gospel to the nations. The prescription presented in this book is one of engaging exposition that is Christ centered, text driven, and Spirit led so that it transforms lives.

One cannot rightly love the God of the Book without a right love for the Book of God. Let us read it, study it, explain it, and obey it for the glory of God and the good of the church. We stand behind our words at the beginning of this book, "Engaging exposition is not an option. It is an absolute necessity for the health of the body of Christ." At its core, Christianity is a religion of the Word. We must never forget this truth. We must never forsake this truth.

---

4.   Walter C. Kaiser Jr., *Toward an Exegetical Theology* (Grand Rapids: Baker, 1998), 235–36.

NAME INDEX

353

SUBJECT INDEX

SCRIPTURE INDEX